T0110212

PENGUIN CLASSICS

AMERICAN PLACES

WALLACE STEGNER was the author of, among other works of fiction, *Remembering Laughter* (1937); *The Big Rock Candy Mountain* (1943); *Joe Hill* (1950); *All the Little Live Things* (1967, Commonwealth Club Gold Medal); *A Shooting Star* (1961); *Angle of Repose* (1971, Pulitzer Prize); *The Spectator Bird* (1976, National Book Award); *Recapitulation* (1979); *Crossing to Safety* (1987), and *Collected Stories* (1990). His nonfiction includes *Beyond the Hundredth Meridian* (1954); *Wolf Willow* (1963); *The Sound of Mountain Water* (essays, 1969); *The Uneasy Chair: A Biography of Bernard DeVoto* (1974); *American Places* (with Page Stegner, 1981); and *Where the Bluebird Sings to the Lemonade Springs: Living and Writing in the West* (1992). Three short stories have won O. Henry prizes, and in 1980 he received the Robert Kirsch Award from the *Los Angeles Time* for his lifetime literary achievements.

He is the author of three novels, *The Edge, Hawks and Harriers,* and *Sportscar Menopause;* a critical study of Vladimir Nabokov, *Escape Into Aesthetics;* and five works of non-fiction, *Islands of the West, Outposts of Eden, American Places, Grand Canyon: The Great Abyss,* and *Winning the Wild West: The Epic Saga of the American West, 1800–1899.*

He has been the recipient of a National Endowment for the Arts grant, a National Endowment for the Humanities grant, and a Guggenheim Fellowship.

PAGE STEGNER was born in Salt Lake City, Utah, in 1937. He attended Stanford University, where he received his B.A. in History in 1959 and his Ph.D. in American Literature in 1964. From 1965 to 1995 he was Professor of American Literature and Director of the Creative Writing Program at the University of California, Santa Cruz, retiring in 1995 to devote full time to writing.

He has been the recipient of a National Endowment for the Arts Fellowship (1979–80), a National Endowent for the Humanities Fellowship (1980–81), and a Guggenheim Fellowship (1981–82).

He is the author of three novels, two works of literary criticism, three collections of essays on the American West, and a natural history of the Grand Canyon, and a history of the American Frontier from 1800 to 1899.

WALLACE STEGNER
and
PAGE STEGNER

American Places

With a New Preface by
PAGE STEGNER

PENGUIN BOOKS

PENGUIN BOOKS

Published by the Penguin Group

Penguin Group (USA) Inc., 375 Hudson Street, New York, New York 10014, U.S.A.

Penguin Group (Canada), 90 Eglinton Avenue East, Suite 700, Toronto,
Ontario, Canada M4P 2Y3 (a division of Pearson Penguin Canada Inc.)

Penguin Books Ltd, 80 Strand, London WC2R 0RL, England

Penguin Ireland, 25 St Stephen's Green, Dublin 2, Ireland (a division of Penguin Books Ltd)

Penguin Group (Australia), 250 Camberwell Road, Camberwell,
Victoria 3124, Australia (a division of Pearson Australia Group Pty Ltd)

Penguin Books India Pvt Ltd, 11 Community Centre, Panchsheel Park, New Delhi–110 017, India

Penguin Group (NZ), cnr Airborne and Rosedale Roads, Albany,
Auckland 1310, New Zealand (a division of Pearson New Zealand Ltd)

Penguin Books (South Africa) (Pty) Ltd, 24 Sturdee Avenue,
Rosebank, Johannesburg 2196, South Africa

Penguin Books Ltd, Registered Offices:
80 Strand, London WC2R 0RL, England

First published in the United States of America by E. P. Dutton 1981
This edition with a new preface by Page Stegner published in Penguin Books 2006

Preface copyright © Page Stegner, 2006
All rights reserved

Chapters from this book have appeared in the following periodicals, in slightly different forms:
"Inheritance" in *American Heritage;* "The Northeast Kingdom," "Crow Country,"
"The River," and "Remnants" in *Country Journal;* "There It Is: Take It" in *Harper's;*
"Life Along the Fault Line" in *Esquire.*

ISBN 0 14 30.3974 1
CIP data available.

Contents

Preface   vii
Foreword   xi

AMERICAN PLACES

Inheritance	1
The Northeast Kingdom	28
Last Exit to America	45
The River	56
Dead Heart of the West	80
Crow Country	93
High Plateaus	113
The New Riders of the Purple Sage	138
The Redwood Curtain	152
There It Is: Take It	166
Life Along the Fault Line	186
Remnants	204
Unfinished Business	221
Bibliography	235
Index	247

Preface to the Penguin Classics Edition

A Note on Writing *American Places*

This book was conceived in the aftermath of a series of special supplements run by *The Atlantic Monthly* in the mid-1970s, one on Texas, one on the Pacific Northwest, and one written by my father and me called "Rocky Mountain Country." As *The Atlantic Monthly*'s editor Robert Manning put it, "It struck us that there could be no better Lewis for this expedition than Wallace Stegner, the distinguished teacher, essayist, historian, biographer, and Pulitzer prize–winning novelist. And what better Clark than Stegner's son, Page, also a teacher, critic, and novelist." What Mr. Manning generously failed to point out (though perhaps implicit in his blurb) was that Stegner's Clark was neither an essayist nor a historian, and unlike the real Mc-Coy was woefully unprepared for the journey. However handy he may have been with the written word, he didn't know anything about the West except California (which is really not the West at all, but west of the West), and he had to lean very heavily on the *pater familias* for inspiration, direction, and revision. One of his more memorable gaffs, one which actually escaped the paternal eye and found its way into print, was a description of the Colorado River winding "through the Grand Canyon into Lake Mead and south along the California border to the Gulf of Mexico." Numerous picky readers wrote the magazine to express their astonishment upon learning that California had extended its boundaries eastward, absorbing Arizona and half of New Mexico and that the Colorado had somehow veered five hundred or so miles toward El Paso and joined the Rio Grande.

On the whole, however, it was a largely successful overview

of a widespread and varied terrain and it inspired John Macrae at E. P. Dutton to think along the lines of a coauthored book, one that would encompass the entire country and would be richly illustrated by the famous photographer, Eliot Porter. But as is obliquely noted in the original foreword to *American Places*, neither Stegner, when approached with the idea, felt competent to write about turf that they did not know rather intimately—which was to say most everything east of the Great Plains except parts of Iowa (where Wallace was born) and Vermont (where both Stegners maintained summer homes). Porter was not interested in merely illustrating the text, nor were the writers particularly interested in providing captions and sidebars for Porter's photographs, so there was a lot of refining to be done before the project was liberated from its incubator.

Eventually we all arrived at the following dodge: "In our commentary on the American land we have guided ourselves by Robert Frost's remark that all art is synecdoche, that all an artist needs is samples." Freed from the confines of inclusion we all went our separate ways, mining our individual experience, writing and photographing places with which we each had strong and personal attachments. From my involvement with "Rocky Mountain Country" I had learned a good deal about writing about the land and its human interactors, and my old man had learned much about my testy reaction to having my prose rewritten beyond recognition. So we got along famously.

Which is not to say that there were not a number of fender benders along the way. John Macrae threw out two of my pieces, and in spite of vigorous protest from both authors insisted on inserting a largely irrelevant chapter from Van Wyck Brooks's *The World of Washington Irving* (it has been eliminated from this edition). In a snit, I threatened to absquatulate from the entire project. Macrae threatened to sue. Porter nearly withdrew his portfolio in a huff over the writers prejudice against Maine; i.e., Maine is not Vermont (not even close). And finally some copy editor took it upon him or herself to revise all of Wallace Stegner's essays, correcting punctuation, tweaking syntax, changing nuance and often meaning, generally red penciling every page until it resembled a case of terminal acne. Needless to say, these improvements were not well received— nor did they prevail.

It might be argued that some of the "test borings" in this volume are dated and therefore of little interest beyond whatever literary merit they possess. But I would demur. The issue of land use and abuse in essays like "Crow Country" or "High Plateaus" may vary in particulars, but the problems are just as relevant in 2006 as they were in 1980. Environmental protection verses reckless exploitation is perennial and ubiquitous and, unfortunately, will never become passé. The Los Angeles Department of Water and Power continues to drain the Owens Valley, as depicted in "There It is: Take It"; Sedona today is an even worse frightmare than the one described in "The New Riders of the Purple Sage"; the limits of tolerance in post dot.bomb Santa Cruz continue to be tested in precisely the same manner as depicted in pre dot.com "Life Along the Fault Line." Anyway, to paraphrase our original forward, *American Places* is less a book about the American land, which does, of course, change, than it is about the making of Americans—a process that will endure at least until there's no one left to read about it.

Page Stegner
Santa Fe, New Mexico

Foreword

In the dust where we have buried the silent races and their abominations we have buried so much of the delicate magic of life.

D. H. Lawrence

It is necessary to say what this book is, and what it is not.

It is not another book of natural wonders, though some of the country it deals with is wonderful; not simply a work of history, and not simply a collection of personal experiences, though it contains some of both. And it makes no effort to cover *all* the regions, topographies, climates, corners, coasts, boundaries, rivers, and lakes of the North American continent.

The plan for this book came from Jack Macrae, the book's editor and publisher. The idea was to create a book about North America's human and natural history with a decidedly personal touch.

Wallace Stegner, born in Iowa and brought up in North Dakota, Washington, Saskatchewan, Montana, and Utah, began his travels in a Hudson Super Six in the Yellowstone country in 1920. Page Stegner, born in Salt Lake city and educated in Massachusetts, New Hampshire, Arizona, Colorado, and California, has had the continent in his blood since his earliest years. Both have crossed and recrossed this land many times. But even though we believe we know much of the North American continent, no two people could cover everything of importance, especially in the personal terms we have chosen to adopt. So each of us, in making each contribution, concentrates on places that he knows well and feels deeply, places he has put something of himself into and derived something of himself from. If some of your favorite places are missing, that is not because we don't know and feel them as intimately as we know and feel others. In our commentary on the American land we have guided ourselves by Robert Frost's remark that all art is synecdoche, that all an artist needs is samples.

There are no cities here. Neither do we concern ourselves mainly with the national parks and monuments and the permanent wilderness areas. Parks are immensely important, but they are not America; they are exceptions to it. And though we agree with Lord Bryce that the national park idea—the willed preservation of natural areas which it might be in our short-term interest to exploit—is the best idea to have come out of the New World, we have to observe that these reservations are only the crumbs from the great greedy banquet. They had to be fought for by people whose public spirit was often called, perhaps correctly, un-American; and even yet millions of Americans do not understand them. They want the wilderness areas opened to recreational vehicles and drilling rigs, and they confuse national parks with resorts.

This book is an attempt, by sampling, to say something about how the American people and the American land have interacted, how they have shaped one another; what patterns of life, with what chances of continuity, have arisen out of the confrontations between an unformed society and a virgin continent. Perhaps it is less a book about the American land than some ruminations about the making of Americans. Again the theme is Frost's: "the land was ours before we were the land's." We are the unfinished product of a long becoming. In our ignorance and hunger and rapacity, in our dream of a better material life, we laid waste the continent and diminished ourselves before any substantial number of us began to feel, little and late, an affinity with it, a dependence on it, an obligation - toward it as the indispensable source of everything we hope for.

Native Americans, though they were often guilty of primitive assaults on the land, principally the setting of wildfires to run game or improve the grass, did feel a reverence for the earth and its creatures. Their descendants feel it still; the earth is at the heart of their religion. And Europeans were not land wasters in Europe. Feudalism, with its system of serfdom that bound men to land, and with its laws of primogeniture and entail, was hard on people but good for land. In Europe and especially in England, which set the patterns of land use in much of the United States, land was a resource, not a commodity. It could not be freely disposed of, subdivided, mined, or exploited. But men who had been good husbandmen in Europe found their sense of stewardship eroding in the acid of the New World's plenty. It has taken us nearly half a millennium to begin to correct what our own plenty generated.

Almost a century has passed since the frontier was declared officially closed, and the era of free land came to an end. In that century we have made the first halting steps, not backward toward the enforced stewardship of Europe, but forward toward a new land ethic deriving from American conditions of freedom. Land *gave* Americans their freedom. It also gave them their egalitarianism, their democracy, their optimism, their free-enterprise capitalism, their greed, and their carelessness. It is an ambiguous and troubling legacy. Only recently have any substantial number of Americans learned enough to want to give back to the land the renewable life and health, the natural continuity that it had in far simpler terms when Europeans and their Iron Age culture first put foot to ground in the New World. But every new generation of Americans inherits the expectations that free land aroused and, even long after free land has vanished, goes hunting on the frontiers that once extended the American Dream and retarded American maturity.

Every chapter in this book can be construed as illustrating a stage in the process of adaptation and naturalization. Some pages are less optimistic than others because in some places exploitation has gone further than in others, or frontier expectations have persisted longer. They vary in tone because we are different people, with different life experiences. Page Stegner's America is, of course, quite a different place from the land that Wallace Stegner knew as a child, and the naive belief of superabundance—common in the nineteenth century—has largely passed among younger Americans except some who have moved up to Alaska. All the chapters reflect the guilt and regret that any American must feel when thinking about what America once was, what it once promised, and what we have done to it. But all of them also, we hope, radiate the love we feel for this country even in its abused and mutilated state. For that is where a responsible land ethic must begin, in the love that people feel for their native earth.

We are talking about land uses; it is only as a home for the human race that the earth has any meaning to a member of that race. But one of the things we acquired when we inherited this continent was power, and power either can corrupt or can teach us responsibility.

Chapters 1–7 and 12 are by Wallace Stegner; chapters 8–11 are by Page Stegner. Chapter 13 was written jointly by Wallace Stegner and Page Stegner.

American Places

INHERITANCE

The rich and the poor are not so far removed from each other as they are in Europe. Some few towns excepted, we are all tillers of the earth, from Nova Scotia to West Florida. We are a people of cultivators, scattered over an immense territory, communicating with each other by means of good roads and navigable rivers, united by the silken bands of mild government, all respecting the equitable. We are all animated with the spirit of an industry which is unfettered and unrestrained, because each person works for himself. If he travels through our rural districts he views not the hostile castle, and the haughty mansion, contrasted with the clay-built hut and miserable cabin, where cattle and men help to keep each other warm, and dwell in meanness, smoke, and indigence. . . . There is no wonder that this country has so many charms, and presents to Europeans so many temptations to remain in it. A traveler in Europe becomes a stranger as soon as he quits his own kingdom; but it is otherwise here. We know, properly speaking, no strangers; this is every person's country; the variety of our soils, situations, climates, governments, and produce, hath something which must please everybody. No sooner does a European arrive, no matter of what condition, than his eyes are opened upon the fair prospect; he hears his language spoken, he retraces many of his own country manners, he perpetually hears the names of families and towns with which he is acquainted; he sees happiness and prosperity in all places disseminated; he meets with hospitality, kindness, and plenty everywhere; he beholds hardly any poor, he seldom hears of punishments and executions; and he wonders at the elegance of our towns, those miracles of industry and freedom. . . . Does he

love a country life? pleasant farms present themselves; he may
purchase what he wants, and thereby becomes an American
farmer. Is he a laborer, sober and industrious? he need not go
many miles, nor receive many informations before he will be
hired, well fed at the table of his employer, and paid four or five
times more than he can get in Europe. Does he want unculti-
vated lands? thousands of acres present themselves, which he
may purchase cheap. Whatever be his talents or inclinations, if
they are moderate, he may satisfy them. I do not mean that every
one who comes will grow rich in a little time; no, but he may
procure an easy, decent maintenance, by his industry. Instead of
starving he will be fed, instead of being idle he will have em-
ployment; and these are riches enough for such men as come
over here. The rich stay in Europe, it is only the middling and
the poor that emigrate.

Hector St. John de Crevecoeur,
Letters from an American Farmer (1782)

Sure you're romantic about American history. . . . It is the most
romantic of all histories. It began as myth and has developed
through three centuries of fairy stories. Whatever the time is in
America it is always, at every moment, the mad and wayward
hour when the prince is finding the little foot that alone fits into
the slipper of glass. . . . Ours is a story mad with the impossible, it
is by chaos out of dream, it began as dream and has continued as
dream down to the last headline you read in a newspaper. . . . The
simplest truth you can ever write about our history will be
charged and surcharged with romanticism, and if you are afraid of
the word you had better start practicing seriously on your fiddle.

Bernard Devoto
to Catherine Drinker Bowen (1940s)

Three centuries of fairy stories, DeVoto says. But the fairy stories
go back far deeper into time than three hundred years. As Atlantis, as Brazile or Antillia or Groenland or the Fortunate Isles,

as the Earthly Paradise or the Garden of the World, as something for nothing, as escape from history or authority or oppression or the grind of poverty, as the promise of social justice, freedom, or the ideal society, America is Europe's oldest dream. "The Atlantic," says Howard Mumford Jones in *O Strange New World,* "hid in its misty vastness many wonderful islands, and these island images, compounded of wonder, terror, wealth, religious perfection, communism, utopianism, or political power, conditioned the European image of America. They floated on the maps of the Ocean Sea like quicksilver globules, now here, now there, now nowhere at all, some of them remaining on British Admiralty charts into the nineteenth century."

America was not only a new world waiting to be discovered; it was a fable waiting to be agreed upon. Preconceptions, some medieval, some as old as the memory of Europe, were part of it before discovery and clung to it afterward. Preconceptions are not readily soluble in observed fact, and they often give rise to insoluble consequences.

Thus Columbus, sailing westward to find the East, found something, and assumed that what he found was what he had gone in search of. So he called the inhabitants Indians, and in spite of all later revisionist suggestions such as Amerinds and Native Americans, they remain Indians to this day. Thus Vespucci, only ten years after Columbus' first voyage, clearly demonstrated that America was not Asia; yet 133 years later, in 1635, when Champlain sent Jean Nicolet to explore among the Nipissings on the way to Georgian Bay and the great interior lakes, Nicolet took along in his birchbark canoe an embroidered mandarin robe, just in case, out there in the depths of unknown forests, by unknown rivers, he should encounter the Great Khan, and need ceremonial dress.

As historians have remarked, America was discovered by accident and explored to a considerable extent by people trying to find a way to somewhere else. Cathay died hard. When the reluctant truth was finally established that neither the northern nor the southern mainland was China, and that none of the islands north or south formed part of Cipangu or the East Indies, restless men representing restless and expanding empires probed for ways through or around it, ways easier than the way Vasco da Gama found around the Cape of Good Hope in 1498, or the way Balboa found across the Isthmus of Panama in 1513, or the stormy way around the bottom of South America that Magellan opened seven years later. There must, said logic and wishfulness in ignorance of any facts whatever, there must be some waterway, some Northwest Passage, that would take Europe conveniently into the South Sea and on to the jewels and spices of the East. In the absence of more than a few fixed points of knowledge, wish became fact, and fantasy turned cartographer.

It is a story staled by generalized repetition, but it is the greatest story in the history of civilized man—how the New World was found, explored, opened, inventories, finally settled. And raped. Rapine was a good part of it, and still is.

When literally nothing is known, anything is possible, and even the greatest explorers can err. It took a long time merely to establish what was island and what was continent, especially in the icy and much-islanded north. By the time Gordillo in 1521 and Verrazano in 1524 had, between them, coasted the Atlantic seaboard from Florida to Newfoundland, they still knew only a shoreline, and that in the most general terms. The density and mass of what lay beyond the shore was inconceivable, and would not become clear for nearly three centuries. Uncounted expeditions would have to go up the St. Lawrence and the Ottawa, out through the Great Lakes, from Hudson Bay up the Nelson and the Churchill to the Saskatchewan, up the Saskatchewan to the Rocky Mountains, over the mountains to the sea. It would take the labor and daring of Nicolet, Du Lhut, La Salle, Groseilliers and Radisson, Henry Kelsey and Peter Pond, Marquette and Jolliet, Vérendrye and Hearne, Alexander Mackenzie and Lewis and Clark, to demonstrate how wide a barrier lay between European wishfulness and Cathay. Because no one in the beginning had any conception of the breadth of the continent, error was sometimes ludicrous. Verrazano, sailing along the Carolina coast searching hopefully for a shortcut to China, looked across a low sand isthmus a mile or so wide and thought the water he saw on the other side might be the Pacific. It was probably Pamlico Sound. He couldn't even see the *eastern* shore of America, much less the western.

Verrazano entered New York harbor, but missed the mouth of the Hudson, the only eastern river besides the St. Lawrence that would have taught him something about the extent of the wilderness that lay between him and the ocean leading to the Orient. Actually it was the St. Lawrence–Ottawa route that led Europeans to the interior, but it took well over a century, and the combined and heroic efforts of Cartier, Champlain, Nicolet, Marquette and Jolliet, and La Salle, plus a generally nameless but indispensable tribe of *coureurs de bois,* before that interior was opened even as far as the Great Lakes and the Mississippi.

And long after the interior had begun to recommend itself to far-sighted people as a source of wealth and a bastion of empire, they kept looking for a way through it. In the 1570s, fifty years after Verrazano, Frobisher was groping through the Arctic ice in search of the Northwest Passage. Ten years after Frobisher, John Davis was forced to turn back from what he thought was the very entrance. And in 1611, a generation after Davis, Henry Hudson, in search of the same passage, was set adrift by his mutinous crew and added to the casualty list of the New World: John Cabot lost without trace in the Atlantic, Verrazano killed and eaten by Carib cannibals, Cabrillo dying of injuries and exhaustion on a remote California island, De Soto buried in the Mississippi, La Salle murdered by his own men in the collapse of his imperial dream, Jesuits sliced up and killed a finger at a time by the Iroquois, settlers dying of scurvy and starvation and wounds at Fort Caroline, Santa Fe, Roanoke, Jamestown, Plymouth, San Diego, Winter Quarters, Jedediah Smith escaping Mojave and Umpqua ambushes only to be rubbed out by a Comanche war party on the Santa Fe Trail.

Renaissance princes steeped in Machiavelli, adventurers, soldiers and settlers, bondservants, pathfinders, dreamers in search of riches and freedom and unthinkable in static Europe, they were of many nations and kinds, but to all of them the New

World was a pillar of fire and cloud, an impetuous dynamism, a throwing-open of what had been closed and locked for centuries. America opened Bastille Europe.

Probably, in the last analysis, the economic motive was the strongest of all that moved the newcomers, and imperial rivalry the next strongest. Think of it in our contemporary terms: without the Russians for rivals we would not yet have walked on the moon. And if the moon-rocks our astronauts brought back had been solid gold, our space shuttles would already be making scheduled runs, and the launching pads would be crowded with emigrants. But setting aside the Aztec and Inca gold, what opened up around the year 1500—the beginning of modern times—was enough to dazzle Europe's imagination. Walter Webb summarizes it persuasively in *The Great Frontier*: North and South America found beyond the mists of the Atlantic, with Australia—Terra Australis Incognita—to follow about a century later; Africa rediscovered and laid open to slavers and ivory hunters; a way found around the Cape of Good Hope to India; shortly afterward, a way found around South America into the Pacific. And every one of these discoveries a source of or avenue to new wealth.

For centuries Europe had been living up to the limits of its land and resources. Its population, periodically reduced by the Black Death, was nearly static. Its faith was both frozen and tested by a corrupt and politicized but "universal" Church now beginning to break up in the Reformation, its social and economic systems strangled in the survivals of feudalism and chivalry, its history crazy with dynastic wars and soggy with blood, its learning only just opening out of scholasticism into the Renaissance. To closed and limited Europe America was, as Webb says, a pure windfall, a once-in-the-history-of-the-world opportunity. Both Reformation and Renaissance, already begun, were enormously enhanced by the discovery of the New World; freedoms only half imagined were suddenly possible. No wonder Europe fell upon America as if it had been Blackbeard's chest. No wonder it brushed aside the Stone Age natives—a nuisance, like mosquitoes. Even if a few Europeans looked upon them as souls to be saved, none for a long time regarded them as men and societies with rights and cultures and a healthy relation to the earth. Europe simply washed over them, a tidal wave of cupidity and hope.

From the point of view of the invaders, a story mad with the impossible, by chaos out of dream. And dream kept opening into further dream, chaos often led on to more confusing chaos. Take the Northwest Passage again. It eluded all search from the Atlantic side, but after Magellan showed the way into the Pacific in 1520, men could dream of finding it from the west, and so invented an opening called the Straits of Anian.

Cabrillo in 1542–1543 explored the Pacific coast as high as 42°5' north latitude without finding the straits he was searching for. After that, Spanish exploration subsided, exhausted by fifty years of intense adventuring. But Sir Francis Drake, having looted the Manila galleon in 1579, sailed up the coast and careened the *Golden Hind* for repairs on a beach north of San Francisco, in the country he claimed for England and called New Albion. He was confident that the Straits of Anian lay only a short distance northward, but did not go farther in search of them. Nevertheless his incursion galvanized the Spanish into new activity, for fear Drake might be right, and England gain an enormous advantage. So Vizcaíno came to see what he could discover, and in 1603, off the northern California coast, the captain in his bunk with broken ribs, the crew so weak and sick they could not work the sails, Vizcaíno's boatswain thought he saw the mouth of a large river just south of Cape Mendocino. Scurvy, starvation, and constant storms gave them no chance to explore it. There is no river where he thought he saw one; either the ship was not where the boatswain thought it was, or what he saw was an illusion of longing and blowing fog. But Torquemada, reading the boatswain's report back in Spain, leaped to the conclusion that he had seen the Straits of Anian, and had it recorded on the map. Characteristically, the mapmaker placed it not just below Cape Mendocino, but near Cape Blanco. Illusion was compounded by clerical error and perpetuated by document, and knowledge was postponed.

It was so easy to err, even without the intervention of wishfulness. Sailors in strange waters, working from nearly total ignorance toward knowledge with no tool except their own observation, could miss even salient features. Verrazano missed the Hudson, Lewis and Clark missed the Willamette, Major Powell on the last great exploration within the continental United States missed the Escalante. Cabrillo and Drake, Pérez and Vizcaíno after him, missed the Golden Gate, opening into one of the greatest natural harbors in the world.

Like other New World dreams, the Northwest Passage flickered along just ahead of knowledge, just beyond the next day's sail, beyond where vision blurred with fog and distance. When you do not know how wide a continent is, or whether it is continent or island, or whether it is a separate land body or part of Asia, and especially when you do not yet have a reliable method of determining longitude, anything is possible. Any bay or gulf may open a broad way to the Orient, any river may lead you to the divide beyond which rivers run serenely to the South Sea. For a while, the James and the Potomac were eyed hopefully. And once the Mississippi was found, it was perfectly possible to think it might flow into the Pacific. Marquette and Jolliet, making their way in 1673 from Green Bay up the Fox River, across the portage into the Wisconsin, and down the Wisconsin to the Mississippi, were by no means sure that the great river they had found would not lead them to the Gulf of California. By the time they turned back at the mouth of the Arkansas for fear of running into difficulties with the Spanish, they were fairly sure where it did flow, and La Salle, going the whole distance nine years later, proved that it emptied into the Gulf of Mexico. But both expeditions, passing the mouth of the muddy, rushing, tree-choked Missouri, looked up that savage stream and wondered if *that* might be the route to Asia.

It was, after a fashion, as Lewis and Clark demonstrated in 1804–1806. But even Lewis and Clark, as sane and organized as they were, had their own illusions about the unknown. They left the Mandan villages in the spring of 1805 confident that the Shining Mountains would be a simple range beyond which the westward-flowing rivers would lead them to the Pacific. What they found was five hundred miles of interlocking ranges, a vast belt of mountains, difficult pass after difficult pass, canyons that frustrated attempts to descend them, rivers that ran in every direction. Only after the greatest labor and hardship were they able finally to make the Clearwater and the Columbia.

As with the Northwest Passage, so with other dreams and fantasies, products of the medieval imagination or simply of the unlimited *possibility* of the New World. Ponce de León, the discoverer of Florida, searched it hopefully for the Fountain of Youth it was rumored to contain. The rumor was probably generated by reports of the great springs, actually underground rivers, that boil up through the flat limestone of the peninsula. No spring revealed to Ponce de León any magical properties; but three centuries later, after reading about Florida in the *Travels* of William Bartram, Coleridge demonstrated the immortality of legend by making one of those springs into Alph, the sacred river, which runs through Kubla Khan's magical gardens, through caverns measureless to man, down to a sunless sea. Perhaps the South Sea.

Poetry is realization of a kind, a splendid kind. El Dorado, the fabled Golden Man whom Walter Raleigh pursued so desperately up the Orinoco, found no such place in poetry, but survives as legend. The Seven Cities of Cíbola and the land of Quivira did not survive, even as legend, the exposure of their reality. Their pursuit brought only bitterness and disappointment, dust and ashes.

When Pánfilo de Narváez tried to colonize Florida in 1528, he died of the attempt, and most of his people with him. A handful, including Ávar Núñez Cabeza de Vaca, survived six years of wandering among the Indian tribes, sometimes as prisoners, sometimes as revered medicine men, and in 1536, having walked across the southern part of the continent and down the Mexican Gulf Coast, they appeared in Pánuco (now Tampico). They brought tales, heard from the Indians, of a land to the north and west where there were seven cities built of stone, with buildings four and five stories high whose doorposts and lintels were inlaid with turquoise.

People still vibrating to the shock waves of what Cortés and

Pizarro had found were not skeptics. Viceroy Mendoza sent a friar, Marcos de Niza, northward to investigate, and along with him the black slave Esteban who had been with Cabeza de Vaca. Esteban went ahead of Fray Marcos, sending back increasingly excited messages of what the Indians along their route told him. He was still ahead when they reached the first "city," but when he entered it, his arrogance and his way of handling Indian women so offended the inhabitants that they killed him. Fray Marcos and his companions watched from a ridge and then fled—"with," the historian Pedro de Castañeda wrote contemptuously, "their habits up to their waists." But not before their eyes had seen what their imaginations told them to see: tall stone buildings, a city "larger than the city of Mexico," doubtless full of treasure.

Fray Marcos's overheated report led to the Coronado expedition, as grandiose a failure as even the Spaniards in the New World ever launched. The company that gathered at Compostela on February 22, 1540, contained 230 mounted men, many of them non-Spaniards, filibusters and fortune hunters from all over Europe. There were also 62 foot soldiers, 1,000 horses, 600 pack animals, thousands of sheep and cattle, four friars with their escort, mountains of suppliers, and hundreds of Indians—a far more powerful force than either Cortés or Pizarro had had for his conquests. It was supported, moreover, by a naval arm under Hernando de Alarcón, with which it was supposed to make contact at the head of the Gulf of California.

This army pursued hallucination up the west coast of Mexico, through the Sonora and San Pedro valleys to near the Gila, and then northeast to the Zuñi town of Hawikuh—in Castañeda's words, "a small, rocky pueblo, all crumpled up, there being many farm settlements in New Spain that look better from afar"—which resisted and was destroyed. No gold or silver could be sifted out of its ruins. Resting the main army, Coronado sent his captains exploring—Tovar to the Hopi towns, Cárdenas as far west as the Grand Canyon, Alvarado eastward past Acoma and the Tiguex pueblos around modern Albuquerque and on to Cicuye (Pecos), where a fast-talking

Wichita Indian from the buffalo plains told the Spaniards the kind of tales they liked to hear, of a land called Quivira, on a great river far to the east that contained fish as big as horses, where Indian kings rode around in canoes with twenty paddlers on a side, ate off golden plates, and took their siestas to the tinkling of little golden bells.

By spring, Coronado had left some of the Rio Grande pueblos in ruins and the rest in a state of sullen submission. He had found no treasure in those poor mud-mortared villages. But there remained Quivira. Under the guidance of the Wichita, whom they nicknamed the Turk because he looked like one, they set out into country that only Cabeza de Vaca's party had ever seen, the southern plains.

Perhaps leading them on so that they could be cut off and destroyed, the Turk kept repeating his gilded tales, embroidering them as the Spaniards' impatience and unbelief grew. At last, far out in the plains of Kansas, in country that Pedro de Castañeda thought was "part of a continuous continent with Peru, as well as with greater India or China," the Turk's stories would no longer wash, and they strangled him on the excuse that he had been heard conversing with the devil in an olla. Then they retreated from Quivira, and shortly afterward from the Rio Grande, and returned in defeat and disgrace, quarreling among themselves and with their leader, to New Galicia. Of the three hundred horse and foot soldiers who started, about a hundred returned. No historian counted the losses among the Indian allies, or among the horses, which may from this expedition have begun to populate the horse heaven of the plains. Of the friars, two elected to stay in Cíbola and save souls, and were killed for their pains.

Not even the most pitiful amount of treasure from all that effort and bloodshed, and though some of the participants reported wonders, including many strange beasts out of medieval bestiaries, Castañeda, a cool observer, saw nothing of the kind. What he did see, and describe for the first time (though Cabeza de Vaca and his companions had certainly *seen* them first), was the plains and the buffalo, no small wonders in themselves.

All that they could see in that country, he said, was cattle, by which he meant the buffalo, and sky. "The land is in the shape of a ball, for wherever a man stands in it he is surrounded by the sky at the distance of a crossbow shot," and "so level and bare that, wherever one looked at [the buffalo] one could see the sky between their legs." There, for almost the first time out of a Spanish mouth, is accurate observation of New World phenomena. He goes on: "Who could believe that although one thousand horses, five hundred of our cattle, more than five thousand rams and sheep, and more than 1,500 persons, including allies and servants, marched over those plains, they left no more traces when they got through than if no one had passed over, so that it became necessary to stack up piles of bones and dung of the cattle at various distances in order that the rear guard could follow the army and not get lost."

Coronado spent two years, 1540–1542, trying to find another Tenochtitlán among the New Mexico pueblos. Blinded by gold, he missed the opportunity to settle the Rio Grande valley, an operation that would have to wait another sixty years. At nearly the same time as Coronado's failure, Hernando de Soto was seeing what could be realized out of Florida. His men too were raiders, not settlers, and their encampments were beachheads, not towns. The Florida that they searched and ravaged was more than the peninsula. It covered much of Georgia, the Carolinas, Tennessee, and Alabama, and before they were satisfied De Soto's men had probed out into Mississippi, Arkansas, and East Texas. As reported by Garcilaso de la Vega in *The Florida of the Inca,* De Soto's campaign through swamps and forests had to be one of the bloodiest in the history of the New World, and it was attended by more hardship, suffering, and death on the part of the Spaniards than any other.

They found as little treasure as Coronado found, nothing but some furs and freshwater pearls that they traded for or seized for lack of anything better. The one thing of importance that they did find, the Mississippi River, was more barrier and threat than anything else. Its 1543 spring flood appalled them. In the same turbid waters, the year before, they had sunk the body of their commander to keep the Indians from learning of his death. Down that majestic current they eventually made their escape. After four years of campaigning, two-thirds of them dead, their horses all killed, the survivors sick and full of wounds, bearded, dirty, clothed in rags and skins, they scrabbled together seven crude boats on the Gulf Coast and made their difficult way to Pánuco.

There their suffering was enlarged by an ironic realization. At Pánuco they found Spaniards tilling the dry ground, scratching out a bare living, making a settlement in country not one-tenth as rich and attractive as that which the De Soto army had passed through in scorn. More: the few furs and pearls they had managed to hang on to struck the Pánuco people as being of great fineness and worth. Pánuco was filled with envy at the richness and wonders these haggard ragamuffins had been privileged to see. But the ragamuffins, embittered at how the lust for gold had blinded them to the good land of Florida, broke out in fighting with knives and swords among themselves, and were hardly kept from assaulting the king's officers who had misled them.

There is a moral here, the same one that Castañeda drew from the Coronado fiasco. Castañeda thought Coronado's retreat from New Mexico a mistake—he should have stayed, and settled the Rio Grande valley. "For although they did not obtain the riches of which they had been told, they found the means to discover them and the beginning of a good land to settle in and from which to proceed onward. And since, after they returned from the land which they had conquered and abandoned, time has made clear to them the location and nature of the region they reached, and the beginning of a fine land they had in their grasp, their hearts bemoan the fact that they lost such an opportune occasion."

Though unauthorized filibusters would raid New Mexico in the 1590s, though Gaspar Castano de Sosa would again conquer Pecos and the Tewa, Queres, and Tigua towns, and though Leyva de Bonilla and Antonio Gutierres de Humaná would carry Spanish ferocity from San Ildefonso clear to the Arkansas River in eastern Kansas, New Mexico would not be officially recognized as an opportunity until Juan de Oñate left the Rio de Conchos in February 1597, with 130 families, 83 wagons, and 7,000 head of stock, and took a direct line through El Paso to the upper Rio Grande. That was the true beginning of New Mexico. It was a beginning made with a reduced and more realistic expectation; a settlement, not a raid.

Reduced expectation was something that other Europeans than the Spaniards did not have to learn by so hard a means, but they all had to learn it. Whatever America might in the end prove to contain, whatever authentic wonders of great rivers, mountains, plains, minerals, oil and coal, deep soil, fertile valleys, canyons so deep that rocks which from the top look no bigger than a man prove to be taller than the great tower of Seville, it took time before they could be seen straight and inventoried in realistic terms. Some gilded expectations would have to be scaled down, some fantasies disproved and discarded, some open-ended possibilities put over onto the impossible side, some biases given up, some purely native matters first understood and then accepted, some civilized accomplishments of the indigenous tribes given credence and respect. It took a long time for Europeans even to grant that Indian civilizations sprang from Indian brains, and not from the brain of some white stranger, some Quetzalcoatl or Welsh Prince Madoc or Nephite out of the Book of Mormon. Some of those myths lingered on and on. In the 1870s Brigham Young sent a Welsh Mormon down to the Hopi towns to see if the Hopi language contained Welsh words that might confirm the legend of Prince Madoc's lost twelfth-century colony. If it did, the Book of Mormon story of the Nephites and the Lamanites, both derived from the Lost Tribes of Israel, would have come into question. It didn't, and the Mormon mind was relieved.

More: the hope of sudden wealth that the discovery of the New World engendered in a human race not until 1500 sanguine about the worldly future has not died. Every mineral and oil strike, every Prudhoe Bay or Overthrust Belt, every boom town from Fairbanks to Rock Springs, demonstrates how easily ignited is the human desire for a jackpot. It burns in most of us, especially Americans, like a pilot light; the mere turning of a valve expands it into a flame. And when it is in flame, we are rather likely to act about as the Spaniards under Coronado or De Soto did.

No one ever duplicated the glittering strikes made by Cortés and Pizarro, but it is largely true, as Walter Webb suggests, that New World wealth fueled Europe's climb out of the stagnation of the Middle Ages, and that modern times in both Europe and America have been times of almost unbroken boom, now approaching or at its end.

The French and English, enviously watching the Spanish loot their American empire, had to settle for something less than Aztec and Inca gold—though Drake alone, in his single small ship, took home from his piracies on Spanish galleons enough gold so that Queen Elizabeth, out of her royal share, was able to pay off the entire national debt and have enough left to found the British East India Company. Drake's gold was only a redistribution of Spanish booty, but actually all Europe benefited from the New World in food plants, especially maize and potatoes, as well as in timber, fish, furs, and much else. For the French and English the more permanent enrichment came from the fish of the Newfoundland banks, from Canadian furs, and from tobacco.

The French got their foothold on the St. Lawrence and expanded it. The English, after the disaster at Roanoke and the near-disaster at Jamestown, consolidated footholds in Virginia and Massachusetts. There is no better way to remind ourselves of the variousness of the American heritage than to remember how different the French and English were in their approach to the new continent, and how different both were from the Spanish. The Spanish, at first looters, became settlers, and imposed Spanish institutions on their territories, including the encomienda system that in practice enslaved the Indians, but they did intermarry—biologically they incorporated themselves into the indigenous population even while they were bending the indigenous population to Spanish ways. The French likewise never made a barrier to intermarriage. Adventurers and woods runners, they came closer to adapting themselves to the continent than any of their rivals, and except for some accidents of history and some pressures from the United States, they might have created in western Canada a *métis* nation like the mixed nation of Mexico. The English, stickers and settlers, did not much intermarry and did not much wander, but what they took and held they changed.

In his *History of the Dividing Line* (1729) William Byrd complained that "our country has now been inhabited more than 130 years by the English, and still we hardly know anything of the Appalachian Mountains, that are no where above 250 miles from the sea." The French, by contrast, had run over half the continent, had discovered the canoe route to the Great Lakes, had found the Mississippi and gone down it to its mouth, had explored the Ohio and the Illinois, had dreamed of a vast inland empire based on the fur trade (a trade that depended on continuing wilderness) with the Illinois and Mississippi rivers as its lifeline and the Gulf of Mexico as its opening on the world.

Had La Salle's magnificent dream been realized, his colony on the Gulf would have been under constant threat from the Spanish to the west, and indeed, Spanish exploration from Mexico eastward through Texas in 1689–1690 was motivated by fear of La Salle's settlement, as the colonization of California in the eighteenth century was motivated by fear of Russian incursions from the north. Empire went to those who got there first and backed their claims with force. Consider La Salle. With that European arrogance which was so innocent it is almost charming, he stopped his canoes at the mouth of the Arkansas in 1682 and took formal possession of the land he named Louisiana in honor of Louis XIV. "On that day," Parkman says, "the realm of France received on parchment a stupendous accession. The fertile plains of Texas; the vast basin of the Mississippi, from its frozen northern springs to the sultry borders of the Gulf; from the woody ridges of the Alleghenies to the peaks of the Rocky Mountains—a region of savannas and forests, sun-cracked deserts, and grassy prairies, watered by a thousand rivers, ranged by a thousand warlike tribes, passed beneath the sceptre of the Sultan of Versailles; and all by virtue of a feeble human voice, inaudible at half a mile."

In nothing was the New World more fabulous than in the justifications Europe found for seizing it—a foot on a strange shore, a boat in a river mouth, a proclamation to wondering Indians, a brass plate, a planted cross. But the dubiousness of imperial "rights" did not make the conflict less bitter. After a century of border wars, France lost Canada to the British on the Plains of Abraham in 1759. The British lost their thirteen American colonies to the rebellious colonists in the Revolution. Louisiana, tossed back and forth between Spain and France, was finally sold to the Americans by an overextended Napoleon Bonaparte for $15 million in 1803, and France was out of the North American competition. Within two years, Lewis and Clark had carried the Americans to the Oregon coast—claimed by America because Captain Gray had taken his ship *Columbia* over the bar into an unknown river for a quick peek in 1792. Manifest Destiny was born of the westward pressures, and clashed with the Spanish in Texas, the British in Oregon, until in 1846, which DeVoto called the Year of Decision, geopolitics operating from the heartland forced out both empires, and the republic consolidated itself from sea to sea.

Any schoolchild now can draw with his eyes shut the familiar shield-shaped map of the nation, but the map itself was the product of recurrent wars, and the jolts and consolidations reflected in a dozen treaties. The Treaty of Paris in 1783 began it, the Louisiana Purchase vastly enlarged it, the Convention of London clarified its northern boundary in 1818. The 1819 treaty with Spain, almost at gun point, defined the western limits of the Louisiana Purchase and relieved Spain of Florida and all the West Coast above 42° north latitude. The Webster-Ashburton Treaty of 1842 adjusted the border between Maine and Canada, and the annexation of Texas in 1845 made official what had been inevitable ever since Texas won its independence from Mexico in 1836. The Oregon Treaty of 1846 settled the long and rancorous dispute with Great Britain over the boundary between the crest of the Rockies and the Pacific, and in the same year war with Mexico effectively eliminated all remaining outposts of the old Spanish empire north of the Rio Grande. The Treaty of Guadalupe Hidalgo and its trailer, the Gadsden Purchase, completed us a continental nation and ended our first long phase.

In the extended effort that led to independence, unification, and completion, most of the myths melted away. California's Amazons receded back into the romance from which they had sprung. Cíbola and Quivira, the Fountain of Youth and the Rio Buenaventura, faded out in the daylight of observation. Such animals as Vizcaíno's men saw on Monterey Bay, with wool that dragged on the ground and horns three yards long, shrank and reshaped themselves into tule elk. But realistic wonders remained, a continent whose riches even by 1846 had been barely touched and only partially discovered. Already penetrated, not quite so vaguely realizing westward as it once had, possessed America lay ready not for *them,* Europeans, but for *us,* Americans, molded by generations of adaptation to successive frontiers, with our unchastened hope and greed and our barely formed responsibility, our democracy and our capitalism and our growing technical knowhow, all products of the frontier; with our gospel of work, our individualism and independence and self-reliance, likewise born of the frontier and the long boom it fostered; and with our carelessness born of plenty, our wastefulness that, once we were past the first stage of settlement, had never known shortage.

The people who inherited the United States in the mid-nineteenth century were as unstoried, artless, and unenhanced as the land of their inheritance, midway between a Europe that had not died in them and an America that was not yet born. But they had already begun to try to answer the question Crèvecoeur had asked before the Revolution: "Who is the American, this new man?"

In a little more than a generation after 1846, Henry James would paint his portrait, significantly naming him Christopher Newman, and combining in him a history of past ruthlessness and an abiding innocence and basic decency. Mark Twain would do his portrait in one-gallus frontier terms as Huckleberry Finn, the quintessential American orphan; and Abraham Lincoln would have embodied his highest virtues on such a grand scale that he would thereafter sit like a demigod above our national life. But no sooner had those trial syntheses been realized than new waves of immigration, drawn by New World opportunity and hope, flooded the nation with new seekers, new races and cultures, new types, and old old memories, postponing a new and higher synthesis, a final consolidation of the American character, into the twenty-first century and beyond.

It has taken a long time. We are older than we think. The four hundredth anniversary of Coronado's grandiose raid passed in 1940. The four hundredth anniversary of the founding of our oldest city, St. Augustine, passed in 1965. In 1992 it will be half a millennium since Columbus and his sailors crowded to the rail to stare at a dark ambiguous shoreline and sniff the fragrant breeze off a new world.

And the continent itself? What we have done to it in nearly five centuries of exploration, raid, settlement, and accommodation—and what it has done to us—is, in its way, a story mad with the impossible. But it is no fairy story. Nor is it finished.

Because we live by human time, and have to measure eternity with foot rulers, the continent we know seems to be the same one that Europeans began exploring in the early sixteenth century. Change may be the law of the universe, but some kinds of change are too slow to be detected in a human lifetime, or even in the lifetime of a nation or a civilization. Even the works of man, Ozymandias to the contrary notwithstanding, can seem eternal. Luxor and Baalbek oppress us with their antiquity; and Josiah Royce has testified that as a boy in the raw California mining camp of Grass Valley he thought the crumbling cabins he saw around him, none of them more than two decades old, must have been there forever.

If things built by human hands can seem nearly eternal, how shall we perceive the changes in the solid earth? We lift up our eyes unto the hills, whence cometh our help. We are reduced to awe by the incessant unchanging sea. John Gould Fletcher, viewing the Grand Canyon of the Colorado, summed it up in a phrase: "It is finished."

He couldn't have been further wrong. If all flesh is as grass, then all rock is as flesh. For all its apparent solidity, it can disintegrate, flow like oil, rise up, sink down, be folded like ribbon candy. Nature abhors an elevation as surely as it abhors a vacuum. The rivers war with the mountains, the ocean with the coasts; continents and sea floors break up and float and are jammed together like ice pans in a spring river. North America and Europe, once joined as part of the ancestral continent Pangaea, drift apart at a rate of 2 or 2.5 centimeters a year. The facing coasts of South America and Africa still plainly retain the curves of the seam where they were parted. The east coast of North America sinks, the west coast rises. With periodic jolts and earthquake shocks, the Pacific plate grinds northward past the North American plate. In 1857, when the San Andreas fault slipped drastically, it moved thirty feet in one bound. Wait long enough, and Los Angeles will be a suburb of Anchorage.

Even the sea, short of the stars our most persuasive image of the eternal, is fickle and fluctuant. Four times during the Pleistocene epoch, water falling as snow was held back and gathered up in continental ice sheets, and the locking-up of so large an amount of the earth's water lowered the sea level substantially, perhaps as much as 300 feet. Shorelines were extended. The moving ice reshaped the land, grinding down elevations and gouging out canyons and carrying along masses of boulders, gravel, and dirt. When it reached its limit and began to recede during a period of warmer climate, it dropped its carried material as moraines, drumlins, and till, and as it melted back along its course it left finger lakes, as in upstate New York, and kettle lakes, as in Wisconsin, and U-shaped canyons, as in Crawford Notch in the White Mountains. Some of the land once depressed by the weight of the ice rose again when the weight was removed. Near Vancouver it has risen 750 feet since the last Ice Age, ten thousand years ago. Around Hudson Bay it has risen several feet in the last few hundred years.

As for the Grand Canyon that Fletcher called finished, it is still in vigorous youth. The river is still cutting its canyon, or would be if we had not damned it and its tributaries. From all the country through which the canyon is carved, once sea bottom on which were deposited two miles or so of sedimentary strata, thousands of feet of solid rock have been worn away by water and wind. Most of the resulting sand and silt have been carried into the Colorado, and dumped by the Colorado at the head of the Gulf of California.

From the canyon's north rim, at Bright Angel, the country is stepped back like a giant tilted stairway, the Vermilion Cliffs about fifty miles back, the White Cliffs ten or fifteen miles farther, the Pink Cliffs ten or fifteen miles farther yet. They are the retreating edges of the strata that once stretched unbroken across the whole region. Except for some residual cameo buttes in the Kanab Desert, between the Vermilion Cliffs and the Kaibab Plateau, those strata are gone, clear to the cliff edges. Off in Monument Valley, to the eastward, spires and buttes stand a thousand feet and more above the red sand plain, the remnants of an almost completely dissected plateau. The Robbers' Roost country in the San Rafael Swell is the remains of a similarly dissected dome.

So it isn't quite the same continent that it was in 1500. Its eastern coast is thirty feet or so farther from Europe, its western edge has slipped almost ninety feet toward Alaska. The volcanoes of the Cascade Range have changed shape and size, and altered the country below them with ash and lava. Along the margins of Virginia, the Carolinas, and Georgia, and on the Gulf Coast, the sea has been busy tearing out, rebuilding, and rearranging the sandspits and barrier islands. Rivers have cut their channels a centimeter or an inch or six inches deeper, the Mississippi, Colorado, and Rio Grande have spread their great deltas wider, the cliffs of the plateau province have retreated (at Bryce Canyon the recession has been measured at one foot - every fifty years—nearly nine feet since Cárdenas and his men first peered into the Grand Canyon in 1540). Along the edges of the Great Basin ranges, the alluvial fans have gone a foot or two on their way toward burying the mountains themselves. Great Salt Lake has risen and fallen through several cycles. The

Appalachians, worn stumps of ancient rock, all that is left of mountains once higher than the Himalayas, have been leveled a millimeter or two closer to peneplain. On the other side of the continent, the Santa Cruz Mountains south of San Francisco have warped themselves several inches higher above the narrow Pacific littoral.

None of this except possibly the deltaic buildup of the great silt-bearing rivers and the volcanic changes in the Cascades would be noticeable to the most observant eye. If we set out to circumnavigate the United States, or cross it east-west or north-south, we will see the same basic continent that the first explorers saw. Starting from the northeast corner, at West Quoddy Head, Maine, we will sail down a coast whose physical outlines have not changed perceptibly since Leif Ericson's time. There are the same drowned river mouths, the same rocky headlands enclosing coves and inlets and snug little havens and harbors. There are the same islands. Reaching off eastward is the submerged continental shelf whose rich fishing banks lured Breton and Irish fishermen from earliest times, and lure Russian trawlers and factory ships now.

Down the coast, Cape Cod, the outer islands, and Long Island are just where the last ice sheet laid them when the continental shelf was exposed by the lowered sea level. All down the inland waterway, rivers from one side and the sea from the other are still working to fill in estuaries and lagoons. Off Key West, colonies of mangroves, seagoing shrubs, are anchoring themselves, becoming islands, attracting soil and sea birds, dying of an overdose of guano, and sending off floating branches to establish new islands. The flat Gulf light still glares with marine mirages, the shoals that betrayed La Salle's careless ships look the same to the eye, however they may look on the charts. Matagorda and Padre Islands screen the Texas shore, curving - toward Mexico.

At Brownsville we begin a two-thousand-mile portage up the Rio Grande—Laredo, Eagle Pass, Del Rio, the stone trough of Big Bend, and on to El Paso where Oñate's settlers crossed into New Mexico in 1597. As along the coast, it is necessary to wear blinders to screen out human installations, but out of the corner of the eye it is the country the Spaniards knew, especially through the ocotillo and saguaro desert from Nogales to Yuma at the mouth of the Gila. In some places, say around Sasabe south of Tucson, it can hardly be distinguished from what Castañeda and Father Kino saw.

The bays and beaches and bold headlands of the Pacific coast are where Cabrillo and Vizcaíno found them. The Channel Islands, mountaintops rising from the sea, still curve alongshore from San Diego to Santa Barbara. The surf is still fierce on Point Conception, which Cabrillo had great trouble rounding. The Santa Lucia Mountains are still, as in Cabrillo's time, "mountains which reach to the sky, and the sea beats upon them. When sailing along near the land, it seems as if the mountains would fall on the ships."

We probably miss the Golden Gate, buried in fog; we may strain our eyes past surf and sea stack searching for some Straits of Anian northward. The Oregon coast is wild and rugged and thinly peopled, the Olympic Peninsula comes grandly down to the sea, clothed in rain forest, and all the islands of the San Juans are exactly where Juan de Fuca first saw them, if he ever did.

After 1,888 miles of Atlantic Coast, 1,659 of Gulf coast, 2,013 of Mexican border, 1,293 of Pacific Coast, there still remain, of America's circumference, 3,987 miles of Canadian border: first the mountains through which Alexander Mackenzie found his way, then the plains dropping in three broad prairie steppes, patterned with dendritic rivers. From Lake of the Woods we follow the old fur route backward down Lake Superior to the Sault, but instead of pursuing the oldest route of continental penetration by Georgian Bay, the Nipissing, and the Ottawa, we go down Lake Huron to the straits at Detroit, through Lake Erie, and down the Niagara past the falls. (The falls have receded somewhat since Hennepin first visited them, because of the undercutting and collapse of the shelf over which they pour, but the eye will not detect the change.) The Niagara takes us into Lake Ontario, and Ontario into the St. Lawrence, whose man-improved seaway would lead us to the

Atlantic if we were not committed to following the border. As it is, we bend north where the St. Lawrence cuts the 45th parallel, and go clear to the St. John River before swinging south again to Eastport and West Quoddy Head, where we began.

Apart from the St. Lawrence, the Hudson is the only eastern river that leads far into the interior. All other routes mean a crossing of mountains. Low as they are relative to the Rockies, the eastern ranges are every bit as effective a drainage divide. From the swamps of the coastal plain, where moss-hung cypresses lift above their bracing knees and the eyebumps of alligators float motionless on motionless black water, the parallel rivers lead westward only a little way—past the fall line, through an occasional opening such as the Delaware Water Gap, into the forested mountains blooming in spring with azaleas and rhododendrons, and up to the divide. There they stop, as according to the Quebec Acts American settlers were supposed to but did not. As we do, they went on down the streams that flow westward into the Ohio and thence into the Mississippi.

Or, more properly, the Missouri. If the historic direction of settlement had been west to east instead of east to west, we would probably be calling the great concave of the continent the Missouri Valley, not the Mississippi Valley, and would recognize both the Mississippi and the Ohio as tributaries of the Missouri, which is the longest river on the continent and one of the longest in the world, and which below the junction completely converts the placid Mississippi to its own wild ways.

Whatever we call it, the great central basin is awesome in its size and simplicity. Hung like a hammock between the eastern mountains and the Rockies, it compels unity as the upthrust alpine center of Europe enforces multiplicity. Eastward it is rolling, fertile country, well watered, once covered with the greatest broad-leafed forests on earth. Westward, toward the Missouri, it flattens, grows more arid, begins to lose its tree cover, until about a third of the way across the Dakotas, Nebraska, and Kansas it reaches the almost mystical line beyond which the annual rainfall is less than twenty inches. From there, about the 98th meridian of west longitude, the short-grass plains begin, apparently almost flat, actually sloping steadily upward, rising nearly three thousand feet between the Missouri and the mountains. This is semi-arid steppe, Dust Bowl country in bad years. It lies in the rain shadow of the Rockies. It is where the West begins. Narrower to the north, wider to the south, that "long hill" of the plains was laid down by swinging rivers such as the Missouri and the Platte. It is a country that strains the eyes and hazes the mind with its distances, a country of big weathers, big sky, exposure without hiding places. It sweeps from southern Saskatchewan to the Staked Plains of Texas, and was once, when it was full of buffalo and the horse Indians who hunted them, the most romantic country on earth.

The Rockies are not one range of mountains, but many interlocking ranges, part of the system that extends from Alaska to Tierra del Fuego. At their broadest, about on the line between Denver and Salt Lake City, they are five hundred miles across. At their southwestern edge they give way to plateaus, and their whole western edge is desert. To the north are the lava deserts of the Snake River plain and the Columbia Plateau, in the middle is the Great Basin with its twisted worn ranges and its dead lake bottoms paved with salt, to the south are the Mojave and the Colorado deserts. As the high plains lie in the rain shadow of the Rockies, the desert basins lie in the rain shadow of the Cascades and the Sierra. Beyond those lies a milder country, watered by Pacific rains and by the rivers that flow westward from the mountains. And at the very rim, last wrinkle in the continental crust, scenic overlook for the last American sunsets, the Coast Ranges stand with their feet in the surf.

On this incomparable continent, unmatched for its variety, soils, resources, and climate, a free people—well, partly free, and trying—have built a nation of 220 million. In our youth as a nation, the habitat was a boast second only to our free institutions, which indeed were derived from it. We loved its rocks and rills, its woods and templed hills. We called it beautiful for spacious skies, for amber waves of grain, for purple mountain majesties. We wrote epics about Niagara Falls. We compared our bountiful continent with Europe, to Europe's disparagement, and our freedom with Europe's enslavement, and our fresh clean start with Europe's suppression by the dead hand of the past. We aspired to crown the republic's good with brotherhood from sea to shining sea.

These are soberer times. What a young American just coming of age confronts now is not a limitless potential, but developed power attended by destruction and depletion. Though we should have recognized the land as a living organism demanding care and stewardship, we have treated it as a warehouse, and now it is a warehouse half emptied. In the centuries of our occupation we have altered the continent immeasurably more than geological forces have. It was bad farming methods, in a country of steep hills and torrential rains, that started the reduction of Appalachia to the sterile clay. It was strip mining for coal that completed what was already begun a hundred and fifty years ago, when Audubon found refugees from West Virginia squatting in the Mississippi River bottoms. The mountains of the Mesabi Range, at Butte and Bingham Canyon, and the plains in the vicinity of Colstrip and Decker have been more changed by human means than any mountain, except perhaps Mt. St. Helens, by any geological force whatever. We have done more damage to the fragile California deserts with off-road vehicles and motorcycle rallies than wind and rain - could have done in five hundred years. When he is after something that he thinks the earth contains—gold, coal, oil, or recreation—the average American moves like a maniac with an ax in one hand and a blowtorch in the other. When he uses a river or lake or marsh or dry coulee as a dump for something he doesn't otherwise know how to get rid of, he can create in a few years, as in the Love Canal, a hazard that may not be cleaned up for generations.

This in spite of the fact that to all intents and purposes America is an incredible success story. Jefferson, flown over the Mississippi Valley above those squares and rectangles of corn, soybeans, winter wheat, and other crops, would be exhilarated at what the American yeoman farmer (or his factories-in-the-field surrogate) has accomplished. Coming to the dry country beyond the Missouri, he would be thrilled, probably, at the lakes that have been made out of rivers, and at the circles that center-pivot irrigation has scribed in green within the square section lines. Just as surely, Alexander Hamilton would think his vision fulfilled in the industrial complexes of Gary and Detroit and Pittsburgh and Youngstown. There is infinite power, infinite productivity, exposed at every mile of a crossing of America. The open question is consequences.

There have always been good stewards in America. Jefferson and John Bartram were both husbandmen in the very best sense, as was Crèvecoeur, and they have had distinguished successors. Some environmentalists have been sentimental, as was G. P. Morris, who wrote "Woodman, spare that tree!," and Gene Stratton Porter, who wrote nature novels about a place called Limberlost. But some have been as hard-headed and scientifically austere as George Perkins Marsh, John Wesley Powell, or Aldo Leopold, and these are the true inheritors of Bartram and Jefferson, the men upon whose teaching and example the future had better build if there is going to *be* much of a future.

Emancipated from history and therefore from forethought, repudiating tradition and social memory along with the ancient tyrannies of the Old World, experimenting with freedom in increasingly anarchic and eccentric ways, this society has worked miracles and at the same time been as greedy and destructive as a hoodlum gang in a liquor store. Given the freedom we have learned and grown used to, there is no external control that is ever going to restrain us and teach us civilization. Nor should there be. The challenge of the New World is still there: to demonstrate that without tyranny and constant policing, this society still in its destructive infancy can learn from its mistakes and profit from its good luck and grow by its own developing tradition. Not only in national parks and wilderness areas but in those private lands where the owner can do about as he pleases, we may please to hold our hands, learn restraint, renounce short-term profit in favor of long-term health. That way, we have a future. The old way, we have only a past, and not a very long one as nations go.

THE NORTHEAST KINGDOM

The first of our procession of four cars turns left at the one-room school beyond Shatney's, and eases out on the track to Long Pond. The second and third cars follow it into the woods, but I stop for a minute to look down the road that continues past the school. It is a road I know; it runs through years of my life. For a half dozen summers in the 1940s we lived in the last inhabited house on it. I follow it in my mind past the next farm—the last operative one, whose housewife used to scuttle for the house when our approaching car caught her at the mailbox; past the abandoned black-silver shell just beyond, across whose windows our late lights used to slide with a furtive, greasy gleam; past two more abandoned places, in our time briefly inhabited by families who stuffed the broken windows with rags, and whose Indian-wild boys prowled the woods carrying an old broken-stocked .22 mended with friction tape; past the entrance to our own place, now surely overgrown; over the hill past another dead farmhouse among gnarled and weather-broken apple trees, and so on down to join Highway 16 at the head of Runaway Pond.

It is a road of failed effort, of lonely, hard, stubborn labor defeated and beaten back. They first cut this track through the timber at the end of the eighteenth century. In 1810 it saw one of the spectacular events of Vermont history, when Aaron Wilson's attempt to improve his millrace by deepening the outlet of Long Pond (not the one we are headed for now, but another of the same name) struck quicksand, and the whole pond emptied itself in one roaring rush through the village of Glover.

Hardly anyone uses the road now. Beyond this point, farms

that produced wool and mutton during the Civil War, and wheat during World War I, and milk after that, have been quietly returning to woods since the 1930s. The last time I visited our own place, I could hardly get to the old foundations for the rose bushes, heliotrope, goldenglow, lilacs, and Virginia creeper, all gone rank and wild; and in the raspberry patch where the barn used to be I came upon bear dung still smoking.

The day is balmy, the breeze fitful and soft; shadows of fair-weather clouds darken me and pass on. It is the kind of day I remember best from our summers here, the high blue weather full of earth smells and grass smells, the dew still glittering off daisies and paintbrush and buttercups and bending grass, the sweet tang of wild strawberries on the tongue, and the expansive sense of work to be done, things to be built. I remember the nights, too: how we used to squirt a flashlight beam out our gable window and pan it slowly around the blackness of surrounding woods, and pick up the eyes—a pair here, a pair there, green, golden, waiting. There never was a darkness more impenetrable, a wildness more patient.

I see that Shatney has planted hybrid corn and built a silo, and has supplemented his big herd of Ayrshires with some red, shaggy, fierce-horned Highland cattle. But his farm lies as it used to lie under the light fingering wind, one of those rocky hill farms of which it is said the Devil emptied his apron into their pastures.

Shatney makes it because of the hard diligence, the capacity for work, that he shares with his whole culture. His cattle are prize cattle, despite the Highlanders' look of belonging outside a Cro-Magnon cave. The pile of pulp along the Long Pond road tells me that the year-round routines go on: haying in summer (I can hear the tractor down in the field that slopes - toward the Lamoille), plowing and liming and manuring and seeding in late summer, pulp-making and wood-making in the fall and winter, sugaring in March, fence-mending on odd days or when the heifers break out, the milking of up to a hundred cows night and morning throughout the year. He lives close to the earth, uses it, understands it, is bound to it. He looks after his land and makes it yield him hay, fodder, garden stuff, milk, maple sugar, sawlogs, and pulp. Like all his neighbors he is an implacable hunter and trapper, hard on the wildlife, but he keeps his land healthy. It is the people in the last stages of un-success who are hard on the land, who log off their sugarbush and skin off the softwood down to the last six-inch balsam and then disappear, abandoning the wreckage to the bank, which will eventually dispose of it to some paper company willing to wait thirty years for a return, or to a summer person who asks no usufruct from his acres and lets them grow up in brush, or, more recently, to a speculator who will hold his open space against the inevitable rise in value.

I cramp the wheels and turn in along Carroll Shatney's pulp pile and follow the others into the woods. A mile or so in, I come up with them where they have been stopped by an im-passable bog hole. We string out along the trail under the bro-ken shade, the women and children bright as butterflies, the men camouflaged in khaki and green.

A generation ago a group like this would have been less likely, though not impossible. There are Hub Vogelman, professor of botany at the University of Vermont and the state representative of Nature Conservancy, and his wife Marie. There are Lewis Hill and his wife Nancy, native Vermonters who run a nursery specializing in plants and trees adapted to this northern climate. There are a half dozen of us, both Vermonters and summer - people, who are interested in the purpose of this excursion, which is to see if Nature Conservancy may want to start a pre-serve in the Gray family's property on Long Pond. And there is a considerable delegation of Grays, two generations of them, who have already given one of Vermont's two Conservancy pre-serves, that on Barr Hill above the town of Greensboro.

The road runs deep in trees, brush, and ferns. Shatney's log-ging has left stumps and slash, but his cutting has been selective, and in this climate the slash will quickly rot and the clearings will spring up in dense hardwood seedlings. This country *wants* to be trees; it is clearings that are hard to maintain. Lewis Hill tells us that when his great-grandparents came here in 1791 the land was all deep woods. Ninety years later, in his grandparents' time, 80 percent of it was cleared and growing crops, and the wildlife had been cleansed out so thoroughly that they saw nothing but an occasional woodchuck. Deer in the 1880s were extinct in Vermont, and only a planting and a long closed season brought them back. Now, ninety-odd years later, 80 percent of this land is woods, not fields, and deer, bear, foxes, coyotes, porcupines, beaver, fishers, skunks, and raccoons have come back to inherit the restored wild. A few years ago a moose came down from somewhere and grazed among the cows at the edge of East Hardwick. As for the deer, Lewis has given up on them. He grows such succulent goodies in his nursery that ten-foot fences, all-night vigils, dogs, and the enlistment of neighbors hungry for doeburgers are all unavailing. He plants an extra share for the wildlife.

We walk in dappled greenish forest shade. The air smells of mold, damp, fungi. Except for the rutted road, which once led to the Rutledge farm, the woods might be primeval, though in the virgin forest the trees were surely bigger, and included white pine, now almost eliminated by cutting and blister rust. Once, those white pines would have matched well with western trees. In one of Robert Frost's Vermont houses, the one in Concord Corner, there used to be a wainscot made of a single pine board nearly four feet wide. There are no such trees any more. The biggest I see are some yellow birch perhaps sixteen inches in diameter.

Nevertheless, the *feel* of this wood is wilderness. There is no sound of chain saw, tractor, car, or airplane, nothing but the buzzing of flies in sunny openings, the quick light voices of children, the murmur of Hub Vogelman or Lewis Hill identifying plants we ask about. And far off in the woods, the pipe of a white-throated sparrow advising his farmer friend to "Sow wheat, Peabody, Peabody, Peabody . . ."

The trees of this mixed northern forest we all know—sugar and swamp maple, yellow and gray and white birch, beech, wild cherry, elm (the old ones all dead), white ash; and white and black spruce, balsam fir, hemlock, hackmatack, aspen, basswood, white cedar in the swampy places. A rich variety, each with its own color and smell and way of growing. You can tell what you are walking under by the shape of the flakes of sun the leaves let through.

We know the commonest ferns—Christmas, cinnamon, interrupted, hay-scented, sensitive, but we need the experts to identify New York fern with its evenly diminishing fronds down the stem, Long Beach fern with its walrus mustaches at the base, polypodies that grow only around or on granite boulders dropped by the ice sheet. We know raspberry, gooseberry, wood sorrel, trillium; but we have to be instructed in bunchberry, with its small red clusters; and Indian pipe, whose white fleshy pipes turn black after being picked; and creeping snowberry with its tiny laddered leaves and tiny white berries and its smell like wintergreen; and baneberry, whose poisonous white berries, Vogelman says, the Indians used to mash up with jack-in-the-pulpit and throw into lakes to stun the fish. All around the Blueberry Rocks, on the east shore of the pond but not within the Gray land, we find mountain holly hanging its red berries over the granite.

From Blueberry Rocks we see only wildness. Not a human habitation, not a road or pole line, not a mark of man's passing. Sunk in its pocket among the hills, this warm, shallow lake, lightly riffling from our cedar shore to the spruce-and-fir shore opposite, has watched humanity go by, and recovered from the visit.

Once a carriage road ran through Skunk Hollow, on the other side. It is overwhelmed by trees now; the only way to walk it is to walk with an aerial photograph in hand, guiding oneself by the slight streak that the air view shows, and by the stone walls that appear and disappear in thick woods. Once the hayfields of the Rutledge place sloped to the water's edge on the north shore. Now, Clive Gray tells me, the Rutledge place is swallowed up like Tikal, and so is the shack that a local minister used to maintain on the northwest shore. Clive is not sure he could find the site of either any more.

This is hard to believe. Thirty-five years ago, when we brought a friend here, hunting a summer place, the Rutledge farm was a big, well-built farmhouse on hewn granite foundations, its windows unbroken, its rooms as clean as if the Rutledges had moved out only the week before. But it was remote, at the end of a road that could not be kept open in winter, and our friend did not buy it. Some years later someone else did, and turned it into the Tamarack Ranch, a resort camp which failed. Now, neglected for more than a decade, it is gone. Its stone walls are hedgerows of chokecherry and mountain ash, and its hayfields are full of Christmas trees.

For years there has been hardly any human activity on Long Pond except some summer camping permitted by the principal landowners, the Igleheart-Merrill-Freeman family. The special spot on the south shore where many of us have taken first our children and then our grandchildren to camp out and catch a boatload of perch and sunfish, is a precarious beachhead only. Left unvisited even for a year or two, that campsite would disappear in the woods, and the road in would become like the Skunk Hollow road, detectible only from the air. What we look out at from Blueberry Rocks is a home for loon and beaver, as lonely a pond as Rogers' Rangers ever camped by on their desperate return from the St. Francis villages in 1759.

Less than two hundred years from wilderness to wilderness. And this is Orleans County, where farming is still a solid way of life, one of the highest milk-producing counties in the state. In Caledonia County there are places wilder than this. In Essex County nearly everything is as wild as this. In Essex County, much of which was never farmed, but only logged, the population after two centuries of settlement is still less than ten to the square mile. Essex County contains towns like Averill, chartered as early as 1762, which have never been organized as towns, and have fewer than two dozen residents. It contains towns like Brunswick and Ferdinand, with neither church nor store. It contains towns like Avery's Gore and Lewis, with no public roads and no known residents. Opened only after the ending of the French and Indian War made it safe, and settled only after the Revolution, this Northeast Kingdom was born of our post-revolutionary frontiering, contemporary with the migration into Kentucky. Manifest Destiny came north as early as it went west. History touched these wild woods early, struggled for a time against weather and loneliness and hardship, and eventually either hung on in stalemate or withdrew.

As ontogeny repeats phylogeny, our family experience repro-
duced the history of the generations before us. We put a lot of
work into our backwoods place, and in the end were forced
closer in, to a friendlier location. What was once a farm is now
a woodlot, what was once a house is an overgrown cellar, what
was once a meadow is a plantation of red pines, many of them
killed or deformed by the hedgehogs. The memories of our
summers on the back road are lost with the memories of Orange King, the previous owner, whoever he was. We heard that
he once grew wheat there, and in his spare time manufactured
out of cedar or white pine the sap buckets and butter firkins
that have since been replaced by metal.

Once, prowling the dense woods a half mile back from the
house, we came upon the old sugarhouse, collapsing, dim, a
cathedral for chipmunks and white-footed mice. Stacked beyond the rusting pan and scattered woodpile were six or seven
dozen wooden sap buckets bound with wythes, the kind that
now excites women on the lawns of country churches where
antiques are auctioned off. They go with hand-hewn beams
and hand-wrought square-headed nails to give a touch of au-
thenticity to electrically heated, wall-to-wall carpeted summer
homes. We took out four, all we could conveniently carry, to
use as wastebaskets. That summer we didn't get back to that
secret silvery high-roofed cathedral in the woods. When we
tried the next summer, we couldn't find it.

So much for Orange King, whoever he. So much for Mary
and Page and Wallace Stegner, whoever they. As for our own
Mud Pond, one of at least a dozen Vermont ponds by that
name, a hushed and hidden patch of water where Page and I
went a few times to fish for chubs and watch the great blue
herons wade the shallows with their spears poised—Mud Pond
is going too. It is eutrophic, a body of water on its way to becoming a swamp and then a meadow. Below it the returning
beaver have dammed the brook and killed several acres of timber, creating such an impassable bog that you would have to be
a mink to get through it.

This reclamation, unlike the human kind that kills rivers to
create reservoirs, does not assert human purposes; it restores

natural processes. All through the three northeastern counties of Vermont, through our forty years' acquaintance with them and our many summers of living in one of them, we have watched the north woods working quietly and inexorably to reclaim themselves, or part of themselves.

History and culture are artifacts of different kinds. One does not necessarily imply the other. The culture may survive and flourish while history is all but lost. Verbalized as stories and ballads, people and their actions become legend, epic, and folklore. Frozen as records, they become history. Either way, if they happen to matter enough to a people, they may last as long as the language itself. But if they are never memorialized in language or monuments, they die with the heads that remembered them, they rot like a birch in wet woods, they sink into the ground. Vermont knows the history of its few great events, and has its folk heroes such as Ethan Allen and his Green Mountain Boys, and treasures its brief period as an independent republic. But the long stalemate with the woods that produced the Vermont culture has been largely taken for granted by the people who have inherited it, and its history is known only to the few.

Lewis and Nancy Hill, members of the county historical society, are among the few. They have an unending curiosity about their country and its life. They know, though many who live on it probably do not, that the road we came out from Greensboro on was once the Norton Road, the main thoroughfare north. They know that the land now belonging to Shatney was granted in 1790 to the first child born in Greensboro. They know when people first came into these woods— about the Bayley-Hazen Road that during the Revolution was cut from Newbury, Vermont, to just beyond Hazens Notch, under Jay Peak, to facilitate an invasion of Canada that never took place. They can trace the road, on the map or on the ground, up the Connecticut Valley to Barnet, across through Peacham, Danville, Walden, Hardwick, Greensboro, Craftsbury, and Albany. Their kind of people, with their kind of cultural self-consciousness, erected the monument on Hardwick Street, opposite the old Stage House whose secret chamber concealed refugees during the War of 1812 and runaway slaves before the Civil War; and the other monument on the west shore of Caspian Lake where Indians killed two young soldiers in 1781. The Hills can tell you how, when peace came in 1783, settlers found their way up the Bayley-Hazen Road and began the daunting job of hacking farms out of the forest. It is a source of pride to them that like the Wilderness Road across the Cumberland Gap into Kentucky, and like the Santa Fe and Oregon and California trails later, their ninety-two miles of forest track were a road of empire.

But even the Hills can tell us little about Orange King. Memory and hearsay take them back as far as their parents' or grandparents' generation, and then blur out. Human history in the Northeast Kingdom is largely lost because it attaches to no great name or great event. It is the collective history of nameless people who took more territory than they could hold and then gradually, generation by generation, had to give it back to the wilderness.

The process built the Vermont character and the Vermont countryside, both justly celebrated. It also left along the back roads, on the dying hill farms, back in the woods, a fringe of - people living below the poverty level, people with many skills and the toughness of badgers, but without the capital, luck, or ambition to get a start and hold it. They are not unlike the - people whom the California Gold Rush knew as Pikes, whom Bayard Taylor defined as "Anglo-Saxons relapsed into barbarism." They live by odd jobs, logging, hunting. Sometimes they are on the town, or on the state and federal welfare programs that, against the will of a lot of Vermonters, have replaced the town. Many of them, coming toward the end of a lifelong losing battle, are dignified, unself-pitying, as enduring as old roots. Some are defective or retarded, many are made lumpish by a bad diet. Some are simply independent, asserting what Frost called their God-given right to be good for nothing.

They are sly, ironic, humorous, watchful around summer - people, at ease only among themselves, sometimes violent, never servile. The necessity for making do has created a race as ingenious as Eskimos. They can toggle up anything, they know

machinery, animals, tools, the woods. At their worst they can
be Tobacco Road hoodlums like those who threw dead coons
on the porch of a black stranger in Irasburg. At their best,
among those they know and trust, they are neighborly, helpful,
and quite astonishingly tolerant of difference and eccentricity.
They judge a man primarily by how he works. And all of them
know who they are. The social commentators, usually outsiders, who point out that the whole Northeast Kingdom is
well below the state and national averages in income, and that
in Orleans County actual hunger exists, should probably work
to improve the statistics but spare their alarm. This is poverty
which has lost neither its independence nor its self-respect,
poverty that half the time doesn't even know it's poor.

Years ago, in company with Phil and Peg Gray, the parents
of the present generation of Grays, we used to take annual
walking trips with a packhorse, choosing the remotest back
roads we could find. In the Lowell Mountains, on the northernmost reach of the Hazen Road, we took refuge one rainy
night in 1939 in a farmer's haymow, and next morning had
breakfast with the farmer and his wife. Both were past eighty.
Their eight children had one by one gone downcountry to find
work. They now had no help, hired or otherwise. The old man
still milked twenty cows, by hand. The old woman kept up a
big garden, a flock of hens, a few geese and turkeys. Her cellar
was full of Mason jars of peas, beans, beets, corn, and apple-
sauce, its bins stocked with potatoes just dug and put down.
They were somewhat flustered to have company. The woman
reminded us of Mrs. Shatney, Carroll's mother, who used to
ambush us at the mailbox when she heard our car coming, and
hold us in talk for half an hour with her hands tucked in her
armpits.

We could detect no self-pity in what this old couple told us,
though we could see that their farm was the last kept-up place
on the road. Everything on the way in was ramshackle, beyond
them there was nothing but woods. Another year or two, until
the winters got too hard, and then they would have to sell if
they could, or simply move out if they couldn't. An auction to
dispose of the cows and the usable machinery, furniture, and

tools, and they would be in some home for the aged. The farm had been their life, they had made it with their bare hands. But no one would have known from their talk that they found it hard to have no sons or daughters who wanted it. They accepted and endured as they had always done.

That was one kind. Very different was the cracked old cackler who visited our camp on Zack Woods Pond and told us, among other things, that the fish were all drownding. So many camper women going in swimming nekkid that the fish got too stiff to swim.

The next year we walked from the valley of the Lamoille past South Maid Hill and around Wheelock Mountain. The road we walked had been a carriage road in 1911, when our USGS quadrangle was printed, but in places we had to hack a patch for the packhorse with machetes. It was three days before we met a living soul, and he was an old man with cataract-blue eyes who was living in his milk shed, his house and barn having burned, and getting into Lyndon every week or two by horse and buggy. He sold us—tried his best to give us—a mess of snap beans and sweet corn, and told us that in his boyhood it was common for people to drive the way we had come, and that in the fall parties used to go out by buggy or car to see the color.

About noon of the next day we had our second human contact, a man plowing with oxen and a bulltongue plow. He turned the plow on its side, left the oxen standing, and came hopping across the furrows, a man with a whiskery face and no teeth, his mouth a delighted black hole. "I God," he said, "I thought for sure you was a camel! I thought you was comin' right out of the Bible, God if I didn't!"

Now a woman came striding down from the house along the drive. She waved her arms as she came; she was saying something loud and unintelligible. The farmer stopped talking, an expression knowing and weary crossed his face, he sucked in his cheeks and closed his toothless gums together, wizening his whiskered jaws. On the other side from the approaching woman, his finger made a brief twirling gesture at his temple.

Then the woman was before us, vigorous, brown-legged,

considerably younger than he. She had eyes as quick as mice and as big as millwheels, and she too was fascinated by our horse, a superannuated Irish hunter seventeen hands high without his pack. The woman walked all around him twice, popping her lips like a fish. She spoke in a poetry and parable. "What is in the pack, a lifeless form? You will be left all forlorn. The French will show no mercy. What did they do in Twenty-two? Who'll be alive in Forty-five?"

She said a good deal more before the man took her by the elbow, and with a hand as firm as a tow-bar led her back to the house. He had offered us camping space in his lower meadow, by the brook, but we did not like the thought of being visited by that Cassandra, and though it was a hot, smothery day, and our legs were dead, we walked another three miles before we stopped.

As for the road we had walked over to make that contact, it was a road even further gone than the Norton Road. We had passed dead farms in clearings that were closing in from all sides. We had snooped through an abandoned one-room school and an abandoned church. We had come upon stone walls that appeared and disappeared in deep woods, with trees a foot in diameter growing out of the piled stones. We had paused in a lost cemetery, still surrounded by sagging barbed wire, its slate and granite and marble stones buried in blackberry vines, mullein, goldenrod, and milkweed. The earliest grave we found was 1812, the latest 1931. Only nine years ago the last burial had taken place there, the last farm had been closed up and left empty.

In August 1978, a friend and I took a walk in the first few miles of that same obliterated road. It is not as obliterated as it was forty years ago. A half mile off Highway 16 we passed a planting of red pine, planted since that trip in 1940 and now all dead of *Sclerorerris* canker: proof that man-made pure-stand forests are more vulnerable than the mixed forest nature developed for this country. One of the formerly abandoned farms was lived in by a family that gave off mixed signals. The mother sounded like pure backroads Vermont, the daughter in tight jeans and T-shirt might have been one of the city dropouts that have been flocking to these woods since the sixties. They said that grandpa and grandma were cutting and skidding tie-logs another mile in: that at least established them as Vermonters and not city folks.

We found grandpa and grandma logging—he riding the tractor, she walked behind to unhook the log chain and carry it, a seventy-pound iron python, back along their rutted skid road. They told us where the cemetery was, and we found it after struggling through a creation raspberry patch. Its feeling had not changed. The stones were even more overrun by brambles, milkweed, mullein, and goldenrod, and some cedars and firs had taken root and grown to ten or twelve feet. But the sky was blue overhead, the wind was hushed there in God's acre. My skin itched with spiderwebs and pollen, my hands smelled of raspberries. Off in the woods a wood thrush and a hermit thrush were competing, the wood thrust always beginning on the same note, the hermit starting anywhere on the scale he pleased. It seemed one of the pleasantest and most restful of all places in the world to be laid away, and it seemed to say what now we hear Long Pond saying—that people had come, and struggled for a while, and gone for good.

But the graveyard did not tell a completely true story, and Long Pond may not either. The insistent *memento mori,* the tale of human intrusion quietly leafed over, is not quite accurate. For one thing, that salty, well-matched, friendly pair snaking out poplar logs represented an activity that is going to go on indefinitely. Trees are what the country produces naturally, and trees are a cash crop. For another, look what had happened to the abandoned schoolhouse after forty or fifty years of abandonment. Its inside was now equipped with four double-decker bunks, a kitchen range, and a table. A sign on the door said "Island Pond Rest Center." What was that? A hippie pad? Mystery. Island Pond was miles away. And rest center for whom? Furthermore, there was the music we heard in the woods, music that did not come from thrushes either wood or hermit, or from Peabody birds, but from the Grateful Dead. Following it, we came to a geodesic dome half finished in a clearing, and near it a van parked under some trimmed-up spruces, with laundry inert on a length of wire.

Nature abhors a vacuum. Land relinquished to the wild, especially at a time when the wild is being overwhelmed in most parts of the continent, inevitably attracts seekers, as Orange King's abandoned farm attracted us in 1938. There is hardly an empty farmhouse in the Northeast Kingdom that has not been taken over and to some extent patched up and renovated. Up in Glover a whole community of Bread-and-Puppet young people create summer Happenings in a meadow for thousands of the bare-backed, barefooted, and long-haired, plus hundreds of the local curious. Their meadow during a performance is as colorful as the Field of the Cloth of Gold. And up at Norton, on the Canadian line in Essex County, is the Earth People's Park, eyed with suspicion by the local people and gingerly avoided by both American and Canadian authorities. By some variant of the Second Law of Thermodynamics, Vermont's returning wilderness is moved in on, even as it returns, by the restless energies of outsiders at odds with what the United States has become elsewhere. What has been happening throughout the emptier quarters of the West has been happening even more swiftly in Vermont—perhaps because Vermont is close to the great concentrations of people in the East Coast megalopolis, perhaps in part because it is convenient to an imperfectly patrolled international border.

Local people cannot say much good for the Earth People's Park except that it probably *started* all right, with draft evaders and flower children and somewhat dewy idealists—committed, it is true, to the drug culture, but as consumers, not pushers. Shortly, however, the park was moved in on by other kinds. That border has from its earliest beginnings had its share of illegal activities. Smugglers' Notch was not named out of mere whim; and during Prohibition Bernard DeVoto, who summered for a couple of years on Lake Seymour, near Morgan Center, made a reputation as a host at Harvard because he happened to know a Vermont farmer with a sugarbush that merged with the Canadian woods. The officials at the Derby Line port of entry now report a considerable monthly haul of drugs and illegal aliens, and they assume that their haul is only a fraction of what gets away.

But the Earth People's Park has shown signs of growing ugly In the 1960s a literary friend saw signs clear down in Mexico: "Trouble with the law? Draft Board after you? Being hassled by the old lady? Come to Earth People's Park, Norton, Vermont." Some saw in that invitation exactly what they were looking for, and in recent years the People's Park has got a reputation as a dangerous place. Some of its residents are reputed to go armed. There have been confrontations and clashes between Earth People and the farmers of Norton. Increases in crime in the region are commonly laid to that dropout heaven. It is the Missouri Breaks of the Northeast Kingdom, and though there are surely some perfectly ordinary and harmless - people there, there seem to be enough hard cases to damage the reputation of the whole place.

The usual back-road immigrants, however, the young people whom Lewis and Nancy Hill call "homesteaders," are another matter. A lot of them are well educated, many of them have trust funds, or families who will supply what Vermont's niggardly woods and fields fail to. They often work their heads off, they are full of idealism and enthusiasm, they are readers and students of history, they make good winter company. Being year-round residents, they instantly acquire a respectability in Vermont eyes that no summer person can expect: it is people who are up to staying past Labor Day who get inside a Vermonter's wariness. As year-round residents, too, they can vote in town meetings in March, and many a town meeting has recently been stirred up in ways it has not known for generations.

Finally, they are Earth People, at least as authentic as any in Norton's park. They are children of the sixties and the first Earth Year. They care about the environment, and know something about it, and they are becoming a force behind Vermont's increasingly enlightened land-use laws. They are against billboards, shopping centers, motorboats, unselective logging, and the smoke and rats of unsanitary landfills. They make the shut-in winters livelier, they reintroduce the notes of hope and growth.

And it is easy to tell the real ones from the imitations. The imitations run around all summer in their vans, undressing on the public beaches and offending the godly with their promiscuity and idleness. The real ones probably live by couples, whether legally married or not, and work, and listen, and learn. The real ones are not caught, some early October morning, with cracks in their houses, no storm doors or windows, no insulation, no bank of brush or tarpaper around their foundations, and a winter woodpile that will last till Thanksgiving. The real ones don't appear barefooted, bare-assed, and shivering in Willeys' store on the morning after the first freeze, frantically looking for shoes and socks and long underwear. The real ones are not grasshoppers but ants, and they are likely to have a part in the future of the state. The real ones don't buy steaks with food stamps, or sell food stamps at a discount to buy beer.

Vermont is a great character mill, and it grinds exceeding fine. It is too rough a country for pretenders, but it will make room for anyone, however odd, if he doesn't put on airs or show himself incompetent or think himself above the homespun and the calluses and the hard-mouthed virtues that Vermonters have come to the hard way, and don't intend to lose.

As for Long Pond, which we have all but forgotten, it may or may not remain dedicated to its natural processes as quasi-wilderness. There are boundary problems; other landowners have differing aspirations for their pieces of shoreline. The next generation may find the pond's future still hanging in the balance.

But I take it as a good omen that many people of many kinds want to see the pond preserved as a natural treasure. The Igleheart clan, "immigrants" of some twenty-five years' standing, successively dairy farmers and then builders, have large holdings on or near the pond as the result of a generation's hard work. They have shown a reluctance to develop in any way that will damage the pond. The lots they offer for sale are removed a healthy distance from the shoreline, and one of their principal attractions is the assurance of a preserved and natural lake. The Grays, who also favor a "natural" as opposed to a "developed" pond, represent the best of the summer people—academics

most of them, with four generations of Vermont summers behind them. The Hills just as clearly represent the most thought-
ful and informed native Vermonters, active in every socializing
aspect of their town's life: 4-H leaders, officers of the historical
society, authors of books on horticulture under the St.
Lawrence storm track, people who are solidly traditional but
open to the new, and friendly up, down, and across the various
layers of the town's population.

Walking out, we have a feeling that we are closing Long
Pond for the winter. Nobody is going to be in there much, now
that summer is ending, unless it is some farm boy trapping
muskrats. Through the winter it will lie locked under four or
five feet of snow, its water frozen clear to the bottom in many
places, its fish driven into the deeper parts to wait for spring.
When spring finally comes, every twig of every tree, every un-
coiling fiddlehead of fern, is going to come on with one idea in
mind: to hide that woods-bound lake even deeper in green.

Up to now, it is the pond that has saved itself. But against
speculators with money—Florida money, California money,
Venezuelan money, Kuwaiti money, Mafia money, whatever
kind of money—it is going to need help. To a certain kind of
eye, Long Pond's hushed remoteness might be transformed into
a vision of a thousand shorefront summer cottages, each with
dock and boathouse; and an inn with a bar, tennis courts, perhaps a nine-hole golf course where the Rutledge meadow used
to slope down to the water's edge.

If Long Pond were in California, that vision would almost
certainly come true. Since it is in Vermont, there is a chance
that something better may happen. For there is something in
Vermont—in its climate, people, history, laws—that wins people
to it in love and loyalty, and does not welcome speculation and
the unearned increment and the treatment of land and water as
commodities. Here, if anywhere in the United States, land is a
heritage as well as a resource, and ownership suggests stewardship, not exploitation.

LAST EXIT TO AMERICA

In Indiana, as you enter Interstate 80–90, the toll booth attendant will hand you a Travelaide packet containing strip maps, a directory of accommodations indexed by interchange, a list of scenic, historic, and cultural attractions on the road west, and the cheerful voice to "discover America." Keep the camera loaded, you might encounter some wild life.

The information is reliable. The gas stations are where they are said to be, the accommodations are as advertised. But after a day and a half or so the traveler will realize that crossing the continent by Interstate he gets to know his country about as well as a cable message knows the sea bottom.

It is not America that you pass through. You get a false impression even of the topography because the contours have been flattened, the grades leveled, gulches filled, hills cut away. What was all that nonsense about wagons having to be double- and triple-teamed on Windlass Hill or the Burnt River grade or the Donner summit? It is clear from the Interstates that America is a country of under three percent grades.

Regional cultures, local differences of human type, life style, dialect, diet? The right of way is wide enough to keep all that at a distance. The tourist dollar is lifted not by competing entrepreneurs but by franchise motels and restaurant chains which make every accommodation the replica of the last one—efficient, clean, stereotyped, and sterile. You drive across the continent and sleep in the same bed every night, select from the same menu, confront the same Indian jewelry and bead work made in Hong Kong.

Regional architecture? You catch an occasional glimpse of a

distant barn or grain elevator. If the Interstate has to pass by a city, it climbs and loops over or around it on ramps and by-passes that make Omaha barely distinguishable from Denver. Since our modern cities are already virtually clones of each other, the lack of variety is accentuated. You can drive straight over Omaha, looking all the time for the Missouri River, and never even know when you're on the bridge.

Wildlife? You won't see any—not even dead. The rabbits, coons, and skunks, the farmers' chickens and stray cats that are elsewhere done to death by speed and glaring lights are strangely missing from the Interstates. On one brief country-road by-pass between Dyersville and Iowa City, Iowa, we once counted thirty-four dead animals, mostly raccoons, in as many miles. On I-80 again, through the same corn country, we did not see another for two hundred miles. Turning off to discover America at Grand Island, Nebraska, we saw eleven dead creatures in less than ten miles of access road. What confines these deaths to the homelier highways? Do the woven-wire fences keep even small animals off the Interstates as the posted signs keep off hitch hikers, or do they sense that there is nothing on that arid speedway worth risking their lives for? I am happy for the animals. The Interstates may be the best thing that has happened to them since the automobile emerged as their deadliest natural enemy. But the absence of their mangled and flattened bodies on this pavement enhances my sense of the unreality through which we travel.

In the projections of those who used to prepare us for the era of the four-day work week, the Interstates used to figure largely. Millions of Americans were to be hurling themselves along millions more miles, demanding thousands more Savarins and Howard Johnsons, hundreds of thousands more Beauty Rests, millions more servings of roast tom turkey with old-fashioned stuffing, millions more containers of Southern fried chicken, billions more hamburgers, beef-burgers, barn busters, Cokes, Seven-Ups. They were to speed through a carefully prepared stage set, and when they arrived at Yellowstone or Glacier or wherever they were headed, they would not have arrived at much of a change, for nearly every major national park in season is essentially one great metropolitan traffic problem through which the millions must be conducted with a minimum of delay or discomfort. I have worked on the master plans for some of those parks, and I know what comes up first. Rising gas prices and falling speed limits alter only the tempo, not the condition.

Thinking dark thoughts as *we* flash by, I mutter to my wife that if our civilization had developed any sensible priorities, we would not be such suckers for the notion that leisure is only for shooting like a rocket down a landscaped tube on the way to some place more crowded and more advertised.

You're exaggerating, as usual, she tells me.

All right. But not very much.

Nebraska is not a state that tourists seek out. They travel through it, stopping only when sleep or hunger overtakes them. That is the way it has always been. That is the way the wagon trains went through, headed for Oregon or California or Zion in the valleys of the mountains. Nebraska, especially the Platte Valley, has always been a roadside.

Nevertheless it was, and is, many a traveler's first introduction to the West. About Grand Island, or a little beyond, you cross that imperceptible line beyond which the rainfall is less than twenty inches a year, and when you have crossed that you are moving into another world, under another light, among another flora and fauna and through another variety of land forms. This is about where the wagon trains of the 1840s and 1850s expected to meet the buffalo. This is where they began to see prairie dogs and horned toads and antelope. This is where they reported the parching of lips and nostrils and were struck by a new dry clarity in the air. This is where they began wildly to underestimate distances.

Except that we no longer expect to see buffalo, antelope, and prairie dogs, none of that has changed. From about the time we passed Schroon Lake in the Adirondacks and dipped down into America's industrial fumosphere on that last transcontinental journey, this was the first air we had breathed that seemed fitted for lungs rather than exhaust pipes. And if there were no buffalo, there were big herds of cattle, big feedlots, a quality of life that was still partly visible even from the Interstate. The benches above the Platte's flood plain, what the pioneers called the Coasts of the Nebraska, lifted the horizon a little on each side of the broad trough through which the river, "a mile wide and an inch deep," braided and shifted among its yellowing cottonwood islands. What we saw, though vastly changed in a hundred and twenty-five years or so, was still bounded by historical features, and full of echoes of a heroic past. Up this water-level highway went buffalo-hunting Pawnee villages, fur caravans, Oregon wagons, California wagons, Mormon wagons, the Irish track-laying crews of the Union Pacific. And close upon the great trail-breaking days came the first phase of the sod-house frontier, the first encounter between American farmers and the dry country.

Plenty to see, plenty to be reminded of. And some of it was being advertised in a way to turn the student of history off. All the way from eastern Iowa we had seen, in strategic pasture corners off the Interstate right of way, billboards advertising Harold Warp's Pioneer Village in Minden. I would not have minded seeing Harold's collection, which I had heard was large, and I had no reason to believe that his pioneer settlement was not authentic. But I dislike the huckstering of history, as I dislike the huckstering of scenery, and I was offended by his billboards, which polluted two hundred and fifty miles of roadside. So we vetoed Minden and turned off instead at Grand Island, Nebraska's third largest city, to stop overnight with friends and refresh ourselves in the Stuhr Museum, a place where history is given the dignity it deserves.

As a collection, what is displayed in the Stuhr Museum is not unparalleled. But without shouting from billboards along the Interstate it demonstrates something: that many Nebraskans are interested in their past, curious about it, proud of it, willing to put themselves out to learn and preserve it. There are more than a hundred museums and historical parks in Nebraska, and they commemorate more than Pawnees, covered wagons, and Buffalo Bill Cody. Three of them—at Red Cloud, Gordon, and Bancroft—celebrate three Nebraska writers, Willa Cather, Mari Sandoz, and John G. Neihardt. The Joslyn

Museum in Omaha is a fine regional resource, both artistic and historical, and has one of the best collections on the transcontinental railroad. The Stuhr, started by a Grand Island farmer who was himself the son of a pioneer, deals with the plains pioneer and the life he created in the wake of the western wagons.

We found it simple, honest, direct, oddly impressive, a regional variant of Cooperstown, in New York, or Shelburne, in Vermont. Its reconstructed town of false-front store, commercial hotel, one-room bank, plank sidewalks, Danish church, railroad station, and characteristic farmhouses is like one of Wright Morris' photographs, or like the town I was a boy in. I recognized the high-laced shoes in the window of the general store as my mother's, I saw three of our old cars among the splendid assemblage of historic machinery housed in a temporary building. I had never driven one of those enormous early tractors, as big as locomotives, but I had ridden binders just like these, and forked sheaves into just these models of threshing machines. And in the indoor museum I recognized all the homely garments and tools and gadgets and household implements that shaped me—that shaped the whole region of the Plains. I had worked those dasher churns and run those early cream separators, carried and dumped those copper boilers steaming with soapy water, watched my mother at those primitive washing machines and the backbreaking tubs and boards that led up to them, and I had seen her in aprons and dresses just like these, and hung around playing in her button box while she sewed for local girls just such wedding gowns as we saw displayed in the Stuhr Museum.

All this homely and touching life gear is housed in a light, airy, fountain-cooled building designed by Edward Durell Stone, set on an island in a man-made lake. For a city of thirty thousand it seemed not merely commendable, it was close to splendid. It offers any youngster growing up in Grand Island a sense of history that I, who grew up without history, have to envy. Children here have a measure of their tradition, a feel of identity, a demonstration of community and continuance. Around the edge of the 267-acre site of the Stuhr is a wooded picnic and recreation ground (man-made, for the Platte Valley in the early days was as bald as a billiard ball except on the islands); and surrounding museum, island, lake, reconstructed village, and picnic ground is the clean, vigorous, attractive little city. I don't suppose it is paradise. I suppose it has its social injustices and its lesions and its scabs. But it is a persuasive and even proud example of a democratic society. If I were electing to grow up again, and could pick the place to do it in, Grand Island, Nebraska, would not be the last place on my list.

Eastern Seaboard cities do not know about towns like this, and sometimes wear superior smiles when they hear their names. Read our contemporary novels and you don't hear about them, unless as traps. Even our dropouts hunt the sunbelt and vacation country. Drive the Interstates and you bypass the Grand Islands. But they continue to exist and even thrive, solid, self-respecting, hopeful, proud of their history and believing in their future, and far less provincial than urban provincials suppose. They are part of America that we have either forgotten or denied or ignored as we headed down our escape routes to Las Vegas or La Jolla, Big Sur or Taos, Carmel or Tucson. But I have a feeling they are here to stay; maybe they are our forming Weimars and Dresdens, our Veronas and our Aix-la-Chapelles. The tourists and their restlessness and anomie, even the Interstates that Evasion runs on, may be gone sooner.

Another trip: about halfway between Juleburg and Denver, in the year 1971, Interstate 80 petered out into U.S. 6, which led us into Denver through an incomparable—well, *too* comparable—ugliness of construction, blight, and rush-hour traffic. The high scarp of the Front Range sat above the Queen City of the Plains and Peaks like a reproach. My wife suggested that Denver was what we deserved for getting off the nice protected Interstate to discover the real America. But she was only being tired and captious. Our motel was a truck stop; diesels idled under our windows all night. We could barely wait for daylight, to get out of there and into the mountains.

But the Rockies were as bad as Denver—worse, because they should have been so much better. Interstate 70 was being rammed through them then, and every feeder road seemed to be under construction in preparation for the 1976 Winter Olympics. We - could not know, grinding through those detours, that the - people of Colorado would rise up and send the Winter Olympics elsewhere—as it turned out, to Lake Placid in the Adirondacks. And so, having watched Los Angeles in 1932, Squaw Valley in 1959, and Rome in 1960 prepare for the Olympics, I took a sour satisfaction in predicting what would happen to the promoters, or to those who inherited their leavings. The mining camp of Georgetown was happily advertising its role in the coming spectacle, like a girl who is going to be raped on TV. "Flagbags," girls in construction stiffs' clothing, waved us through crawling single-lane traffic under blasted mountainsides and through bulldozed gulches. Under their hard hats their faces were too delicate for the place and job. They sniffled in the cold and stamped booted feet in the road, emancipated into a job that a traffic light could have done as well. I gave them grave greeting as we passed, welcoming them into full partnership in our social insanity and our environmental guilt.

On the shores of Dillon Reservoir, part of a project that delivers western-slope water to the eastern slope so that Denver may continue to grow, many-storied buildings had sprouted: condominiums for Denverites bent upon escaping their city. The high valley was scarred with roads and construction, the air smelled of diesel exhaust and smoke. Only a little while, and there would be another city here which would have to be escaped in turn.

By the time we had got as far down the Colorado as Glenwood Springs, we were sick of those mountains, sick of this culture, sick of our species, sick of ourselves. So what did we do? We escaped, naturally, and by car, of course. We took a thirty-five mile detour in order to have lunch in Aspen. We knew it as a little city which, protected by wealth and a quite special foresight, had escaped the worst sorts of exploitation. Leisured and cultivated people had made it a home for music, drama, and the dance, and had there developed a higher cuisine than that of the Interstates. So we turned up Roaring Fork and took aim at the 14,000-foot pyramid of Snowmass, sitting like a front sight at the end of the canyon's notch.

Aspen was less well kept than we remembered it, there had been much building, the visual charm that was once discreetly protected had been somewhat marred by signs. Still, a pleasant town, beautifully cradled in the mountains. The leafless aspens gave the slopes a pale white-violet tinge, the sky was dark and faultless, the Maroon Bells were a serene nobility to southward. We located a little open-fronted eating place we once knew, and lunched on a salade Niçoise, a French roll, and a bottle of cold Chablis, none of which would have been available on the Interstate; the food there would have been as advertised, "the same as you would find in your home town."

Even in that fall season, after summer and before skiing, Aspen was crowded, almost exclusively with the young. Everybody's sick or runaway or dropout child seemed to be there, either joining us in flight from American civilization or drawn by a wistful hope of action or pleasure. It looked like the panhandle of Golden Gate Park on a fine morning, or a mass happening at somebody's Free University. The historic old Jerome Hotel had a "No Bare Feet" sign on its door and was crowded with young people, many of them barefooted. The washrooms were dirty; the lobby and dining room were full of Kit Carsons and Wild Bill Hickoks.

I wonder if there is much hope for the pleasuring grounds such as Aspen. Evolving from mining camp to ghost town to sanctuary of privilege and taste, modern Aspen had become a beautiful little museum in which Americans who had the means could play frontier, play unspoiled America, play Culture in the Hinterlands. It was an innocent game and a charming one, but it had been moved in on by counterculture barbarians by 1971, and since then has been increasingly taken over by the entrepreneurs and the pleasure-circuit riders and the beautiful - people. Nowadays, ten years later, there are so few dropouts in Aspen that the lodges and restaurants can't find dishwashers. Aspen once again is only for those who can afford it. It is also on the way to becoming a cultural junk heap, a rootless resort, one of the things we are best at making. Or so it seems.

In any form, whether as privileged sanctuary, dropout heaven, or pleasure-circuit pit stop, I couldn't defend it. It was either trivial, ugly, or unreal. I couldn't make a case for it as a community, the way I could make a case for Grand Island. An aging puritan, I muttered my own convictions under my breath, into the teeth of Aspen and the whole resort world and the whole pleasure principle.

We look pretty good when we are at work, on work we like to do. We look even better when we unite in work that lifts our spirits and our hope. We look best when we have to dig in and look disaster in the eye and hold it off. We are never so hateful as when we are filled with hate, never so unattractive as when we are idle and bent on pleasure. For pleasure, a splendid by-product, is a contemptible goal. Yet it is the goal that this civilization teaches us all, especially those predestined to be casualties and victims, to seek.

Maybe it is time some Jeremiah came down from Snowmass and told young and old that what they are escaping when they come up here is often worth fleeing from, but what they come seeking is frivolous.

And so back to the Interstate, discovering America at seventy miles an hour.

The unexamined life is not worth living, but it is precisely the life toward which Americans as a people desperately yearn. As much as any of our institutions, as much even as our proliferating resorts, though in the direction of a compulsive mobility rather than a compulsive pleasure-seeking, the Interstates are symptom and symbol of life resolutely turned away from, hushed up, hidden, barred out, painted over, evaded. Those multiple ribbons of landscaped paving, I thought as we turned back onto one, mark the graves of two hundred million unexamined lives in an unexamined civilization.

Or was I exaggerating, as usual? Perhaps there is a saving remnant, the unnarcotized two percent for whom our pervasive amnesia of the spirit is a provocation to precisely the kind of self-examination it is designed to put to sleep. Grant two percent, grant five, grant ten. Call it 180 million unexamined lives. I could still be depressed. And anyway, by the time one has got through making the concession, our equally unexamined fertility will have built up the population far enough to justify the original estimate.

Let it stand. Two hundred million unexamined lives.

Our night's destination that day in 1971 was Grand Junction, but we mistrusted what the Interstate might have done to it since our last visit, and so turned off into the little peach-growing town of Palisade, under the Book Cliffs. For eight dollars (and *there* is a measure of change!) we found a small, clean, adequate room in a ma-and-pa motel run by a decent old farmer and his decent little fifteen-year-old granddaughter. Dinner came out of our picnic basket. We were blessed.

After eating, we took a little walk, simply to touch base with the earth again. The sun was still on the upper half of the gray, stepped cliffs, but the sunken pocket of the town was in shadow, and heavy with trees. Dusk was rising like smoke from the ground, along with the exhalation of wet lawns. In the twilight, lawns and trees burned with the vivid, intense green that one seems to see only in such irrigated western oases as this. Up the street a screen door banged, and a man came out and turned off the sprinkler. A boy pumped by, standing on the pedals of his bicycle, going somewhere in a hurry. We watched the high school football team in stained practice uniforms clump on noisy cleats across the road to the gym. Then we went back and to bed and to sleep in the least expensive, most humanized, most satisfactory place we had slept in all across this much of the continent— the only place that in recollection I can tell from all the others, the kind the system is systematically crowding out.

As I drifted toward sleep I was thinking that so long as our efforts produce a world less and less fit to live in, our roads will be as they are now—routes of flight that arrive nowhere, Kafka roads that recede forever into Siberian wastes of the spirit, without rest and without end, and with only comforts in place of satisfactions. And I had an envious perception of something in the little town of Palisade, something in the little city of Grand Island, that is missing from the lives that the most visible Americans lead. I thought I understood why so many American novels (which *do* examine American lives) are elegiac in tone. From Fenimore Cooper's *Last of the Mohicans* to Larry McMurtry's *Horseman, Pass By*, they mourn lost possibility, lost peace.

The last image in my mind, just before I fell asleep or just after, during that rapid-eye-movement time when the mind twitches like a dreaming dog, was the Indian pictograph that our friend Dean Brimhall once projected for us onto his wall, down in the Capitol Reef—that quintessential statement, surrounded by the handprints of asserted identity, made by some Anasazi perhaps a thousand years ago on a protected and protecting cliff: the man standing stiffly, his arm outstretched, and from his hand a growing tree, and in the tree a hummingbird.

There was a man who did not have to run from his home canyon, whose house was contentment and sanctuary rather than restlessness and disgust, who consumed no transportation and pursued no pleasures beyond the pleasures of work and family and tribal association. There was a man who never had to *learn* how to give himself to his land of living.

I saw him in the shade of a cliff, by a water-seep green with maidenhair and redbud, examining his simple, enviable life. I know he examined it: that tree growing from the protective hand, that hummingbird vivid in the tree, proved it. The picture he left behind him lured me toward resolutions I would probably not be able to keep. But I thanked him just the same.

THE RIVER

What possible charm can we attach to any of these towns other than that the Mississippi flows past them, touches them? What is John Deere at Moline? French and Hecht at Davenport? Standard Lumber at Dubuque? Ah, we love and cherish these mammoth enterprises because they are by the river. What is left of glamor at Read's Landing? A store with Rice Krispies—and the river. McGregor, Iowa is all tired out, but the river keeps it on the map. Lansing, Iowa would be worse than South Dakota— but it's on the river, and in the evening it's better than Lake Louise.

Richard Bissell, *A Stretch on the River*

Hernando de Soto was an explorer only by serendipity. His principal occupation, during his raid that lasted from 1539 to 1542, was torturing Indian chiefs to make them reveal the hiding place of gold they did not possess, and burning their towns when they couldn't tell him. But the great river that he stumbled across somewhere near modern Memphis was more important than any gold he might have found in what he called Florida, or any that he had actually acquired as one of Pizarro's captains in Peru.

Look at any map that does not obscure it with roads and boundary lines, and observe how it reaches into the north, the east, especially the west; the great tributaries forking into lesser ones, the lesser rivers into streams, the streams into creeks, the creeks into brooks and rivulets and runoff coulees, draining the whole enormous interior basin from the crest of the Appala-

chians to the crest of the Rockies. Two-thirds of the rain that
falls on the continental United States, as well as some that falls
on southwestern Canada, falls within that basin and finds its
way down those coulees, rivulets, brooks, creeks, streams, and
tributaries into the Mississippi. Rain that fell on the Milk River
ridge in faraway Alberta helped swell the tide in which De
Soto's body, hidden in a hollow log and weighted with its armor,
was secretly sunk to keep the Indians from taking out their hatred on it. Rains from those far northern prairies, months after
their falling, joined the rains of half a continent that flushed
first the log-coffined leader, and later Moscoso and the survivors, out into the Gulf of Mexico, expelling them like sewage
from the country they had violated.

Flowing from western mountains, eastern mountains, and
northern height of land to the delta, from north-temperate to
semitropical, from mixed northern forests to cypress swamps,
from wheat to sugar cane, the Mississippi ties North and South
together as East and West, with only airlines and Interstates for
a bond, can never be tied. It drains the heartland and in the
long run will unite it. William Gilpin, that John the Baptist of
Manifest Destiny, based a whole theory of geopolitics and national unity on it. Three empires fought over it for generations
before its valley was inherited by the mongrel republic. In the
adolescence of the republic it was the major communications
link between free and slave; in the crisis of the republic it was a
principal battleground. It has been a highway of settlement and
of inter-regional migration. From its riverine culture have derived many of our most significant writers, including two of the
greatest, Mark Twain and William Faulkner. In 1861 an ex-
captain of infantry cashiered for drunkenness gave up clerking
in his brother's store in the river town of Galena, Illinois, and
emerged into daylight to become the greatest general in his
country's history. Ulysses S. Grant was a very American figure,
not least in the weaknesses that made him one of his country's
worst Presidents.

The valley of the Mississippi contains not only more of
America's mass, but more of what America is about, than all
the other regions put together. He who grows up on any branch

or twig of that river system may feel that he grows up isolated, provincial, or limited, but for whatever it is worth, he grows up American.

Creator, destroyer, highway, sewer, the Mississippi is also a dream and a myth. For a time it imposed itself as a boundary across the flow of America's westward movement; briefly, it seemed a line at which settlement might stop, or at least pause. Then almost at once its tributary the Missouri, and *its* tributary the Platte, led the nation on west. The Mississippi stayed put, generating its own north-south dream that was made immortal in *Huckleberry Finn*. Europe troubles the East Coast, Asia troubles the West, but nothing troubles the Mississippi. It is a life river, it is autonomic like pulse or breathing. Nineteenth-century British travelers inspecting the bizarre democratic experiment were absolutely right in making a Mississippi River trip part of their itinerary. Along the Mississippi and Ohio they found the newest, brashest, most ignorant, most hopeful, most egalitarian America. It did not always please them, but they knew they were not seeing any pale echo of Europe.

Through the first three quarters of the nineteenth century, the river held the gaudiest parades the young republic put on. Rafts, broadhorns, and keelboats gave way to steamboats; and steamboats, with their gilt and crystal, their belching stacks, their spittoons and bars and gamblers and calliopes, their impromptu races, their careless fatal accidents, their lonesome whistles heard from around far bends, touched every river town from St. Paul to New Orleans with color, life, adventure, vulgarity, violence, possibility, magic.

Then war closed the river; then the railroads supplanted it. It went on flowing with its old force and its old mystery, but - people had forgotten. Boys might still dream of going down it on rafts, but few actually made the trip. Visitors came less frequently, towns went to sleep. Tributaries such as the Galena, once busy with lead-carrying steamboats, silted up. No smokes showed above the trees of distant points, no whistles brought - people to the riverside.

Since Mark Twain sang its swan song in *Life on the Mississippi* the river has regained its importance in our lives but lost its hold on our imaginations. It inherits the unfashionableness of the region it drains. For those who do not know it, the great interior valley is only a long tedium between the two coasts, not heartland but hinterland. A stereotype nearly as old as the twentieth century says that insensitive Midwesterners are full of brag and that sensitive ones feel the cultural inferiority of their region, and live in it wistfully or resentfully, and look upon the life of other regions with envy.

In our hierarchy of acceptabilities, urban is sophisticated and desirable, wild is fashionable, but rural—Jefferson, Bartram, Crèvecoeur, and other American gospels to the contrary notwithstanding—is dull. And despite its Chicagos and Detroits, in the nation's thinking the Middle West counts as rural. To East or West, an Iowan is seldom an Iowan; he is always an "Iowa farmer." Once I heard two fledgling Ph.D.'s at Harvard discussing the jobs that had been offered them. "Oh, God, not *Iowa!*" one said to the other.

In the Mississippi Valley, according to the stereotype, live the original hundred-percenters, preserving a native conservatism and xenophobia behind intracontinental spaces and within such centrifugal spheres of influence as Chicago *Tribune* opinion and Ohio State football. Away back in the time of the literary revolt from the village, when condescension achieved the status of revealed truth, Glenway Wescott defined the Middle West as a state of mind of people born where they do not like to live, and Sinclair Lewis defined the midwestern village as dullness made God.

Some of this was never true. Some of it has changed—or perhaps it is our minds that have changed.

The fact that I was born on a farm in Winnebago County, Iowa, gives me no status. But when my wife tells people that she is from Dubuque, she says the name a little challengingly, knowing that the only thing most people know about Dubuque is that *The New Yorker* is not written for an old lady from there. And she takes pains to mention that Dubuque is on the Mississippi, another fact they are unlikely to know. It was a good town to be born in and grow up in, and she lived there without noticeable cultural undernourishment until I induced her to move. She learned to swim in the Mississippi when the undammed current was strong enough to carry a swimmer halfway to Quincy before he could struggle back ashore. Some of the romantic nights of her youth—and mine—were spent on the excursion boats that in the early 1930s still operated out of Dubuque, Davenport, and other towns. Old sternwheelers converted into floating dance floors, they were equipped with big bands and drew big crowds of young people.

On such night-time excursions it was customary for the captain to get his blazing palace up into some dark reach, away from the lights of any town, and abruptly shut off both lights and engines. The band stopped, the wheel rolled over and died, all noise and conversation came to a halt. You could hear the watery stillness. You were afloat on the dark river in the middle of the dark continent, in touch for a brief theatrical moment with the force and mystery of that mighty flood.

A minute, perhaps, of flowing dark. Then the searchlight awoke on the pilothouse and probed a smoking hole in the night and picked out, far downstream, a jungled point. From the point it swept up the black wooded face of the bluff, then down to the living surface of the water, then restlessly wide to find an island, then clear across to the bluffs of the opposite shore. Following that probing light was like standing and breathing shallowly while a doctor holds a stethoscope to your chest. Young men found it a good time to put their arms around their girls.

The searchlight went out. A moment of total black, a feeling like breakdown, like panic. Then the boat's lights blazed on, the band burst out, the held breath was released, the wheel resumed its lazy roll, the minute of mystery was over. But not forgotten. Those captains knew what they were doing.

It was inevitable that nostalgia, loyalty to the region where we were born, and curiosity about what time has done to the timeless force of the river, would eventually bring us back, and put us aboard one of the two overnight steamboats still operating on the Mississippi. We choose the *Delta Queen* over her big new sister ship the *Mississippi Queen* for purely sentimental reasons. She is older, smaller, more intimate, more like what we remember. Though built originally for the Sacramento River, she remains the most authentic way to see the Mississippi. We are not deterred by the Coast Guard's reservations about the *Delta Queen*—she is wooden-hulled, and hence not fireproof, and she operates under annual permits of exemption, and has to extract waivers of damage claims from her passengers. But anything that the Secret Service will O.K. for the President is safe enough for us. As a matter of fact, for all the battering of her fifty years of service, she is a lovely old boat, a living memory of the great days.

We have just finished dinner, a bounteous buffet, when the *Delta Queen* stirs and moves. We feel the tension between wheel and current, and go out to stand at the stern above the big red slow homemade-looking wheel and watch the Twin Cities slip behind. A high bridge moves over us and stands in the sky, arching the city lights. Ahead of us a great quiet darkness begins to grow, swallowing the clustered lights of towns, the single lamps of farms, the headlights of cars. In the shirt-sleeve night we watch it a good while. It looks as if it might last. Finally, leaving the boat to push on steadily into the dark that flows around, over, under, and behind, we go to our cabin, big enough for both of us if at least one is in bed, and fall asleep to the comforting tremor of the wheel.

When we awake, the pre-dawn light is pure and gray, faintly pink ahead and to port. Farms, their lights pale and overtaken, hug the shore under the bluffs. The river is very wide, perhaps three miles. From the USGS maps I brought along I determine that we are in Lake Pepin, about which I possess two pieces of information: (1) Read's Landing, at its foot, was once the assembly point for the great log rafts from the upper-river pineries; and (2) in 1922 a local youth named Ralph Samuelson invented water skiing here. Neither fact changes the early look of Lake Pepin, or obscures the realization that we must have loafed along all night. It is reassuring to have made so few miles. Some ancient relation to earth and water has been reestablished, as it is on any river trip, and time is set back to its natural speed.

Having coffee with the early birds in the Texas Lounge, we watch Minnesota rotate past to starboard, and Wisconsin, more distantly and slowly, rotate past to port. During breakfast we pass under the bridge at Wabasha. The river narrows, the bluffs crowd in, and we tuck into Lock No. 4 at Alma. The town, like so many upper-river towns, is strung out, two streets wide, on the shelf under the bluffs. There is the usual North-European-looking brick church. Nothing much is going on. There is a clean, quiet look, the lawns are well mown, flowers are banked against the houses, many bird houses perch on poles in front yards. Whatever Alma, Fountain City, and other such little towns once were, they are now a forgotten, almost secret part of America, sunken, hidden away, linked to the world only by the river, whose traffic stops here only to negotiate the lock.

While we lock through, townspeople lean on the railing, ten feet away, to ask if we've got any presidents aboard this time. There is a lot of shirtsleevy kidding, laughter, friendly waving as the lower lock opens and we ease on through. I remember scenes very this when the weekly train came through Eastend, Saskatchewan.

Now the river that was a lake is an archipelago. The flood plain curves between bluffs that are noble without being quite grand. The channel weaves from one side to the other, leaving on the inside of its bends mazes of sloughs and string islands. There are no farms, no fields, no cottages, only these low green islands choked with growth and edged with white beaches where an occasional houseboat is tied up. It cannot have looked wilder or more beautiful when Father Louis Hennepin, that sacerdotal liar, went upstream as a captive in a Sioux ca-noe in 1680.

If they were open to private use, the islands would be a jumpy habitat, for even with the flood-control dams, the river constantly rearranges them. But they are not open. Everything in the flood plain is federal property. The Corps of Engineers supervises flood control and navigation, and since 1924 the 284-mile stretch of river from Wabasha to Rock Island has been protected as the Upper Mississippi River Wildlife and Bird Refuge. In the broad sloughs, many of them marked on the map as "stump fields," we see blue and white herons, egrets, rafts of ducks. In spring and fall there would be thousands of Canada geese migrating to or from Labrador. I hope they give an occasional honk of thanks for the enlightened policy which, however late, has preserved them a habitat and a flyway.

At Lock No. 5, under the high bluffs of Latsch State Park, we hang around waiting for three upstream tows, which have the right of way, to lock through. A whole Mississippi documentary goes by while we wait: tows big and little, riding high and empty or low and loaded; houseboats, most of them probably rented for the weekend; speedboats; pontoon boats crowded with families in swimming suits; fishing skiffs; and here in the pool above the dam, sailboats. These waters are uninhabited, but they are not unused. We exchange a few words with a sunburned Englishman who is happily rowing from St. Paul to New Orleans, and with two youths in a leg-powered paddleboat, who are less happy. The dams all but extinguish the current for long stretches, and the wind blows so steadily upstream that they seldom get a rest from pumping. So much for the lazy Huckleberry Finn dream in 1979.

Numerous as pleasure boats are, it is the barge tows that dominate the river—vast acreages of rusty iron as wide and long as several football fields, pushed by four-story tugs that lean into their work like strong horses leaning into the collar. The barges have won back much of what the railroads once took away. A single barge—and we see many tows that are three barges wide by five long—can carry as much as an ordinary freight train, and for that matter could carry the train too, and sometimes does, piggybacking the cars sideways. The crews loafing on the front barges give us demonstrations of handstanding and grandstanding, but they impress us less than the immense tonnages these tows move. It is the commerce of an empire that goes up and down the river.

After lunch Captain Blum instructs us in whistle signals: one toot, a port pass; two toots, a starboard pass; three toots, reverse; short-long-long, fog; short-long, the *Delta Queen*'s identifying signal. We have no immediate use for this information, but you never know. Captain Blum tells us that, growing up in

Cincinnati, he had no intention of becoming a river man, and fell into it, so to speak, by accident. If a similar accident befell us, it would be useful to know that we should not fall into it off the stern just after three toots.

At Winona we tie up for a couple of hours and wander through the Levee Plaza, an urban-renewal sort of area where a flea market is in progress and Winonians are selling each other their old junk. This is a good-sized and livelier town, and its United Methodist Espicopal Church, with four Neuschwand-stein towers, looks like something designed by the Brothers Grimm. Less bizarre is the *Julius C. Wilkie,* run permanently aground as a steamboat museum, the common fate of superan-nuated sternwheelers.

The swing bridge at Winona is open; so is another a couple of miles below. High-tension lines crossing the river are hung with orange, yellow, and white balls, as a warning to low-fly-ing aircraft. On the high bluffs of the Wisconsin side, the after-noon light turns twin silos into a Rhine castle. It is hard to believe in the prairie that rolls away from that rim clear to the shore of Lake Michigan, and rolls away from the Minnesota rim until it flattens out across the wide Missouri. The farms, towns, and cornfields up over the horizon are as unreal as Oz.

The slow wheel turns, the pleasure boats dart or drift around us, the tows plow by. We cruise through sloughs that the map marks as the Delta Fish and Fur Farm, we pass Trempealeau Mountain, a remnant of bluff left isolated in the middle of the flood plain, we lock through Lock No. 6 at Trempealeau with the calliope playing. Sometime during dinner, bingo, and the evening dance we lock through No. 7, opposite La Crosse, and nose into a maze of sloughs and islands. After we are in bed we feel that we are in still another lock—that would be No. 8, at Genoa—but it has been a long day, and we sleep through this one.

This is indeed a life-river. Waking on it can be like having a walk-on part in the Creation.

We awake to absence and stillness, missing the steady tremor of the wheel, and go out on deck to find everything shrouded in fog. We can see nothing off the rail—can barely see the ropy surface of the water, whose current seems to be going the wrong way. Maybe we have been captured by Big Eddy, the river god whom we knew on the Colorado. But going around to the port side, we see ghostly trees reaching out of the mist, so close we can almost touch them, and a line drooping in the water. We are tied up to a tree, our bow upstream.

Not a sound. Not even the Texas Lounge is awake. It may never awaken. Fog as thick as this may never clear. This may be eternity. We may sit here, soundless and motionless, until Gabriel gives us two toots for a starboard pass.

A half hour, and the boat is awake. Another hour, and we have finished breakfast in the marvelously bright, warm dining saloon. But on deck it is still hushed, shrouded, muffled, damp, and chilly. Then, standing on the stern, we are aware that something—not a breeze, not a brightening, nothing that can be identified—has happened. What we are tied to has defined itself as a muddy shore, a wall of woods. There is a throbbing on the air—how long has that been going on?—and the fog moves and swirls, wisping upward. The throbbing has taken over, it comes from everywhere, directionless.

"Look!" Mary says, and points astern. The blunt end of a tow, three barges abreast, has appeared out of the swirls and marblings of fog. It is not moving. It recedes and disappears back in the mist, who knows how many barges long, backed undoubtedly by a tug whose four layers of wedding cake are totally lost. This behemoth must be tied up to the same island we are tied to, an island probably smaller than itself.

The throbbing grows, the mist swirls and wisps upward, a gray clarity spreads across the surface of the river. Then abruptly, a couple of hundred feet away, a huge shape emerges, growing in definition like the image on a negative in the developer: a tow, plowing downstream at an insane clip, the fog parting for its passage. The throbbing is loud, close, and ominous. Two barges surge by, then two more, two more, two more, all high and empty, showing six feet of rusty hull above the water line, and finally the snorting tug. It gives us short-long-long, as if it didn't trust us to recognize fog when we're buried in it, and shoves its thousands of tons of burden downriver, into the mist, gone.

But its passage has done something. The gray clarity has spread wider, and the fog lifts like a curtain revealing a stage set. We are surrounded by tows, two upstream, two down, one plowing past, one just below us, tied to our island. Another island defines itself to starboard, then all at once what has been happening has happened. Eternity has been breached; time has begun again. Vanishing wisps of fog fly upward toward widening rifts of blue. Bluffs loom over us, the river is clear, the sky without a cloud. The captain, leaning down from the pilothouse, informs us that we have spent the night at Bad Axe Bend, Mile 674, opposite the Minnesota-Iowa line, fifty-one miles above Prairie du Chien.

Bad Axe Bend I know something about. It is an ambiguous place for creation to have occurred. In 1910 the *J. S.* burned and sank here in one of the last great steamboat disasters. But Bad Axe Bend was hexed before then, for in 1832 more than six hundred Keokuk men, women, and children were shot down here like jack rabbits caught in a drive, to end the disgraceful Black Hawk War. Merely to hear the name of the place gives us bad vibes. We are glad when the *Delta Queen* takes in her line and rotates out into the channel and resumes her run downriver. I see by the map that we are passing Black Hawk Memorial Park. It should have crepe hanging from every tree.

Now we have Iowa to starboard, Wisconsin still to port. Lansing, Iowa, appears: limestone houses, church spires against high bluffs, and away up above the town a highway overlook crowded with parked cars and the bright shirts and dresses of - people watching the *Delta Queen* swim by. We wonder how the Creation looked from up there. Maybe better than Lake Louise.

Now Lock No. 9 at Harper's Ferry, and a river narrow between high bluffs, with ribbons and tatters of water and island filling the flood plain, and finally Prairie du Chien.

This is a discovery place, the most historic town on the upper river, and unlike some discovery places it can still communicate the thrill of visible history. From Wyalusing State Park, on the south bank of the Wisconsin, or even better from the bluffs of Effigy Mounds National Monument across the Mississippi, you can oversee the great meeting of rivers, and with only a little narrowing of the eyes, see Marquette and Jolliet, with their three companions in two canoes, floating down from the east looking for the "great water" the Indians had told them of. What Marquette and Jolliet had in mind was the Pacific Ocean, but that does not diminish the importance of the great water they found, just here, in 1673.

Well into the nineteenth century, Prairie du Chien was a fur-trading center inhabited mainly by French Canadians. Now the old waterfront is essentially a park and museum, for the Corps of Engineers has been moving the residents to higher ground so as to avoid having to raise the dam. The Brisbois House, a National Landmark, is closed, but the Villa Louis, built by John Jacob Astor's local agent for his bride, is a museum run by the Wisconsin State Historical Society. So far as we can see, nobody is up in the new town. Everybody is down here, picnicking, jogging, and making tours of the *Delta Queen* while the *Queen*'s passengers tour Villa Louis and the Astor fur warehouse.

Sunday on the river. A wine-and-cheese tasting is in progress on the green. The cheeses are superb, the wines could stand a little more work. Though this cliff-bound reach of river may look like the Wachau, it doesn't taste like it. We intimate as much to Fred La Pointe, the president of the Prairie du Chien Chamber of Commerce, who comes aboard to ride with us down to Guttenberg. Wait, he says. Give us time.

Seen from the river, with their splendid bluffs behind them, the little towns on the Iowa shore—Marquette, McGregor, Guttenberg—are as picturesque as anything between St. Paul and St. Louis. Even with the sun low above the rim and the towns in shadow, they excite Mary with recollections, for these were the towns of Sunday excursions in her childhood. In the morning, front-lighted, their steeples like tall candles, they would show even better.

But they are not lively towns. Marquette and McGregor have a good deal going through them on the highway, which here runs along the shore, and across the Marquette bridge, the only crossing between Lansing and Dubuque. But the streets are somnolent in the late afternoon. As for Guttenberg, it went quietly to sleep a long time ago, and is not likely to awaken, or realize any of the high aspiration that went into its founding.

Even more than other American regions, the rich farmland of the Middle West attracted idealists and perfectionists—Owenites, Icarians, Hutterites, Amanites, socialists and Christian communists of many varieties, pentecostal sects pursuing New Jerusalem with the same hope of sectarian isolation and social asepsis that brought the Pilgrims to Plymouth Rock. New soil, new social compacts. New frontiers, new moralities and religions and political systems.

The whole Turkey River valley, which joins the Mississippi a few miles below Guttenberg, was a province of the perfected society. Up the Turkey a few miles, French and German Christian communists founded in 1847 a colony called Communia. In 1850 a dozen Scottish families established a cooperative colony at Clydesdale. At Spillville, up near Decorah, there flourished for a good while a colony of Bohemians, including the Bily brothers, notable carvers of wooden clocks; and among the Bohemians, for a short period in the 1890s, lived Anton Dvořák. It is Iowa's boast, in the best American tradition of going well dressed in borrowed clothes, that Dvořák's *String Quartet in F Major* and the final movement of his *New World Symphony* were both written in Spillville.

Earlier than any of these Turkey River communities was Guttenberg. It was founded in 1845 by a group of German intellectuals who in a glow of aspiration named their town after the inventor of movable type. But what happened to the town's name—first mispronounced, then misspelled, then added to the map in its corrupted form—is not unlike what happened in general to imported culture and millennial dreams in America. Their purity was tainted by contact with unwashed neighbors, internal discords multiplied, young people were lured away, enthusiasm waned, and after a generation or two or three what was to be a rural Athens was only another sleepy village from which the liveliest intelligences and the most ambitious talents yearn to escape.

The country westward from Guttenberg, seen from any high point, is a vision of rural opulence out of "America the Beautiful"—white houses, red barns, silver silos, hayfields with great rolls of hay, fields full of grazing dairy herds. But the best Guttenberg itself can show is a certain threadbare tidiness. The church is big and solid, with double spires, but the streets are nearly empty, the riverfront warehouses of local limestone are closed, nobody is stirring around the commercial fishing dock, the lock and dam don't seem to have brought any business. Like the river, the Milwaukee Railroad seems to run *through* the town, not in any real sense *to* it. Without any significant industry, Guttenberg has only the limited future of a farming center, and perhaps as a bedroom community for industrial towns such as Dubuque.

Our anachronistic steamboat swims through the lock, navigating between nostalgia and faded idealism, past the mouth of the Turkey, where in 1780 the British captured an American fur barge during the only Revolutionary War battle fought in Iowa. In the dusk, before going down to dinner, we search the darkening water in vain for the thing that Marquette reported seeing along here: "a monster with the head of a tiger, a sharp nose like that of a wildcat, with whiskers and straight, Erect ears; the head was gray and the Neck quite black."

Explorers always have the best of it. They get to see things before the wonder has worn off. Nevertheless we look forward to Dubuque in the morning: a reunion with Charlotte Robinson and other old friends, a look at familiar tree-heavy streets, a ride on the Fourth Street elevator, a treat of smoked sturgeon, which has it over smoked salmon as far as salmon has it over carp. We are not hunting the future or an ideal society, only the present and the real one.

Whatever Glenway Wescott said, these are not people born where they do not like to live. Except for Mim Bissell, who came here as a bride and learned Dubuque from a houseboat,

all of them were born in Dubuque and all of them live here con-
tentedly. They are all people of means, and could live where
they choose. They choose this river town where their families
have lived for four or five generations.

The house we are having a drink together in is known as the
Octagon House. A National Landmark, one of the famous
houses in the Middle West, it was designed by John Francis
Rague, the pioneer architect who built the Old Capitol in Iowa
City, the first Illinois capitol in Springfield, the old sin in Madison,
and other midwestern monuments. It dates from 1857, from time
of Eddie Chalmers' great-grandfather, Edward Langworthy, one
of four New England brothers who all built Dubuque houses
about the same time. Eddie has been telling us about them and
their pioneer practicality. Because bricks were hard to get on
the upper Mississippi in the 1850s, the Langworthy brothers
built their own brickyard. Because gas had not then reached
from the lower town to the bluffs, they started their own gas
plant. There is something cheerfully frontier-American about
that coping with difficulties. We understand how the Langwor-
thys became one of the most prominent families in town.

As befits a prominent family, this is a great house. The ceil-
ings are thirteen and a half feet high, the rooms are grandly
sized and grandly furnished. One of the pier glasses in the parlor goes clear to the ceiling, and came up from New Orleans by
steamboat along with much of the other furniture. Most of
what we see now is the original furniture, though some of it has
had to be rescued from modernizers. A rocker that Eddie
Chalmers obtained from a relative who was about to give it to
the Goodwill turned out to be the piece on which the Lincoln
Rocker was modeled. The square rosewood piano, given years
ago to the Presbyterian church, was on the way to the dump as
a wreck when Eddie intercepted it, sent it to a rebuilder and re-
finisher, and reinstalled it in its ancestral place.

Eddie calls our attention to the carpet. It had already been
worn threadbare by three generations when Eddie and his sister
were children, but nobody could bear to take it up and replace
it with something less loved. When Eddie's Aunt Edith died, she

left the old house a new carpet, on condition that it exactly duplicate the old body Brussels. It took Eddie several years of consulting with carpet factories before he found one willing to accept the challenge. The Alexander Smith mill agreed to build a special loom, and on it weave an identical replacement for what had served in the Langworthy house since 1857.

The stairs in this house are unique. Like an oversized stile, they run straight up from the front door and straight down again from the upstairs hall into the kitchen area. That arrangement allowed servants to come and go freely between the first and second floors without competing with the family or being knocked over by the five generations of Langworthy children whose bottoms have shined the old solid-walnut banisters to a satiny glow. The back stair is now equipped with an inclined track to which is attached an invalid's chair. This allows Eddie, who walks on canes, to move at will upstairs and down, and frees his wife Mary from having to be an attendant nurse.

It is continuities such as those observable in the Octagon House that give a city such as Dubuque its character. Dubuque does not destroy its modest past or its antiquities, but goes on living in and with them, even generating a certain pride in them. Eddie Chalmers has enriched his own sense of history by having to explain his house to the visitors to whom it is open on scheduled days. At least of the old families of the town, families who made it big in railroads or steamboats or lumber or sash and door factories, a certain richness of association is generated, and it rubs off on successive generations. My wife is not envied for having been one of the few among her childhood crowd who broke the pattern and moved away, nor does she feel superior to those who have remained, as if this were some Winesburg, Ohio. The stability of the place, the slow pace of change, are a comfort and a reassurance to her.

Going around town, she finds most things just where she has expected to find them. It is not the survivals, but the occasional change, that disorients her. The Majestic Theater, for instance, is disastrously gone, swallowed up in an urban-renewal sort of development called the Five Flags. She should be reminded of

Dubuque's history, of the dominance first of Bourbon France, then of Spain, then of England, then of Napoleon's France, and finally, in 1803, of the United States. But history, under five flags or not, cannot compensate for the obliteration of images formed in her impressionable years, when the Majestic Theater was indulgently opened to crowds of teen-agers. She would never like the Five Flags, if it produced the *Ring* with Flagstad or played *Don Giovanni* every Thursday night with Cesare Siepi. It takes a trip to the top of the Fourth Street elevator, an inclined plane with deftly separating tracks where ascending and descending cars pass one another, to restore her to equanimity; and after that an hour on top of the buff, overlooking the little-changed panorama of the harbor, the bridges, the river, the far bluffs where Illinois and Wisconsin meet on the other side, before the loss of the Majestic can be assuaged away by the familiarities that remain.

To learn what is going on on the river, Charlotte has said, we should go down and see George. So, following directions, we cross the Illinois Central bridge, turn right, turn right again at an Exxon station, and follow the road to an open gate. Beyond the gate the road is dirt, deeply rutted but dry. A pickup and an old car are parked under the trees. Where sun and shade meet, constellations of gnats rise and fall. The line of houseboats hold down their reflections in the brown, apparently currentless water. On the tip of the island a man is working on an outboard clamped to the rail of a float. There is a lazy, Septemberish buzz, punctuated by small metallic sounds. The light is the brown light of eighteenth-century English landscapes.

From George's dock in the middle of the line of houseboats a motorboat and a pontoon boat hang dead asleep. A brown and white dog rises from the float and comes wagging, starting a quiver of ripples. We step from dock to float, from float to deck. George opens his door and invites us in.

His boat is mainly one light, cool room with a galley in one corner. Behind the galley are a small bedroom and the head. The open windows let in the smell of river past the shelves of potted plants. All the windows are tightly screened, and all, George points out, are double glazed: the bugs are sometimes bad, and in winter it gets cold down here. He opens a hatch and shows us the furnace in the hold, working off the same bottle of gas as the parlor heater and galley range. Everything is shipshape. Except for the yielding under the hull, a waterbed instability, we might be in a mobile home. It is about that size and of comparable spacesaving neatness.

It is neat because George is a contractor, and handy, but also because he wants to marry Charlotte's daughter, Little Charlotte. Some Dubuque mothers are suspicious of houseboat living; it has a certain raffish connotation and smells of Budweiser. Since we are old family friends of the prospective bride, George is anxious that we find his place clean, comfortable, even romantic.

I remark that the Chandler Slough community is not the sort of decrepit shantytown I remember, and I take out the Dick Bissell book I have been carrying around, and read him Bissell's description of a "development": *Get two big cottonwood logs and nail some rotten boards across them for the float, leaving a few nails sticking up in various places. Con some gas company into the gasoline end of the deal including a great big sign. Now get yourself a secondhand drink machine that is out of order, but don't put any Out of Order sign on it, and jimmy it so it will take and keep the coins but deliver no pop. Throw around about 300 empty quart oil cans, rusty gas cans, a busted washing machine, lots of empty beer cans and pop bottles, etc. A kiddy's tricycle with one wheel missing is not a bad idea. When all is ready, go to Albert Lea Minnesota to visit your wife's folks, but leave the key to the gas pump and the oil shed with Bud Moody who tends bar at the Pastime Tavern. Leave a sign on the pump that says, "Open. Get key at the Pastime."*

Where has all that gone? I want to know. Chandler Slough is as tidy as a middle-class suburb.

Gone for good, George says. Ever since the first settlement the Mississippi bottoms have been a handy dump-ground, the river a handy sewer. Now the Engineers and the Wildlife

Refuge are systematically returning the sloughs and islands to their natural state. A slovenly lessee of a cottage or houseboat site risks having his lease terminated. Even good housekeepers have been getting only year-to-year renewals.

The lease of the Chandler Slough Association still has two years to run. It was obtained a quarter century ago by George's father, who formed a corporation and subleased space to friends for a dollar a front foot a year. Most residents live on their boats the year round. They can cut no trees, and can build nothing on the shore. The Association uses the small rent money to keep the dirt road passable.

Accompanied by the dog, also named George, we go out and board the pontoon boat for a little tour. We have seen dozens of these pontoon boats as we came down on the *Delta Queen*. A friend of George's bought this one for fifty dollars because its pontoons were rusted out. He blew them full of liquid Styrofoam, and now the thing couldn't be sunk with a bomb. It is nothing but a deck—a carpeted, railed, canopied, motorized patio. Steering, George does not squat on a thwart and move a tiller with his backside, but reclines at ease in a porch swing and twirls an old automobile wheel. Mary and I occupy wicker chairs forward. The dog lies down with his nose in the bow wave, and dreams of sturgeon.

We wind for a quarter of a mile through a narrow passage between banks overhung with trees and vines, and emerge into the river. At once we feel the current. Here, only a mile or so below Lock and Dam No. 11, the Mississippi is no more than a half mile wide, and runs with something of its old force. Upriver are the Illinois Central bridge and the highway bridge paralleling it, and farther up, the high Wisconsin bridge overlooking the dam and lock. Spread between them, poking up brick steeples and packed with roofs from river to bluffs, is Dubuque. Across from us, below the mouth of Catfish Creek, a tow is fleeting up, and on the bluff above the creek the round tower of Julien Dubuque's grave oversees everything that passes.

Dubuque, a Canadian fur trader, came down from Prairie du Chien in 1788, married a Fox woman, and started mining lead here on Catfish Creek. Later he obtained from the Spanish governor general a grant of land twenty-one miles long and nine miles deep along the Iowa shore. When he died, his Indian friends planted him on the bluff and closed the mines to other whites, even the St. Louis Chouteaus who had bought part of Dubuque's grant. They did not hold off the whites long. By 1828, eighteen years after Dubuque's death, there were twenty-two steamboats carrying lead from here to St. Louis; and as late as the Civil War years, 95 percent of the lead mined in the world was coming out of the limestone region where Iowa, Wisconsin, and Illinois meet. The old shot tower on the Dubuque waterfront is a relic of the days when bullets were molded by dropping molten lead through a screen into water.

All the mines are quiet now, even those stirred to brief activity by World War II. Galena, on the Illinois side a few miles downriver, is a bedroom and tourist town. Mineral Point, Wisconsin, makes something out of its past by selling Cornish pasties on the old miners' row called Shakerag Street. Dubuque, having converted to lumber mills during the time of the great log rafts, and to sash and door factories after that, has converted again to John Deere and the Dubuque Packing Company, and remains a major fleeting station in the barge traffic, and its principal upriver wintering place where the river is closed by ice.

No development mars the restored quiet of Catfish Creek. A man in a skiff is fishing under the Burlington bridge that crosses its mouth, but there is nobody up the creek itself. This jungly tributary was probably much more populous in 1788, when Julien Dubuque moved into the Fox village. I can see no change whatever from the time when we were last here, with Dick and Mim Bissell, at least thirty years ago. It is the kind of quiet stream, lifted out of time, that boys dream of. At any moment we might meet Dick as a boy, rowing down from his family's place. Or Huckleberry Finn, squatting on the bank cooking a catfish held on a stick over the fire.

We go up as far as the bridge leading to the gravel quarry on Horseshoe Bluff, and then turn our patio around and ease down through the serenity of woods touched by fall, and angle across the Mississippi to the Illinois side and enter Crooked

Slough. There are about as many Crooked Sloughs on the Mississippi as there are Mud Ponds in Vermont, and they are about as similar as the Mud Ponds are: a maze of channels among islands whose brush still wears the trash of the last high water. I ask George if people ever picnic down here. No. I ask Mary if anybody did when she was growing up. No. It is easy to see why. To land and sit down amid that tangle of nettles, poison ivy, blackberry vines, and tall grass would be to invite a cloud of mosquitoes, and risk a month of oozing, itching chigger bites. A Mississippi island sounds better in print than it is in fact. I imagine that Jackson Island, where Huck and Jim hid out, was much like these. If it was, then Mark Twain was as guilty of romantic misrepresentation as he accused Fenimore Cooper of being.

Crooked Slough leads into the wide quiet water of Frentress Lake, where we pay a courtesy-and-nostalgia call on Bissell's old houseboat, *Hernando's Hideaway,* now retired. She hangs a little forlornly on her slack anchor line, her captain dead, the good old days long past, nothing lively going on any more. Ah, there, oldtimer. Do you remember an afternoon when, happy on beer and good company and the unaccustomed river freedom, I played a French horn solo from your deck, and scared up every mallard and mudhen within two miles? I who do not play the French horn?

Frentress Lake is lined with two-faced sheds where weekend boaters rent berthing at prices much higher than the Chandler Slough houseboaters pay—$100 to $125 a season, George guesses. There are hundreds of boats of all kinds, resting up for the weekend. This is the true river life now, the life of weekend recreation, since the dams have backed the river into a series of great pools. The Frentress Lake marina is the middle-class one, George says; the classy one is below Eagle Point, next to where the *Delta Queen* tied up yesterday. Clearly George feels superior to both. The houseboat culture is purer, less self-indulgent, more self-reliant, the modern successor of the old shanty culture. There is virtue and self-respect in not selecting the days when you commune with the Mississippi. You take it the year around, complete with its gnats, mosquitoes, Mormon flies, chiggers, poison ivy, and nettles; with its spring rises and winter cold, and its sultry July nights when you can hear the corn growing clear up at Balltown.

Fur traders and squatters once built their cabins in the bottoms for the best of reasons. The river was the highway to everywhere. Raft, canoe, skiff, broadhorn, steamboat, came by the door. People cut trees and made rafts of them and floated them to St. Louis or even to New Orleans, and came back by foot or by steamboat. (The trees, then as now, were Uncle Sam's, but that hindered no one.) The bottoms were full of game and small fur-bearers, the river full of catfish, sheepshead, and sturgeon. Civilization was far off. And if the climate was harsh and the pests bad, if the June rise periodically carried off pigs, cows, and cabin together, those hazards were a small price to pay for the total freedom of the life. Audubon, Timothy Flint, Thomas Nuttall, every early traveler on the Mississippi and its major tributaries found those gaunt malarial squatters far in advance of organized settlement. Mark Twain painted their group portrait in the residents of Pokeville, their characteristic individual in the "acclaimed man" of *The Gilded Age*. They were notorious for a crude hospitality and also for outlawry; they lived almost as precariously as the Indians they displaced. Mrs. Trollope, visiting their cabins on the Ohio, found their standard of living below that of the lowest European peasant, and their celebrated liberty an abomination. "All the freedom enjoyed in America, beyond what is enjoyed in England, is enjoyed solely by the disorderly at the expense of the orderly."

Spoken like a Dubuque mother.

In steamboat years there was work cutting and stacking wood for the boilers. After the railroads killed the steamboats, the river settled into the torpor from which it has never fully recovered. During Prohibition, moonshiners and bootleggers made good use of the islands, but the handwriting was on the wall even before Repeal. The coming of federal regulation and the navigation-and-flood-control dams meant the taming of the wild river and the constriction of the old freedom; it also meant the partial cleaning up of the old careless pollution.

Heading back out through the maze of waterways, we pass survivors of the earlier, cruder river-bottom life: a cottage on six-foot stilts, apparently abandoned; another with nothing left but the privy, which wears four numbers that George explains are not a street address but the lease number. Farther on we pass a cottage built on oil drums and anchored by cables to two trees. At high water she can simply float off and lie tugging at her painter. No sign of life in any of these places; perhaps they are already condemned.

The fact is, except for the tows and the weekenders, the Mississippi, at least along this stretch, is not a lively place. Even former high-toned communities such as Shawandasee, on a high bluff a few miles downriver, where the cultural elite of Dubuque used to gather for summer tennis and poetry readings and amateur theatricals, are moribund. But that was only the cultural elite. The money elite of Dubuque have customarily maintained summer homes on the lakes of northern Michigan or Minnesota. Though they often keep boats on the river, sometimes pretty fancy boats, they have left the sloughs to the fishermen, the weekenders, and the people with a little muskrat blood in them.

Where the channel turns at the foot of an island, a sign says "No Water Skiing." Young hotdoggers have caused accidents, coming too fast out of blind waterways. On both sides of our boat the trees hang, nearly touching, unstirred by any wind. A turtle slides off a log and disappears at once in the murky water. The dog stands up and wags his tail. George cuts the motor, and we ease in toward his dock. When we bump the tire that hangs over the edge as a buffer, ripples shiver outward. The dog jumps onto the dock. For a minute the rest of us sit there.

Listen to that quiet. The man who was working on his outboard has gone away, or inside. No radio is playing anywhere, no traffic noise makes its way into the hush, though the slough is barely a mile from East Dubuque and no more than ten minutes from Dubuque itself. Tamed or not, the river preserves its integrity, it out-waits human busyness. Chandler Slough is a real place, as few places are any more.

George looks at us, estimating our reaction. "You think she can stand it?"

"I think she's lucky," Mary says.

DEAD HEART OF THE WEST

On the face of the Wasatch Mountains, in Utah, and on the faces of the tormented desert ranges westward, there are lines of terraces like the grades of abandoned roads. The highest is a thousand feet above the floor of the valley. Up there the soil is underlain with flattened, polished pebbles: the beach of a great lake that in glacial times pushed against the eastern wall of the Great Basin. It made fjords of the Wasatch canyons and a great bay of Cache Valley, where the city of Logan now lies. Westward it spread more than a hundred miles, submerging low mountains and making islands of high ones. Northward it reached four arms into what is now Idaho; southward, a long bay almost touched what is now Arizona.

This was Lake Bonneville, a freshwater sea as big as Lake Michigan. Stand on its highest terraces and count the ledges which, at various stages of water, waves driven by the prevailing westerly winds cut into the mountainous shore. Some are so faint that a heavy growth of grass obscures them, some so broad and deep that they indicate a stable lake level over hundreds or thousands of years. And away westward twenty-five miles or so, against the foot of brown mountains and islands, you can see what is left of that inland sea—a thin line of quicksilver, of lead, of improbable turquoise, of deep-sea cobalt, or of molten metal, depending on the condition of the sky: Great Salt Lake.

It is a remnant only, one-tenth the area and one-sixtieth the depth of its parent, which first reduced itself catastrophically by overflowing and cutting a channel through Red Rock Pass in Cache Valley, and then dried up spasmodically and irregularly over many centuries. We know from the layers of hard salt under the clay of its bottom that it has more than once dried up completely, only to be given new life by a rainier cycle. The country around it, once rich with vegetation, has for thousands of years been a barren desert. The once-sweet lake, having no outlet except evaporation, is in periods of low water saltier than the Dead Sea.

Fly over it and see it as the residual puddle it is, set in borders of white salt or putty-colored mud from which rise worn mountains half buried in alluvium. Drive toward it, say along Interstate 80 from Wendover, on the Nevada line, and you cross for scores of miles the ancient lake bottom, the concrete-hard Bonneville Salt Flats, where land speed records are regularly set and broken.

All approaches except that from the mountainous east must brave a desert bleaker than Arabia. The Western Pacific comes east across the salt desert and circles the lake's south shore. The Southern Pacific offers the best of all approaches—straight across the desert to Lakeside and from there across the Northern Arm and Bear River Bay by the combined trestle and fill of the Lucin Cutoff. A splendid way to approach it by car, and to see it at its loneliest and most beautiful end, is to turn off U.S. 83 west of Brigham City and take the back road through Promontory, Cedar Springs, and Kelton to a junction with U.S. 30 just east of the Grouse Creek Mountains.

Everything about Great Salt Lake is bizarre and contradictory. Remnant though it is, it is still the largest lake west of the Mississippi. In a land where water is more previous than diamonds, this lake seventy-five miles long and fifty wide provides not a single oasis. It offers no refreshment and only beauty in place of recreation; and though it has been on the map longer than America has been a nation, large parts of it remain unvisited and almost unknown.

It is a desert of water in a desert of salt and mud and rock, one of the most desolate, and desolately beautiful, of regions. Its sunsets, seen across water that reflects like polished metal, are incredible. Its colors are of a staring, chemical purity. The senses are rubbed raw by its moonlike horizons, its mirages, its parching air, its moody and changeful atmosphere.

Unknown though it is, its name is familiar the world over, and millions have sampled the two thrills it offers tourists—sunsets and non-sink swimming. This last is feasible only at the lake's south end, where Sunset Beach, Black Rock, and the now defunct Saltair resort are clustered. Swimming in Great Salt Lake is less recreation than an "experience." A hundred and thirty years or so of it have created a body of lore, passed on from the knowing to the uninitiated.

It is impossible to sink, as advertised. But it is also very difficult to swim, because the buoyancy lifts your feet higher than your head. You could drown while floating like a cork. If you want a life preserver, tie a weight to your ankle to keep you right side up.

Unless you are fond of a sensation like sulphuric acid in your eyes and lye in your throat and nostrils, keep your eyes and mouth shut and out of the water. If you want to rub your eyes, suck your fingers clean of salt first.

Swimming in the brine is exhilarating, but you will be uncomfortable later unless you shower in fresh water. If you don't, you end up crusted with salt like a herring.

Don't dive. In 1924 I saw a high school boy from Illinois disregard the warning signs and take a running dive off the Saltair pier. When we fished him out, his neck was broken. He might as well have taken a running dive into soft cement.

G. K. Gilbert, when he studied old Lake Bonneville for the U.S. Geological Survey in the 1880s, predicted that Great Salt Lake would dry up as Mormon irrigation took more and more water from the Jordan, the Weber, the Bear, and the smaller affluents. His prediction could still come true, but for the nearly hundred years since his study the lake has simply fluctuated. After the all-time high of 1873 there have been peaks in 1885, 1910, and 1924. Since the all-time low of 1940, the level has stubbornly started to climb again.

But even if it should rise again to the 1924 level, which is when I knew it best, Great Salt Lake is never likely to become a casual and populous resort. At best it is glaring hot in summer, mosquito-haunted in late autumn, when unused irrigation water fills the sloughs along the eastern edge, and bleak in winter. In spring the larvae of the brine fly, one of the few forms of life that breed in the lake water, wash up on shore in a layer that Captain Stansbury, who surveyed the lake in 1850, described as looking like dried cow dung and having a "sulphureous" smell. Boating can be dangerous because of the weight of the salt waves, and the water is corrosive to outboard motors. There is not a picnic spot, not a tree. If you tried to water-ski, and took a spill, you could break bones.

When I was fourteen I sold hot dogs and hamburgers at Saltair, the resort built on pilings at the lake's south end. It was the old Saltair, since burned down, rebuilt, burned again, rebuilt, and finally abandoned. In that year, when the water was six feet higher than at present, swimmers climbed down ladders from their dressing rooms into breast-deep brine. Later, they had to chase the receding waters across the flats in little cars. Still later, there was an attempt to dike up a swimming hole around the pavilion, but it did not work well.

But in 1924, memory tells me, the lake air was hot, rich with the odors of popcorn, spun candy, and frying meat. The whole pavilion, even the potted palms, glittered with an airborne deposit of salt. Salt gritted underfoot. The pilings, pink below the water line, were crusted white above. At night, because the water cooled more slowly than the land, the air stirred with a land breeze drawn down from the Wasatch. It strengthened as darkness came on, bringing the hint of cool heights, and more than a hint of salt flats along the water's edge. Everything was louder and brighter at night: the roar of the roller coaster and the squeals of girls, the glitter of thousands of lights, the barbaric noises of what we proudly called the Coney Island of the West.

Sometimes we could slip away from the stand for an afterdark swim, moving quietly among the reflected green and blue and lemon-yellow lights on the water's surface. Cradled in water warm as milk, we felt the sting of brine in every cut, and over us washed the secret shore breeze tainted with its smell of the flats. To me it was an enchanted place.

It was natural that a desolation as forbidding as Great Salt Lake should come slowly into knowledge. Fathers Escalante and Domínguez heard about it from the Utes of Utah Valley in 1776. They did not visit it, but Miera put it on his map—by ear, with the fictitious Rio Buenaventura flowing out of it - toward the Pacific. For a half century it changed shape, size, and position at the whim of creative mapmakers. Then, toward the end of 1824, young Jim Bridger floated down Bear River in a bullboat and dipped his hand in the water at the mouth of Bear River Bay and found it salty. He was the discoverer, but he thought he had found the Pacific Ocean.

Other mountain men had a hand in its exploration. Jim Clyman, hunting for beaver streams that he might as profitably have hunted in hell, led a party that circumnavigated the lake in a bullboat in 1826—a feat so heroic that few have tried it since in any sort of boat. In 1827 Jedediah Smith and two companions crossed the desert from California and barely made it to water near the lake's southwest corner. In 1833 Joe Walker, a Bonneville man, took forty trappers around the Northern Arm and onto the Humboldt River, thus demonstrating that Great Salt Lake had no Rio Buenaventura draining it. And in 1843 and again in 1845 John Charles Frémont, with Kit Carson, Basil Lajeunesse, and others, visited the two largest islands and explored the route across the desert that would become known as Hastings' Cutoff—one of the tragic roads of the West.

The Mormons who in 1847 began building their Kingdom up against the well-watered slopes of the Wasatch have their own rich history. Great Salt Lake itself has little except the thin lore of its islands and the records of the wagon trains and railroads that tried to break through or around its terrible deserts. It was neither resting place nor destination nor an interlude of water transportation, but a daunting barrier. The Bartleson wagons that made the first wheel tracks in this country fought their way across the Promontory Mountains, around the Northern Arm, and southwest across the desert (a route I have recommended for modern wheels) until they had to give up at the foot of the Pequop Mountains. Later wagons learned to go roundabout northward, *away* roundabout—from South Pass over the Bear River Divide to the Bear, down the Bear to the Portneuf, down the Portneuf to the Snake River at Fort Hall, up the Raft River from the Snake, and across country to the Humboldt. But Frémont's route across the salt desert was urged upon the Donner-Reed party in 1846 by the fast-talking promoter Lansford Hastings. Worn out from laboring through the Wasatch, the party lost so many horses and mules and oxen on the seventy-five-mile waterless stretch from the south end of the lake to Pilot Peak that they never recovered the strength and heart that might have taken them across the Sierra before the snows. Those who died prepared their death here.

In many ways the north end of Great Salt Lake is more interesting than the south. On the north, both history and high ground come close to the water's edge. From there is the best access to most of the islands. And there in Bear River Bay, at the mouth of the lake's principal affluent, is one of the two concentrations of life this bitter sea can show. It is such a concentration of life as can be seen in few places—a place so swarming with wild fowl that it makes all the more impressive the desolation out beyond.

As you go west from Brigham City out onto the delta of Bear River, the hayfields give way to saltgrass, marshland, and tules. In a ditch beside the road a black and white western grebe dives. An egret watches you pass. A great blue heron flaps off with his crest feathers flattened backward, his neck folded tight, his legs trailing; he looks as big as a Navy trainer.

You go past the Bear River Migratory Bird Refuge buildings and out onto the dikes that divide the marshes into five great freshwater ponds. At every yard the birds thicken. A wedge of geese honks over, the sky is darkened by a driving flurry of teal. Clear to the horizon, the lead-colored water flickers with the white, tipping tails of feeding pintail. White islands in the distance turn out to be massed hundreds of pelicans or whistling swans; above us, pelicans are wheeling in wide circles. The canals are alive with grebes, avocets, snowy egrets, glossy ibis, black-necked stilts, night herons. The air vibrates with the swift zigzag flight of snipe, phalaropes, sandpipers. The shallows are almost obscured by teal, canvasback, spoonbill, gadwall, Canada and Ross and snow geese, California gulls, black-crested cormorants. Among the tules flit dozens of yellow-headed blackbirds, birds I have not

seen since Saskatchewan—which is just where they and a lot of
these autumnal ducks were hatched. It is a place to set a bird-
watcher wild. Where else could you see fifteen thousand
whistling swans in one flock? Green-winged teal or pintail a half
million at a time? Canvasback by the hundred thousand?

You see essentially what Jim Bridger saw: he reported millions
of ducks here. So did Frémont when he visited the Bear River
delta in September 1843. So did Captain Howard Stansbury,
coming through with his division of the Pacific Railroad Surveys
in the 1850s. Gunners, the diversion of Bear River to irrigation,
the drying-up of the marshes, and bad outbreaks of botulism
threatened to leave this bird heaven as barren as the salt flats outside, until the establishment of the Bear River Migratory Bird
Refuge in 1928 saved it. The water is now controlled, the
marshes are diked and safe. Botulism is still sometimes a threat,
but even that can be dealt with, given care and effort. Every
year, thousands of sick ducks are picked up, cured, banded,
and released. One pintail saved from death in Bear River Bay in
1942 turned up less than three months later on Palmyra Island,
three thousand miles away in the Pacific.

This is a wonderful place. It deafens and cheers us with the
whistle of wings and the squawking of an extravagant overflow of life. It is one of the few places on the shore of Great Salt
Lake that are easily accessible, open to the public, and sure to
please. Six thousand duck hunters shoot here every fall. On occasion, licensed trappers thin the muskrat population, and licensed fishermen seine the carp. But mostly it is sanctuary, a
feeding and resting ground for millions of birds.

When I was younger, I used to shoot in these marshes. From
here on, I shall only watch. Far better than shooting is to watch
a western grebe swim up a canal with her babies on her back,
or a thousand Canada geese waddle like barnyard fowl along a
dike, or a flight of unwieldy pelicans fight to take off.

It is hardly Great Salt Lake at all, for the ponds within its
dikes are fresh. But there is a seasonal interdependence with the
lake. Thousands of gulls, pelicans, and cormorants nest on
Gunnison, Hat, Egg, Whiterocks, and other lake islands, and in
spring they swarm on those barren rocks as in other seasons

they swarm here. The gulls sometimes feed on the brine fly larvae, but for the cormorants and pelicans there is not a scrap to
eat in all the lake's expanse. They nest on the islands only for
safety, and fly to the Bear River marshes or into the fields and
ditches eastward to feed. Students eating bag lunches on the
high school lawns of Salt Lake City are visited every spring by
hungry gulls, and gulls follow plowing farmers as cowbirds follow a herd. These are the gulls to whom the grateful Mormons
erected the monument in Temple Square, the birds that appeared like a host from heaven to gobble up the 1848 plague of
crickets, and give the nation one of its early lessons in biological pest control.

Let us work closer to the lake and the islands. We can take a
historic route and examine a couple of ghosts on the way.

U.S. 83 goes north of west out of Brigham City. At Corinne,
among green farms, we meet the first ghost, a sleepy village
that from 1869 to 1903 was one of the most important towns
in Utah, a division point on the railroad, the hub of a freight-
ing network to the Montana and Idaho mines, the site of a big
smelter, the home port of an unlucky series of ore-carrying
steamboats, the stronghold of the anti-Mormon population, a
boom town with big ambitions and thirty saloons.

Quietly it lies on the banks of shrunken Bear River. What it
fought has taken it over. When it wore itself out, Mormon
farmers bought it up and leached the alkali and sin out of its
soil and made farmland of it.

Pass by Corinne, turn off on U.S. 83 along the north shore of
Bear River Bay. This is a good paved road leading only to a
point in history. We are paralleling old railroad grades—two of
them, side by side. For dozens of miles through here the Central Pacific and the Union Pacific refused to meet, because
with every mile of track went a prize of land. So until they were
recalled to sense, they went on building, getting farther and farther from their meeting place. Ruins of that old competition,
both grades are without ties or rails now.

The road leads up a dry pass to a saddle, where now are the
reconstructions and the interpretive machinery of a National

Monument. It is worth visiting, but I liked it better when it was a real ghost, when there was nothing but a stucco marker, when you could let the engine die and listen to the wind blowing through this gap in the yellow hills, a dry sound as melancholy as the ruined shacks, broken fences, scattered boards and broken glass and snarls of barbed wire that were then the only relics of the town of Promontory. Then it was a ghost as dead as Baalbek.

This is the place where Leland Stanford swung his hammer on the golden spike (and missed it the first time, irreverent witnesses said). Here, on May 10, 1869, America became a continental nation, and men waved bottles of champagne from the cowcatchers of facing locomotives while Chinese, Irishmen, politicians, railroad officials, Mormon dignitaries, gamblers, and sinful ladies from Corinne cheered. Here happened the single most symbolic hour in the West's history.

Disappointed visitors used to scribble caustic remarks on the old stucco monument and in its register, but for me Promontory has always been an impressive spot. Its wind is full of history.

Along the east side of the Promontory Mountains, which thrust down into the lake for thirty-five miles, there is a road— not a good road, but good enough. What one sees from it is spectacular. Eastward, Bear River Bay is ringed with glaring salt flats except where a tongue of pale turquoise curves up toward the Bird Refuge and the river mouth. An orange-headed worm of train creeps toward Ogden along the straight line of fill across the bay. Beyond it and the low hump of Little Mountain surges up the Wasatch, violet and rose, one of the most beautiful of ranges.

As we curve around the tip of Promontory Point to parallel the railroad, the lake is there, vast, blue as vitriol. It is a color that only desert seas have, the color of the Persian Gulf or the Gulf of Aqaba. Its shallowness, the light bottom, the glazed desert sky, the borders of snowy salt, give the waters a light, pure, mineral brightness.

Across a five-mile channel is the turret-crowned hill of Frémont Island, and beyond that the higher and more rugged hump of Antelope. The railroad, which used to be a single track on a trestle, is now double-tracked, and crosses the Northern Arm on solid fill. The old trestle, besides being slow and rickety, was subject to fires and also, oddly enough, to ice jams. Though the brine never freezes, it sometimes gets so cold that fresh water, flowing in on top of it, freezes instantly, and piles up as icebergs and floes, sometimes thirty feet high.

Only from a boat do you realize how big Great Salt Lake is. The scale of everything around it is so vast that the real dimensions are lost. But stand beside the end of the trestle at Saline and look west, and you can see the rails dipping to the curve of the earth. If you can arrange a boat ride to one of the islands, say Gunnison, you can prepare for two hours of steady cruising at eight knots.

Notice the wake. The water cuts like gelatin, stiffly, and the wake does not widen and roll, but falls in nearly parallel folds. Streaks of bubbles scum the surface like the suds of a detergent. The pinkish specks in the water are brine shrimp, smaller than a housefly but said to be edible if one wants to take the trouble of seining them up. No one does, though a company in Ogden seines them for fish food.

The launch plods on, the great sky flaws a moment with cloud, the water changes instantly from turquoise to vitriol, to lead, back to turquoise. Ahead, Gunnison Island has lifted its northward-facing cliff higher out of the water. Alfred Lambourne, who in the 1890s tried to turn this island into a vineyard, thought it had the profile of a crouching lion.

No need to land on Gunnison Island. Its barrenness is amply visible from the lake, and its history is all subsumed in that bizarre adventure of Lambourne's and in the story of the guano diggers whose enterprise ruined his plans. The remnants of two stone huts are still there. The vines have been dead for three-quarters of a century. The guano has proved unprofitable. Besides the huts, nothing remains except a book, *Our Inland Sea* (originally *Pictures of an Inland Sea*), in which Lambourne recorded in prose-poetry his fourteen months of isolation. He claimed to be the only person ever to live for love on one of Great Salt Lake's islands. It is an odd distinction, but he is entitled to it.

As we go back along the old trestle we face the boomerang curve of Frémont Island and the far peaks of Antelope. The water glares like aluminum. A train pokes along the fill and passengers stare down on us curiously. We wish we had the stuffed carp that a former trestle-tender, Bob Goodnow, used to tow behind his boat to astonish the rubbernecks.

The train and the boat are the only life, the only movement. We see not a single one of the fabled herd of Great Salt Lake whales, not a whisker of the Great Salt Lake Monster, not even a bird cutting the bright air or riding the metallic water. There is a dreamlike, paralyzed intensity to the stillness and the emptiness of lake and sky.

Yet we have hardly landed before three separate black squalls spring up between Frémont and Carrington islands. Lightning licks out of them, the south grumbles with thunder. Before we have the launch swung into its cradle under the trestle, the wind is hammering against us and the heavy waves are pounding the causeway. We are instructed in why boating in small boats is a touchy pastime here. The wind can spring up as if by spontaneous generation, and brine waves hit a boat as solidly as if it had run into a rock.

It is five miles from Promontory Point to Frémont Island, which can be visited only with the permission of Charles Stoddard, who leases it as sheep range. Three-quarters of an hour by boat, an eight-hundred-foot climb, and you are on the turret that led Frémont to name this Castle Island. Here the past has left a small mark: a seven-inch cross scratched on the rock by Kit Carson when he came here with Frémont in 1843.

Look around at three hundred degrees of bright aquamarine, glittering salt, brown mountains. Between outcroppings of dark slate, the treeless slopes are gray, old gold, sage green. It is utterly still—not a bird's cry, not a sheep's baa, not the chirr of a grasshopper, not the rustle of wind in grass.

No one has ever found any great use for the islands, even for Antelope, the largest, though now and again people have tried. On Antelope, which at low water is not an island at all, but is accessible by a causeway, the Mormon Church used to run blooded horses. They are gone. So are the sheep that for a

while were pastured there. Only the buffalo that were planted
on Antelope in the 1890s are still resident. I remember the ex-
citement when, late in the 1920s, Hollywood came there to
stage the buffalo hunt in the film of Emerson Hough's *Covered
Wagon*. When the film made its bow at the Paramount Theater
in Salt Lake City, the theater served buffaloburgers at the door.

Those activities hardly constitute human use. There is not
much on any of the lake's islands for tourists, either—nothing
but solitude and a desolate beauty. Simply by their bristling in-
hospitality, the desert lake and its desert islands have saved
themselves from us, and gone on about their natural business
(at least during this geological epoch) as barren wilderness. It
does not even seem that they need our protective legislation.

But it would not do to be too confident of that. This is a
country of mirages. Periodically, plans are generated to extract
chemicals from the lake and its shores. The MX missile, if it is
ever put on its underground tracks, will be making its endless
movements of evasion and deception through the desert to
westward. Land as open and uninhabited as that which surrounds Great Salt Lake is always recommending itself to the
military mind as a bombing range or a testing site. It is one of
the great ironies that this most desolate heart of the West, if
MX is installed as projected, could become the Number One
target in the United States, or the pushbutton of Armageddon.

Absit omen. As we drive back along the Antelope Island
causeway and across the flats we leave behind the unfamiliar
close-range island with its one ranch house in a clump of trees.
The outlines begin to restore themselves to what I remember
from my years in Salt Lake City, to the bony profile we used to
see from the ancient beach terraces up along the eastern edge of
the city.

Distant, tawny and amethyst in the late light, with the west
foaming into a sunset and the lake glittering along its foot, Antelope Island announces the inhospitable Great Basin desert
that stretches from the Wasatch to the Sierra. Difficult and in-
tractable, it has so far resisted human encroachment and remained stubbornly itself. Until now, it has been something
superlative and useless, immune, to be looked at only, part of

the visual composition that John Muir called one of the great views on the continent. By refusing to be bent to the uses of the tourist or any other industry, it has kept itself halfway safe. One guesses (hopes) that the deployers of the MX missile may find the lake and its surrounding desert as refractory as other entrepreneurs have. If it does, all Americans should cheer.

For in maintaining themselves against us, Great Salt Lake and the salt desert teach us to acknowledge limits. Another hundred years, and we may come to recognize this as a holy place. Another thousand, and its dry silence may remember us no better than it remembers the Gosiutes who lived on jack rabbits, lizards, and pine nuts around its borders, or the Fremont-culture Indians who left their touching artifacts, instruments for the maintenance of the hardest living in the world, in the caves near Black Rock.

CROW COUNTRY

From the ridge above the valley of the West Rosebud we can take our choice among three very different views. All three speak to me in personal as well as regional terms; it is as if they were gathered here to remind me. This is not my native country, but everything in it tells me who I am.

Behind us, surging up to block the whole west, is the highest, wildest, most beautiful mountain barrier in Montana. The ridges and valleys between the main range and us are inconsequential to this view. We look over them, straight into a million acres of the Beartooth–Absaroka Wilderness.

Yesterday, coming over the Beartooth Scenic Highway from the Lamar Valley in Yellowstone Park (many people think it the most spectacular highway in America, and they may be right), we looked across from the 11,000-foot comb of Beartooth Pass and saw not a town, not a ranch, not a cabin, not a road or pole line, not a smoke, only miles beyond miles of forested mountains, shark-tooth peaks, the turquoise sets of lakes, bare stone, snow, wildness, serenity, the blue of distance. Historically these mountains have not been inviting. Exploration, exploitation, and settlement all passed around them: up the Yellowstone Valley to the north; or across Union Pass and the Tetons to Pierre's Hole and the upper Snake River country; or farther south, across South Pass and down the Bear, where the fur trade and the wagons of the Oregon, California, and Mormon emigrations made a road that in season carried tens of thousands of people. None came across here. These mountains say Stop, or Go Around, Not Come. They block off, they divert, and they protect. It is only from a distance, from out on the plains, that their snowy peaks invite.

I spent part of my youth backed up against such a range, the Wasatch in Utah, and it taught me the feel of safety. A man can tuck back in against mountains the way Hemingway used to tuck back into a corner stool at Sloppy Joe's, his back covered and all danger in front of him. The Nez Percés and Flatheads and Shoshones, mountain Indians, must have felt a great easing of watchfulness when they got back from their annual buffalo hunt out on the plains.

The view eastward is the mountain barrier's utter opposite. Across the low bench of the West Rosebud's valley we look into emptiness, beyond made visible. The land falls away, rolls, spreads to the high, even, rounding horizon. We can see the curve of the earth, though in the haze of that long view the line between land and sky melts and blurs. There are smokes out on the plains, an occasional hot wink from the windshield of a car too tiny to be seen, distant intimations of settlement and activity. But there is not enough visible detail to interfere with the impression that from the very porch of security we are looking out on something demoralizingly large, simple, and scary. The plains not only expose your little identity, they tempt and threaten it.

On the hundred eighty degrees of horizon I see only one irregularity: a brown humpy line at the far edge of the world, just south of east. That has to be the Pryor Mountains, in the Crow Reservation south of Billings. The image abides in my head as surely as it impresses itself on my retina. For a half dozen years in my boyhood we lived out on a plain like that, as exposed as prairie dogs under a sky full of hawks, and on days when heat waves withered the air they lifted into sight a mirage that we knew was reality—the outline of the Bearpaws fifty miles to southward. Seen from out on the flats, mountains did not mean the security they came to mean after we moved to them. They meant longing, wonder, mystery; they became a lure and a destination. The Mountains of the Moon, my mother called them. We often talked of going there. In all our years on the prairie we never made it, but the sight of that range breaking the prairie skyline starts a beckoning in my head now as it did then.

The third view from our ridge is just as full of intimations that might interest Carl Jung. Right below us, sunken, tight, miniature in big country, the West Rosebud kinks and races through its belt of cottonwoods and willows. Strung along it for a mile or so is the Bench Ranch. Its house, barns, and corrals, its several old homestead buildings, its hayfields with their stacked bales, its Red Angus cattle as solid as boulders against the opposite slope, make up a picture that is intimate and humanized. It means neither exposure, nor longing, nor the impersonal protection of the mountains, but people, sanctuary, something that men have made for their safety and comfort in an indifferent universe. It too starts echoes in my head: when we came in from our Saskatchewan homestead at summer's end, after a long day of jolting across the flats, we dipped down into a green, rivered valley not unlike this, and were snug for another winter.

There is another, more literary relationship between us and the Bench Ranch. Susan Heyneman, who knows every cow, calf, and bull by name because it was she who named them, reads a lot of books during the shut-in winters. She has read some of mine, and perhaps ten years ago, in what may have been a moment of nomenclatural desperation, she paid me a compliment I did not deserve, and named a Red Angus bull Stegner. Many of the blocky shapes in the hillside pastures are Stegner's get, and down in a corral by the creek, shut away from his beloved and loving cows and irritated by his solitary confinement, is Stegner III, who weighs 1,800 pounds and has a reputation for breaking fences. The Bench Ranch not only reminds me who I am, it flatters me exceedingly, and at least for the four-legged branch of the family, it is home.

I doubt that character and conduct are much shaped by landscape, climate, or geography. We manage to breed saints, brutes, barbarians, and mudheads in all sorts of topographies and climates. But what country does to our way of *seeing* is another matter, at least for me. By and large, I do not know what I like, I like what I know. I respond to the forms and colors and light I was trained to respond to, I acknowledge what revives my memory. But only when I have submitted to a place totally.

Any earth I have shoved around with a bulldozer will be impotent to stir me. The more power I have and use, the less likely I am to submit to anything natural, and the less spiritual power natural things will have over me.

For that reason I bless the poverty and powerlessness of my family in my youth. We submitted to the Saskatchewan prairie not because we wanted to but because we had no choice. We - hadn't settled in undeveloped country because we loved undeveloped country or responded to its rhythms. We had settled there to mine the earth for wheat, and we destroyed some natural rhythms and would happily have destroyed more to make a good crop. Nevertheless I bless our unsuccess and our relative helplessness. Like Aldo Leopold, I would hate to be young again without wild country to be young in; and if I were to give my grandchildren my patriarchal blessing, in the Mormon manner, I would tell them, Be as powerless as possible. Submit whenever you can. Don't try to control the earth beyond the absolute minimum. Work with the earth, not against it. For the earth does not belong to you. You belong to the earth.

Once this was Crow country—and the Crow country, said an early, eloquent spokesman, *is a good country. The Great Spirit has put it in exactly the right place; while you are in it, you fare well; whenever you go out of it, whichever way you travel, you fare worse. If you go to the south, you have to wander over great barren plains; the water is warm and bad and you meet with fever and ague. To the north it is cold; the winters are long and bitter and there is no grass. You cannot keep horses there and must travel with dogs. What is a country without horses?*

On the Columbia they are poor and dirty, paddle about in canoes and eat fish. Their teeth are worn out; they are always taking fish bones out of their mouths. . . .

To the east they dwell in villages; they live well but they drink the muddy waters of the Missouri. . . . A Crow's dog would not drink such water.

About the forks of the Missouri is a fine country; good water, good grass, plenty of buffalo. In summer it is almost as

*good as the Crow country, but in winter it is cold; the grass is
gone and there is no salt weed for the horses.*

*The Crow country is in exactly the right place. It has snowy
mountains and sunny plains, all kinds of climates and good
things for every season. When the summer heats scorch the
prairies, you can draw up under the mountains, where the air
is sweet and cool, the grass fresh, and the bright streams come
tumbling out of the snowbanks. There you can hunt the elk,
the deer, and the antelope when their skins are fit for dressing;
there you will find plenty of white bears and mountain sheep.*

*In the autumn when your horses are fat and strong from the
mountain pastures you can go down into the plains and hunt
the buffalo, or trap beaver on the streams. And when winter
comes on, you can take shelter in the woody bottoms along the
rivers; where you will find buffalo meat for yourselves and cottonwood bark for your horses, or you may winter in the Wind
River Valley, where there is salt weed in abundance.*

*The Crow country is in exactly the right place. Everything
good is to be found there. There is no country like the Crow
country.*

Thus Chief Arapooish, or Rotten Belly, to Robert Campbell
of Smith, Jackson, and Sublette, sometime about 1830. Somehow Rotten Belly's remarks reached Washington Irving, who recorded them in his *Adventures of Captain Bonneville, U.S.A.* But
what Rotten Belly was talking about was not the present Crow
Reservation on the Big Horn. The Crow country of Rotten
Belly's panegyric was bigger than Switzerland, and just about as
spectacular.

The first U.S. treaty with the Crows, that of 1825, made no
mention of territory, but the second, in 1851, defined a Crow
homeland that stretched from modern Yellowstone National
Park far out into the plains to about present Miles City, and
from the Yellowstone Valley far southward into what is now
Wyoming. It took in not only the Absarokas and Beartooths,
but the Big Horns and Wind Rivers and all the wide country in
between.

Even for a tribe generally friendly to whites, such a territory

was sure to strike some whites as over-generous, and other Indians as desirable. Because by the 1860s it contained the best
buffalo range left in the West, the Sioux encroached on it from
the south and east, the Blackfeet from the north. Gold strikes in
Idaho and western Montana brought miners to probe all the
ranges of the northern Rockies. So in 1868 a new treaty relieved
the Crows of the eastern end of their buffalo plains and all the
land southward in what would shortly become Wyoming Territory, below the 45th parallel. That left the tribe a triangle, six
million acres or so, whose eastern leg was the 107th meridian,
whose southern leg was the 45th parallel, and whose hy-
potenuse, running northeast from Yellowstone National Park,
was the valley of the Yellowstone.

The first Crow agency was built on Mission Creek. In 1875
it was moved to the site of modern Absarokee, where Butcher
Creek flows into the West Rosebud a few miles from our picnic
ridge. But by 1880, mineral strikes in the Beartooths and the
stocking of the northern ranges with cattle had convinced
many whites that valuable country was being wasted on a
bunch of gut-eating savages. Granville Stuart, one of Montana's pioneer cattlemen, expressed a common opinion when
he wrote in his reminiscences, *Forty Years on the Frontier,* that
the reservations served only "as breeding grounds for a race of
permanent and prolific paupers." Though Stuart had an Indian
wife, he despised the Crows, and when he was locating his
ranch he passed up the best cattle range he had ever seen in his
life, because it was on the Crow reservation, and located farther north, in the Judith Basin.

Others did not in that fashion bite off their noses to spite
their faces. They forced Plenty Coups and other Crow chiefs
into a new cession that cut off the western point of the Crow
triangle and excluded them from the Absarokas, west of Boulder Creek. By 1883, Crow Agency had been moved once more,
to its present site near Hardin, and the Crows had been pushed
clear out of the mountains onto the pine-dotted broken plains.
The country tight up under the Beartooths was opened to white
settlement in October 1892.

It has been ranching country ever since, the sort of ranching country that the romantic imagination would have to invent if nature had not already done so. Rotten Belly was right: there *is* no country like the (old) Crow country. In this magnificent foothill region folding down to the plains from its backdrop of wilderness, it is hard to feel anything but gratitude to the earth, jut for being as it is. The Beartooth mineral strikes, though they threaten this ranch country now, have been a long time developing. The mountains to which the Crows came for summer pasture and summer coolness have remained as wild as any in the lower forty-eight states, and the ranching foothills are corrupted hardly at all by tourism and resortism.

And observe a cosmic irony. Out on the plains, the tamer country onto which the Crows were forced in the 1880s turns out to contain six billion tons of strippable low-sulphur coal. An equal amount lies under the grass of the Northern Cheyenne reservation next door. The "permanent and prolific paupers" own very valuable resources, while whites inherit the foothill ranch land to which the Crows, given their choice, would probably have clung. The modern Crows can grow rich, if they choose to adopt white styles of exploitation and destroy their traditional way of life and forget their mystical reverence for the earth. Meanwhile the whites who now live in the heart of the old Crow country, as well as many who own or lease range within the present reservation, fight against the strip mines and power plants of the energy boom, and in the face of rising land costs, high money costs, high machinery costs, high labor costs, and uncertain beef prices work their heads off to remain pastoral.

Western cattlemen have had a reputation as feudal barons, as usurpers actual or potential of the public domain. Some have been, some still are, or would like to be. But few, nowadays, would carelessly abuse their fee-simple land as they once abused public land, and as some holders of grazing leases still do. And many, like the Heynemans and their neighbors, have developed a respect for their harsh and beautiful earth that Rotten Belly would recognize.

Glenway Wescott's definition of the Middle West as "a state of mind of people born where they do not like to live" could probably be applied, in 1979, to more regions than the Middle West, and to many of our great cities. It can't be applied generally to the Rocky Mountain West—not yet, at least—and it can't be applied at all to Sweetgrass, Stillwater, and Carbon counties, Montana. They are a long way from the Sun Belt, they yield a grudging living to a limited number of people, their winters are ferocious, their springs late, their summers lyrical but soon overtaken. Nevertheless the people around our picnic fire could not be bribed to live anywhere else.

All are natives except for Jack Heyneman, who came from California. Susan Heyneman grew up on her father's immense Padlock Ranch down in old Crow country, under the Bighorns, near Sheridan, Wyoming. After Vassar, Barnard, and an unsuccessful eastern marriage, she came back west and married Jack, himself recently widowed. From the three marriages there are five boys. The two oldest are working as hayhands this summer down on the Padlock. The three youngest are all around, tearing up the picnic site playing hide and seek. The picnickers lean aside to let them pound through, and pass the mustard or the wine bottle on the lean. Sitting with a wooden salad bowl like a metate in her lap, her braids over her breast and the firelight on her strong profile, Susan looks like an Indian woman. She also looks like a woman who after trouble has made it home.

The picnic includes two courting couples who will be married within a few months. Betty Morse lives in Absarokee, where her father homesteaded and where his real estate office handled nearly every land sale in the area for thirty-five years or so. Her friend Jim Fletcher, a third-generation Montanan born in Billings, has just given up graduate study in the classics at San Francisco State and is setting up a guiding and packing business for safaris into the wilderness from Big Timber or Monroe. Chris Holman is a character like Molly Wood in *The Virginian*—teacher of a one-room school, one of the few remaining, over at Nye, against the foot of the mountain. Her friend Jim Bollingen, also out of *The Virginian,* is the Heynemans' single hired hand, or has been. (In less than a year, it turns out, he will be again.) Tomorrow he is leaving to become foreman of a corporate, absentee-owned ranch forty miles north of here. His imminent departure throws a little cloud over the picnic, the shadow of a possible future.

Romantically handsome, long, slim, a soft-voiced, long-eyelashed tatterdemalion in runover boots and Levi's out at the knee, Jim likes being a cowboy—likes the work and likes the image—but he is uneasy about what he may be getting into. He can't, as everyone agrees, turn down a job that nearly doubles his pay; yet he is half apologetic, as if he were betraying some trust, or being bought out. He worries that he may find himself taking orders from people who don't know one end of a cow from the other. He is afraid that, like a corporate outfit in Arizona he has heard of, they may try some nutty stunt like putting cowboys onto motorcycles. He wonders if they want to produce beef, or only tax writeoffs.

Is that the future? We want to know. This is obviously country where people and the land get on well together, where the prevailing economy not only doesn't harm the land, but with good management may sometimes improve it. The life here is rich, strenuous, and satisfying. Can that condition hold? Does the family ranch get absorbed into the corporate ranch owned by a bank or by a limited partnership whose primary goal *is* tax writeoffs? And will the corporate ranch stick to cattle, or will it turn to more profitable uses for the land—dudes, summer cottages, subdivisions, vacation condominiums? Can country like this remain a difficult but satisfying workground that enlists body, brain, and heart, or is it inevitably going to get turned into a playground, with every deterioration that becoming a playground connotes? What is to prevent entrepreneurs from coming here, as they have come elsewhere, and building a Big Sky or a Ski Yellowstone or a Sun Valley? Is cattle-raising the highest economic use for this land, or is it an anachronism and an indulgence? Can the family with a few hundred acres and a hundred head of cows still make it?

While we sit watching the late afternoon light stretch eastward across the ridges, and twilight begin in the green bottoms of the West Rosebud, they tell me what they think. This is a subject that they all take seriously. Ranching is one of the few western occupations that have been renewable and have produced a continuing way of life. These people don't want tourists or resorts, they don't want Bide-a-Wee cottages along the creeks. They discount sheep not because they hate sheep—the antipathy of cattlemen to sheep is largely mythical, at least in Montana, and historically many cattle ranches have run sheep to get them through bad beef years—but because sheep bring on a coyote problem which even friends of the coyote admit is serious. As for ski lodges, the newly designated wilderness area in the heart of the mountains keeps them out of there, at least. The local people, by and large, applaud the reservation of the wilderness—everybody except the boosters who wanted to push a highway through along Boulder Creek and make Big Timber another (God save us) Gateway-to-Yellowstone like West Yellowstone and Gardiner. There are some ski developments around Red Lodge, but they don't stray far from the pavement of U.S. 212.

Dude wrangling? Jim Fletcher is headed that way. The dude market is probably more dependable than the beef market. But most of these folks would find dudes less attractive animals than cattle, or even sheep, and the season is short. Given their preference, our picnickers would take exactly what they have now; a neighborly community of ranches, big, middle-sized, and small, scattered along the valleys of the swift foothill creeks, and tied together by narrow unpaved roads beside which wild roses, sometimes only inches high, ruffle in the summer wind.

They do not kid themselves. Theirs is a holding action, perhaps a rearguard action, and it could easily lose. Many forces, economic and social, work against the subsistence ranch. They hope that something—some stabilization of beef prices, better management techniques, new combinations of effort—will save the way of life they all articulately love. But they aren't unanimously hopeful.

Betty Morse is pessimistic. She says the subsistence ranch is not an economic unit, never was, and never can be. Her father, after all, sold off a lot of family ranches in his time, and the Bench Ranch itself, which at three thousand acres is of the middle size, was built up out of failed homesteads. The only way to get by, she says, is to be big. In that judgment she echoes John

Wesley Powell, the first and greatest student of the West, who in his *Report on the Lands of the Arid Region* in 1878 advocated "pasturage farms" of four full sections, 2,560 acres, to replace the hopelessly inadequate 160 acres allowed under the Homestead Act. Even four sections are not enough, Betty thinks. The Padlock, where Susan Heyneman grew up, is one ranch that is almost always in the black; the Lazy E–L, just over the hill on the East Rosebud, is another. Good management, maybe. But good management may be possible only on spreads like the Lazy E–L, which owns 30,000 acres, or the Padlock, which is *big*.

Both of those ranches were built up years ago, when land was cheap. No one could assemble such a dukedom now, and if anyone did he could never expect it to produce enough income per acre to pay a fraction of its cost. It takes twenty acres of this upland range to pasture one animal for half the year. It takes a lot of hay to feed him through the other half. All here agree that this land, well watered, beautiful, cool in summer, is worth much more as real estate than as cattle range. If you own only a few hundred acres of it, your debt is going to grow, and eventually your family ranch is going to be bought up by some rich man as a playground, or turned into a dude ranch, or consolidated into some larger unit, perhaps a corporate ranch that can play the tax-writeoff game.

Jack Heyneman agrees, in general. When he came to Montana from Berkeley, possessed of a little capital, a little ranching experience in California and Nevada, and a degree in range management from the University of Wyoming, he was looking for a place just big enough to support his family comfortably. While he worked as an "irrigator-irritator" in Three Forks, he spent his spare time driving around the state, looking and falling in love with what he saw.

Ranch hunting, he says, is the best job in the world. You see all kinds of lovely country, everybody wines and dines you, extends you credit, values your opinion, and likes your company. He knows a Nebraska cowpuncher who every year takes a three-week vacation, free, hunting a ranch in Montana. Jack did not stretch out his own search. He gave up the pleasures of ranch hunting when he found exactly what he wanted, on the West Rosebud near Fishtail.

The ranch he put together was modest, and as a cow-calf operation whose marketable product was steers, unprofitable. So he grew, adding neighboring homesteads as they came up for sale. "Why grow?" I want to know. "What good does it do to grow if you're losing on every steer you send to the feedlots?"

"Well," Jack says with his crooked smile, "we were trying to do it on volume."

In his zeal to make an economic unit, and his enthusiasm for the ownership of land, he nearly lost everything. Trying to save one fine piece from a subdivider, he overextended himself, and after three years lost it. Wryly, he cites compensations. While he was trying to hold the piece, Montana passed a law prohibiting the subdivision of ranch land into parcels of less than twenty acres. So that particular land, though no longer owned by the Heynemans, is still ranch land.

Jack's life here has been a long love-grapple with a hard country and an uncertain occupation, and he wears the marks. When I first met him, I thought he must have been kicked by a horse—a *big* horse, a Belgian or Percheron shod with ice calks. His jaw is dented, and a great scar runs from it down across his neck and disappears under his shirt. But it was not a horse, Susan says. It was a tractor that rolled down a bank with him and pinned him like a squashed bug. Unable to free him, and sure he would die any minute, she squatted beside him in the snow for an hour and a half before the ambulance arrived. She and the doctor from Absarokee somehow kept him alive during the two-hour ride to the hospital in Billings. He had no right to survive, for his face and jaw were broken and his chest and one lung crushed, and one arm was torn nearly off at the shoulder.

He uses that arm now as if it had never been hurt. Except for the scars, and perhaps his air of steady quiet, he seems not to have been changed by the accident. And perhaps he had always had that composure. He is a man who inspires confidence, one you would want on your side.

The Bench is truly a family ranch; the family are all working parts of it. Susan is a full partner. Though she can pull calves, inoculate for blackleg, doctor foot rot, and do the other ranch jobs, she is primarily the keeper of the records. Of the boys still at home, Tom, at eight, is still too young for anything but light chores, and Jim, at sixteen a sensitive, shy boy, "different from the others," as Susan says, may not be born for ranching. With Jim Bollingen gone, he will be his father's chief helper through the summer. In the fall, following a practice common among Montana ranch families who can afford it, he will go away to prep school—Shattuck School, in the Middle West—and perhaps to another life. But of John, eleven, there is little doubt. He is an all-purpose ranch Superkid, a 4-H'er, a great egg-producer and calf-raiser, a bull-rider and bronc wrangler who prefers to ride backwards, or upside down, without saddle, bridle, or hackamore. A reader like all the rest, he saves books for the snowed-in winters. Now, in full summer, he is a cheerful, breezy, extroverted presence with enormous vitality. Going home after the picnic, he leads the other boys on the run, going downhill like a falling boulder, and is at the gate minutes before the jeep. Here is one who will be fully competent to take over the ranch. Privately, Susan thinks he may be off flying airplanes or climbing Everest; in the end it may be Jim, the sensitive one with a love for the country, who will continue the ranching tradition.

Isolation troubles none of them. Except for a few days at a time during heavy snow, they can get out to Billings, Red Lodge, Big Timber, Livingston. In the fall Jack and Susan sometimes show their Red Angus at stock shows. This year they will trail some of Stegner's offspring down to the Cow Palace in San Francisco. Susan keeps the lines open to bookstores and libraries in Billings and Sheridan. She has her separate log cabin, known as The Hague, where she can retire to think, write, or draw, visited only by a gray thoroughbred brood mare named Luna, with her new foal, whom we are invited to help name. (Moon Goddess names occur to us. Astarte? Sin? Or how about Nokomis—Daughter of the Moon, Nokomis? None of our suggestions strikes a spark. Naming is Susan's specialty. Months later, we get a framed photograph, the filly's beautiful clean bony head silhouetted against her mother's flank, and learn that she is called Astrid, after a character in one of my novels whose father conducted some sinister biological experiments. Astrid's father, it seems, was named Shady Fellow. But Astrid's mother has now been bred to a son of Swaps, and that will introduce some class into the family tree.)

And what of the economics? Time, thought, trial, and error have resulted in adaptations that, at least in good years and for an outfit this size, work. There is little resemblance to the movies or to the oldtime open-range cattle business. There *is* no open range—the place is fenced like a Kentucky horse farm. There is no roundup, no chuck wagon, no bunkhouse; during Jim Bollingen's year of flirting with the corporate ranch there is not even one cowboy or hayhand. Jack and Jim Heyneman cut and bale the hay, though sometimes, as this year, they contract the stacking. I have watched the contract crew in the field with its forklift. The bales tumble from the baler, the forklift scoots after and scoops up a load, raises it up as an ant raises a captured insect with its forelegs, scoots across to the stack, slides the bales aboard, pulls in its arms, and scoots back for another load while two youths with hay hooks muscle the bales into place. Not much like the stacking we used to do by hand, or with a beaver-slide.

There is no roundup because the Bench makes no steers. There is branding, but not in one annual carnival of bawling, dust, and scorched hair and there is an extra refinement in the pedigree number that every calf has tattooed in its left ear. Stock is not sold en masse, but an animal or two at a time, a young bull here, a cow with calf there, and at a high price. The buyer trucks away his purchase himself, carefully. And the breed is Red Angus because the records of Red Angus, a mutant identical except in color with its black progenitor, are better and fuller than those of any other breed. The strain is so new that a buyer knows exactly what he is getting: he can trace it back to Adam and Eve.

Every bull with his harem is in a separate pasture; the heifers and bull calves are by themselves. One large pasture is generally rented, sometimes to the Padlock, which trucks several hundred steers north in spring, runs them on Bench grass for the summer, and trucks them back in the fall. The Bench is paid not per-head per-month, but by the weight gain, an arrangement that can be tricky, for cattle lose weight rapidly when moved around. Jack swears they even lose weight just being - driven over the hill to the Top Hat's scales. Nevertheless, in an ordinarily good grass year, this pasturage deal will pay both the Bench and the Padlock. Aesthetically it is less attractive. Beside the Red Angus, which are beef to the heels and whose hides shine in the sun like wet pipestone, those Wyoming range steers look like scruffy country cousins.

By being flexible, the Heynemans have found ways to make the life they love support itself and them. Others have found other ways, not so fully self-supporting. Over on the other side of the Absarokas, south of Livingston, Tom McGuane maintains a small ranch, where he raises and trains roping horses, with money he makes writing novels and movies. Up at Greycliff, just where the old Bozeman Trail enters the Yellowstone Valley, Hunt McCauley is developing a ranch partly on his earnings as an agricultural consultant to the United States and various foreign countries. (Shortly after our visit to the Heynemans, Hunt will buy Stegner III from the Bench, and put him to work creating a herd of Angus-whiteface crosses called Red Baldies.) Since he was trained as a veterinary, has great hay land, and is very knowledgeable about the economics of the family ranch, Hunt ought to be able to make it go if anyone can. Most of all, he wants to keep that land open, fronted by the Yellowstone River and with gorgeous views of the Beartooths and the Crazy Mountains, and pass it on intact to his children.

And there are the Heynemans' close neighbors, each with his own adaptation, some of them imaginative. Just over the ridge is the Top Hat, owned by Dave and Marge Branger—he a big joking man, she plump and amused and chain-smoking. They are good and successful ranchers, and they have tried almost everything. For ten years they raised reindeer, from breeding stock which they imported from Nunivak Island. They sold reindeer to zoos and to other breeders, and sometimes rented them out to department stores to enhance the Santa Claus exhibits. Dave insists he made money on reindeer but just got tired of them. Jack Heyneman says he wouldn't call Dave a liar, but he'd like to see his books.

After reindeer the Brangers tried llamas, which they gave up because the males are very mean, and bite and fight and attack - people. Having been chased through a California pasture once by a wall-eyed Andean cameloid, I second his judgment. Llamas were not a good choice. They are not only mean, they are insane.

Following the llamas' short tenure, the Top Hat pastures held elk. Dave says they got him in bad with the Fish and Game people, who didn't even want to *recognize* what he was raising. When a bull elk gored and killed a valuable thoroughbred stallion, he closed out the exotic wildlife and concentrated on Black Angus and thoroughbred horses. Locally, he is to the Black Angus what the Heynemans are to the Red. As for his horses, they have raced not only on county fair tracks throughout Montana, but on some tracks known around the world.

Dave says categorically that the family ranch conceived as a cow-calf operation is an impossibility, a lost cause. He says sheep are out unless 1080 is taken off the proscribed list so that coyotes can be controlled. Dudes don't appeal to him as ranch stock. That leaves the solutions he and the Heynemans have found—cattle and horses, but blooded stock.

We have also talked to Bill Mackay, who leases the forty-six square miles of the Lazy E–L from the other branches of the Mackay family, and manages them in their common interest. This ranch too is a family ranch, but a long way above the subsistence level. It was built up by Bill Mackay's grandfather, who came out from New Jersey in 1901, when land was cheap, and who until he got the place onto a paying basis supported it with infusions from his brokerage business. His photograph hangs on the wall of his grandson's office—a tall young man in chaps, six-shooter, and leather wristlets, a Wild West figure of the kind and vintage that we know from the career of Teddy Roosevelt.

As might be expected, Bill Mackay is less uneasy about the

future of ranching than smaller operators are. He expects the
beef business to be cyclical, and he is big enough to ride out the
lows of any cycle. But even he does not run a traditional cow-
calf outfit. His is a pasturage ranch, not a breeding ranch. He
buys calves—weaners—and sells yearlings, and makes his profit
simply on the point spread, on the usufruct of the seasonal
grass. He is not the slave of the market because in years when
steers are cheap, so are calves; and because, if he has to, he can
hold his yearlings off the market when the price is too low.

Like Jack Heyneman, he is convinced that grazing is the best
and highest use of this land. Like Jack, he is a specialist, though
of another kind, and a careful manager: for all those forty-six
square miles of the Lazy E–L he needs only two hired hands.
Like his neighbors he is dubious about the future of the subsistence ranch. The only person he knows who makes it on those
terms is Chris Branger, a relative of Dave's, who with 1,400
acres and 120 cows manages to support his wife and two children. But Mackay is also skeptical of some forms of specializa-
tion. He doesn't much like sheep—they would be a come-down.
He is against dudes and tourists out of sheer distaste for the play
ethic as opposed to the work ethic. And he is against thoroughbred horse raising because he thinks horses a cutthroat business.

But he is even more antagonistic to the industrial intrusions
that threaten the pastoral life, to the strip mines and the power
plants, to the mineral developments of the "Stillwater complex"
dominated by Anaconda, Johns-Manville, and Chevron. The
fact is, this "big" rancher, who might be expected to have many
of the attitudes and attributes of the old range barons, is a mili-
tant environmentalist. He wants the country left in grass—an
attitude that the unfriendly could construe as the conservatism
of someone who has it made, but which I construe as the con-
servationism of someone who has learned to respect his native
country in essentially Rotten Belly's terms. One small instance:
Where the oldtime pattern was to throw onto the range as
many animals as it could carry, and sometimes more, Mackay
rests one entire third of his range every year, thus deliberately
restoring something like the conditions of the old buffalo

range, which because of the wide migrations of the herds went unpastured for long periods, and so stayed healthy.

Like the rest of the Rocky Mountain states, Montana has traditionally provided too few jobs for its sons and daughters, and has exported manpower to California and the East. But I have never met anyone who, having grown up in this country, did not leave his heart behind when he went away. Now there is danger that what nostalgia remembers may not always be there. Ranch life in the foothills of the Beartooths is as vulnerable as the old hunting life of the Crows. Eternal vigilance is the price of its continuity.

Bill Mackay is chairman of the Carbon County Planning Commission, which with luck will have a good deal to say about land use in the area in the future. He has also served as president of the Northern Plains Resource Council, an association of ranchers formed to resist the strip mines and power plants of an energy-hungry economy, and to force modifications of the leasing policies of the Bureau of Land Management. The NPRC is tough, stubborn, and politically powerful, and it has had some success in stalling what at first looked as if it might be a walkover. The territory it first had to defend was out in the rolling plains east of Billings where the great coal deposits lie. Now it also has to fight the Stillwater complex in its own back yard, for Anaconda, in alliance with Johns-Manville and Chevron, is proposing to drill an exploratory adit at the site of the old Mouat mine, near Nye, and drain off the waste water into the Stillwater River, or into a settling pond from which it will seep who knows where. Jack Heyneman also fights that one, as president of the Stillwater Protective Association, which is in effect a local branch of the Northern Plains Resource Council. Every rancher in the area looks with apprehension at Billings, which displays the hectic energy, the growth, the hype, and the fouled air reminiscent of an earlier stage of Denver. Every rancher wonders what happens to the water and the grass if the Stillwater complex, with its cobalt, platinum, and silver, its smelter, its adits with their waste water, goes ahead without resistance. These ranchers grew up under the shadow of Anaconda, and its record does not reassure them. If it operates in their area, they want it controlled.

For grass, the Heynemans and Mackays insist, is the steadfast, satisfying basis of this country's economy as well as of its social and cultural organization. In fighting for it, ranchers find themselves in somewhat surprised alliance with environmental groups, never until now their favorite people, and even with the Northern Cheyennes, once widely dismissed as permanent and prolific paupers. There is a true union of interest here, but it is also a union of feeling: ranchers, environmentalists, and Indians cherish land, miners and energy companies tear it up and shove it around and leave it dead behind them.

The sun is three-quarters down behind the Beartooths. The last light reaches out and lays a long pink band on the pastures east of the creek, with their solid dots of grazing Angus. A ray fifty miles long leaps eastward to touch, just for a moment, the far brown hump of the Pryor Mountains. The ray lifts, and the hump is gone. The air is hazy with pine pollen, fragrant with pine and woodsmoke. The light, soft, gentle, nostalgic, fades by the minute. We rise and start gathering the picnic gear and carrying it to the jeep.

Tomorrow on the Bench Ranch is another day in a succession of strenuous days. In the morning two cows with calves must be cut out for a buyer who is coming to truck them away. Stegner III, segregated temporarily from his harem, has walked through his fence again and rejoined them, and must be got back to the isolation he does not enjoy. There is hay down that Jack wants to see baled and stacked before rain comes along and spoils it. At eleven a Pakistani vet (Montana is like that—people are few but various) is coming to look at Luna's foal, which was born so knock-kneed that the Heynemans are worried about it. And some way has to be found to get a neighbor to spray his pasture, luxuriant with leafy spurge. Spurge is a flowering weed that spreads by rhizomes. From the neighbor's untended pastures it is already pushing against the fences of the pastures that Jack has sprayed to the fence and beyond.

Work to be done, the chores of an unremitting but satisfying stewardship. The raising of Red Angus breeding stock is no such slavery to animals as, say, dairy farming, but like any kind of animal husbandry it involves continual responsibility and care. The boys, already bolting down the hill to beat the jeep to the gate, have been brought up in that tacit knowledge, and they are learning the skills that must accompany it. Ten or fifteen years from now, if the threats can be kept at arm's length, one or more of them will perhaps be running this ranch, exercising the same stewardship and working as their parents have worked to keep this island of sanity and naturalness in a far, loved corner of what was once an incomparable continent.

HIGH PLATEAUS

The Aquarius [plateau] should be described in blank verse and illustrated upon canvas. The explorer who sits upon the brink of its parapet looking off into the southern and eastern haze, who skirts its lava-cap or clambers up and down its vast ravines, who builds his camp-fire by the borders of its snow-fed lakes or stretches himself beneath its giant pines and spruces, forgets that he is a geologist and feels himself a poet. From numberless lofty standpoints we have seen it afar off, its long, straight crest-line stretched across the sky like the threshold of another world. We have drawn nearer and nearer to it, and seen its mellow blue change day by day to dark somber gray, and its dull, expressionless ramparts grow upward into walls of majestic proportions and sublime import. The formless undulations of its slopes have changed to gigantic spurs sweeping slowly down into the painted desert and parted by impenetrable ravines. The mottling of light and shadow upon its middle zones is resolved into groves of Pinus ponderosa, *and the dark hues at the summit into myriads of spikes, which we know are the storm-loving spruces.*

The ascent leads us among rugged hills, almost mountainous in size, strewn with black bowlders, along precipitous ledges, and by the side of cañons. Long detours must be made to escape the chasms and to avoid the taluses of fallen blocks; deep ravines must be crossed, projecting crags doubled, and lofty battlements scaled before the summit is reached. When the broad platform is gained the story of "Jack and the beanstalk," the finding of a strange and beautiful country somewhere up in region of the clouds, no longer seem incongruous. Yesterday we were toiling over a burning soil, where nothing grows save the ashy-colored

sage, the prickly pear, and a few cedars that writhe and contort
their stunted limbs under a scorching sun. To-day we are among
forests of rare beauty and luxuriance; the air is moist and cool,
the grasses are green and rank, and hosts of flowers deck the turf
like the hues of a Persian carpet. The forest opens in wide parks
and winding avenues, which the fancy can easily people with
fays and woodland nymphs. On either side the sylvan walls look
impenetrable, and for the most part so thickly is the ground
strewn with fallen trees, that any attempt to enter is as serious a
matter as forcing an abattis. The tall spruces (Abies subalpina)
stand so close together, that even if the dead-wood were not
there a passage would be almost impossible. Their slender
trunks, as straight as lances, reach upward a hundred feet, ending in barbed points, and the contours of the foliage are as sym-
metrical and uniform as if every tree had been clipped for a
lordly garden. They are too prim and monotonous for a high
type of beauty; but not so the Engelmann spruces and great
mountain firs (A. Engelmanni, A. grandis), which are delight-
fully varied, graceful in form, and rich in foliage. Rarely are
these species found in such luxuriance and so variable in habit.
In places where they are much exposed to the keen blasts of this
altitude they do not grow into tall, majestic spires, but cower
into the form of large bushes, with their branchlets thatched
tightly together like a great hay-rick.

   Upon the broad summit are numerous lakes—not the little
morainal pools, but broad sheets of water a mile or two in
length. Their basins were formed by glaciers, and since the ice-
cap which once covered the whole plateau has disappeared they
continue to fill with water from the melting snows. Early in autumn the snows have disappeared and the lakes cease to out-
flow, but never dry up.

   C. E. Dutton (1880)

The skyline here is special: not the toothed peaks of the Rockies, not the worn, contorted shapes of the Great Basin ranges,
not the long, level, cliff-edged mesas of the Southwest, but
raised horizons bounding both sides of the broad San Pete and

Sevier valleys—whale-like shapes, gently undulating, with round-ing knobs and promontories. The higher slopes, on this late September day, are patched with golden aspen; along parts of the rim are intimations of fir forest.

Brought here blindfold, I would know I was in the desert West by the smell of sage and dust and brittle weeds. Given a glimpse of the ground, I would know from the raw earth and the tufted, clumpy vegetation—bunch grass, bunchy sage, bunchy junipers, the bunchy yellow-flowering rabbitbrush whole profusion is a sure sign of overgrazed range—that I was west of the 100th meridian. Allowed to see the sky, I might guess from the dark-ness of its blue and the whiteness of the cumuli that float across it that I was in Montana, Idaho, Colorado, Wyoming, New Mexico, or Arizona. But give me the briefest look at the hori-zons and I would know I was in Utah, in the high plateaus.

Nowhere else in America are such great blocks of nearly level strata lifted so high above broad, deep valleys. Nowhere else would we see forests along such lofty rims. Reaching southward from the end of the Wasatch Mountains in three chains, widening and gaining altitude as they go, the plateaus are as high as many western mountain ranges, but they know no timberline. The Aquarius, for example, is forested all across its 11,600-foot summit, a thousand feet above what would be timberline in the Colorado Rockies of the same latitude.

From almost anywhere along their western edge, these ele-vations are so plain that it takes a while to see that they are also grand. From many vantage points they show none of the level crests and bold cliffs that would reveal them to be unmistak-able plateaus. They loom without asserting themselves. Once I drove my aunt, fresh from Iowa, through the Sevier Valley where the Sevier Plateau rears 5,600 feet over the town of Richfield in one unbroken wall, its last two thousand feet sheer lava cliffs, and my aunt, good soul, was reminded of the bluffs in the county park in Fort Dodge.

Nothing now reminds me of Fort Dodge. This is country where I spent the summers of my adolescence, and what I see is enriched by geology, history, and memory. Standing by the car in the autumn sun I can feel, like a radiation, the aloofness with which this country greeted human intrusion; and like the warmth of a stone on which the sun has shone for a long time, the effect it has had on its settlers. The plateaus remain aloof and almost uninhabited, but the valleys are a collaboration between land and people, and each has changed the other.

The map we spread out on the hood is the product of two hundred years of white exploration and occupation, plus uncounted centuries of Indian use. Utes, Spaniards, mountain men, Mormons, and government scientists have all contributed to it. The Utes left their names on the Pavant, Tushar, Markágunt, and Paunságunt plateaus, on valleys like the San Pete, on towns like Koosharem and Paragonah. Few Spanish names remain, either from the Escalante expedition or from the Spanish Trail that was heavily traveled between 1829 and the 1850s; but the Sevier River is a corruption of their Rio Severo, and their passage is recorded in places like Spanish Fork, Escalante, and the Virgin River. Nephi, Moroni, and Mt. Nebo take their names from the *Book of Mormon;* Mormon hierarchs and pioneers gave their names to St. George, Burrville, and Cannonville. Frémont is all over the map, as a town, a river, and a pass, but Jedediah Smith, who was far more important in the exploration of the region, is uncommemorated. Mormon settlers exercised their right to be conventional in such place names as Richfield and Mt. Pleasant, and the equally Godgiven right to be earthy in Hell's Backbone, Cohab Canyon, and Mary's Nipple and Molly's Nipple. (Mary and Molly may have been the same lady, but if so she was some lady: the parts for which she is remembered are more than a hundred miles apart and of greatly different size.) The Powell Survey and U.S. Geological Survey parties of the 1870s and 1880s left on the map a Secretary of War (Mt. Belknap), a Secretary of the Interior (Mt. Delano), and many government scientists (Mt. Hilgard, Mt. Dutton, the Henry Mountains). They also left on many features names that would not likely have sprung to the lips of Ute, Spaniard, or Mormon (the Aquarius Plateau, the Waterpocket Fold, Smithsonian Butte).

Unloading history on my patient wife as we turn off U.S. 89 and up the Fairview Canyon road across the Wasatch Plateau,

I retrieve from the attic of my skull the fact that it was exactly two hundred and three years ago to the day—September 23, 1776—that Fathers Escalante and Domínguez came down Spanish Fork Canyon into Utah Valley. The map of the expedition's wanderings that was made by Bernardo de Miera y Pacheco first established this country within the known world, and put Great Salt Lake, though inaccurately and by hearsay, in approximately its proper place. After Escalante, the region was unvisited for half a century, until Jedediah Smith made his first exploration down along the western rim of the plateau country (the eastern rim of the Great Basin, on the route essentially followed now by Interstate 15) in 1826. He came again the next year. Beginning in 1829, New Mexican muleteers carried blankets and woollens along the Spanish Trail to California, and drove great herds of horses and big California mules back to Santa Fe. We will meet the Spanish Trail on the other side of the Wasatch Plateau, and follow it down through Castle Valley, back across Wasatch Pass, and down Salina Canyon into the valley of the Sevier; and we will touch it again near Panguitch, and follow it down Dog Valley into the Great Basin; and pick it up again when we come back over the great hump of the Tushar and down into Circle Valley; and follow it backward down the Sevier on our return.

That doesn't mean much to me, my wife says in effect. Why don't we forget the map and look at the country?

After a few miles, our road is dirt, and we have it to ourselves. The fishing season is over, the hunting season not yet begun. The fall colors that in Colorado or New Mexico would have - people out in aspencades have lured nobody up here. The two pickups we meet are obviously locals on local business. We pass a ski ranch, half-finished, deserted, with no visible lifts—a poor-boy project. Then we turn a corner and are engulfed in sheep, a moving, blatting mat of wool and black faces, pushed along by three dogs and two riders, and followed by an RV, the modern descendant of the oldtime sheepwagon.

To John Muir, sheep were hoofed locusts. The West has suffered from their sharp hoofs and nibbling lips, and parts of the world are deserts because of them. Yet here they seem right. They revive some echo of Old Testament pastoralism, they confirm our taste for the unchanging. I recall the envy I used to feel when, at spring and fall times of moving the flocks, Mormon schoolfellows got out of school to spend important days "down to the herd." Similar vacations at beet-thinning time never intrigued me, but sheep had in them something adventurous, touched with the romance of movement and wild country.

Under the slopes that glow red, gold, and apricot, whose fabric of little white-boled trees twinkles and flaws in a wind so clean and chilly it waters the eyes, Mary and I are both reminded of a time years ago in the Pindus Mountains on the border between Greece and Yugoslavia. It was this same fall season, yellow leaves were turning the air to gold, and the Vlachs, migratory shepherds, were bringing their sheep and goats down from the mountain pastures. They immobilized us as we are immobilized now; we sat and let them flow around us and past. The Vlachs were picturesque, as these Mormon herders are not. They had their women and children with them, and the women spun yarn on twirling spindles as they walked. But these Mormons are weathered in the same way, as weathered as stones. Their eyes meet ours with the same careful incuriosity as they pass in their ancient pastoral routine. With no more than a change from Levi's to some other costume, they - could be Vlachs or Baktiaris; they could step back two thousand years, or into other countries and other mountains, and be at home. Give them another hundred or two hundred years in isolation and they might even be picturesque.

On top of the Wasatch Plateau, above nine thousand feet, the air is the kind that automobile tourists expect only on mountain passes. But there is no pass here, there are no peaks around us, only a rolling, grassy plain edged with rounding ridges covered with aspen and ponderosa pine. If this plain were in Nebraska, the horizon would spread to the limits of vision established by the earth's curvature. If it were in Montana, it would lift to the blue of distant mountains. But here we have the sense that just beyond any ridge the edge drops away. We are literally on a roof. It feels wonderfully high, open, sunny, and big. The wind blows off no contiguous land, but straight out of the sky.

Along the top, which is barely six miles wide, wriggles a dirt trail ambitiously called Skyline Drive. Though tempting, it is obviously not designed for rented city cars. So we bear off southeastward, and soon we are in a canyon, descending. Huntington Creek makes its appearance; the walls rise, a strong red. Through a gap to the east we catch glimpses of pale desert mottled with cloud shadows. Then within a half hour we are down, and leveling out. Looking back, we see the plateau as a towering red rim—no trouble recognizing it as a plateau from this side—broken by the wide canyon we have just emerged from, and farther south by the canyon of Ferron Creek. Southeastward, across Castle Valley, the San Rafael Reef marks the edge of the San Rafael Swell—Robber's Roost country.

Now two vignettes, one of the past, one of the future, face one another across the road. On the left, a pond formed by a dirt dam, and on the pond white ducks and mallards—wild and tame coexisting comfortably—and at the end, under cottonwoods worn smooth by rubbing stock, a pair of horses sleeping away the afternoon with their heads across each other's necks and their broom tails switching flies. On the right of the road, a power plant into which a conveyor belt carries coal direct from the mine mouth. From a tall stack, smoke trails across the desert sky. The local history, the local dilemma: Castle Valley in a nutshell.

This Huntington plant is not big. Neither is the Hunter plant at Castle Dale, a few miles down the valley. Together, they probably represent neither a significant source of jobs for local people, nor a serious threat to the environment, nor an alarming intrusion on the integrity of the valley towns. It might be possible to justify both of them as appropriate technology, though I would hate to argue the point with Ed Abbey. It is the 3,000-megawatt monsters that can't be justified, and the drawing boards are full of them.

This road, Utah 10, is an intramural road. All the cars and trucks wear Utah plates and red Utah dust. But there are signs of change. Castle Dale has an elaborate new motel. Ferron and

Emery, cowtowns when I knew them, villages with pole corrals, are still cowtowns, but two signs on the outskirts of Ferron seem significant. One says "Town Zoned—Building Permit
Required." The other says "Green River Ordinance Enforced."
In a place like Ferron, zoning can only have been made necessary by migrant construction workers with trailers—perhaps
the ones who built those power plants. And the Green River
Ordinance, which puts constraints on vagrants and peddlers, is
never enforced against locals. The town fathers must have read
some handwriting on the wall.

Now, below Emery, Interstate 70 comes in from the east, and
at once we are no longer intramural, but in the company of
California, Michigan, Tennessee. I-70 has put us back on the
tourist track, and also on the track of history. Just here, two
branches of the Spanish Trail joined. From the crossing of the
Green River, now Greenriver, Utah, one came across the San
Rafael Swell on the approximate line of I-70. The other, which
Captain J. W. Gunnison chose when he made his 1853 railroad
survey along the proposed Central Route to the Pacific, turned
northwest from the crossing as far as the Price River, then bent
left and came south through Castle Valley, as we have just
done. From their junction here, the united trails went over
Wasatch Pass, between the Wasatch and Fish Lake plateaus,
and down Salina Canyon to the Sevier Valley (one variant
reached the Sevier by way of Fish Lake, Grass Valley, and East
Fork Canyon), and thence up the Sevier to Dog Valley, where it
broke down into the Great Basin near Paragonah. Once out in
the desert, travelers faced five hundred harsh miles with only a
few watering places such as Las Vegas before they could look
down into the green of the Los Angeles basin.

It was never a road for wheels or a route for rails, but it was
a trade route of the first importance, "the longest, crookedest,
most arduous pack mule route in the history of America," as its
historian Le Roy Hafen says. Across twelve hundred miles of
mountains, plateaus, and deserts it linked the two areas of
Spanish settlement in the West, and as an extension of the Sante
Fe Trail it was a transcontinental route before any other. Until
the Mexican War broke up Spanish isolation, and the Gold

Rush redirected travel out the Platte–Bear–Snake–Humboldt line, this unlikely thoroughfare swarmed with summer activity.

I would like to have been a magpie in a piñon, to spy on one of those camps of New Mexican muleteers. I wish I could have sat on some rimrock to watch one of those enormous herds of horses and mules, sometimes thousands of animals in a herd, streaming eastward. Sometimes they were driven by others than their rightful owners. The Ute chief Walkara, his brother Arrowpeen, and the technologically unemployed mountain man Pegleg Smith were all notable horse thieves on the Spanish Trail in the 1840s. All brought their stolen herds to the sanctuary valleys among the high plateaus. I like to think they may sometimes have refreshed them in Circle Valley, where later would be born another highly publicized thief who made equally good use of that difficult country. A Mormon boy christened George LeRoy Parker, he was known professionally as Butch Cassidy.

Interstate 70 carries less colorful traffic than the Spanish Trail used to, and is far tamer and less beautiful than the Fairview-Huntington road over the Wasatch Plateau. In Salina Canyon we are overtaken every few miles by double-van coal trucks doing seventy downgrade. The town of Salina, which Captain Clarence Dutton a hundred years ago called a "wretched hamlet," was better than that when I knew it—was actually a pleasant little irrigated sugarbeet-and-alfalfa-growing oasis like the other Sevier Valley towns. Now it has lost its virginity to the boom. We try four motels before we find a bed. Across the road, while we carry in our bags, a helicopter settles down in a whirlwind of dust and noise, and disgorges men khaki. Phillips Petroleum, the motel clerk says proudly, part of a seismo crew exploring across the valley, in the Pávant. The girls who sells me a couple of beers is so busy trying to catch their eyes that she forgets to give me my change.

All evening, all night, the coal trucks whip past. Five mines have opened in Salina Canyon since the Interstate was completed. Our tax dollars at work making things nice for the energy companies. The trucks hail to Delta, on the Western Pacific out in the desert, or to Salt Lake, Las Vegas, even Los Angeles. Musinia Peak, the flat-topped white landmark knob that crowns the

southern end of the Wasatch Plateau, may look down on those
speeding behemoths as imperturbably as it once looked down on
Spanish mule trains, Ute slavers, government geologists, and
Mormon train robbers, but we are not so philosophical—we have
not learned Aldo Leopold's trick of thinking like a mountain. We
are up very early, eager to be gone.

Our escape route takes us back up Salina Canyon for a few
miles, among the coal trucks. Then we turn off up the Gooseberry, into the Fishlake–Manti National Forest, and are all by
ourselves. There is no other car on this dirt road, though we see
a couple of trailers asleep by the creek—perhaps boomtime
squatters of the kind that Ferron has zoned itself against. Color
begins to appear on the slopes tilted ahead of us, the Fish Lake
Plateau lifts steeply. The higher we go, the rougher and more
beautiful it becomes. The roof is like that of the Wasatch
Plateau, an eroded, rolling plain bounded by low ridges patched
with aspen and ponderosa. As we switch back and forth, still
climbing, the scattered aspen color consolidates itself into
dense planes and slopes of gold, peach-red, and orange. Behind
us, Musinia Peak climbs with us, swimming up as serenely as
the moon. The distance is filled with long tabular shapes.
Ahead, seen and lost again behind promontories, are Mt. Terrill, Mt. Hilgard, and Mt. Marvine, all about 11,500 feet high,
and to the right is the stern rim of the Fish Lake Hightop, the
flat summit of the plateau, higher than any of the residual
peaks. When we get out and stand in the morning quiet, high
above the colored slopes and level with a red-tailed hawk that
has warmed its wings and begun to soar, I find myself trying to
breathe like a mountain.

There is no best season for the Fish Lake Plateau. Gorgeous
as it is in September, it is just as gorgeous in early July, high
spring there, when the meadows are so dense with flowers that -
every step crushes dozens. The botanist who worked with Dutton's survey party at the end of the 1870s identified more than
nine hundred species of plants up here, and the first time I drove
Mary over this road, forty-six years ago, the only surfaces not in
flower were the ruts under our wheels. We went for miles to a

soft multitudinous tapping, the sound of flower heads in the trail's crown knocking against the bottom of the car.

For a good while this superlative mountain is as we remember it and want it. Then, coming down toward the Mt. Terrill ranger station, we meet a seismo crew drilling holes beside the road. That ominous touch is succeeded by a pastoral one— hundreds of fat Herefords, Black Baldies, and Red Baldies grazing along Frying Pan Flat. Above them is the high blue fair-weather sky that even steers must appreciate. Behind them the Hightop slopes steeply up through gold of aspen to black-green of fir before it stands on edge in lava cliffs. Around the flat, as visually striking as Christo's nylon, and a good deal more functional, goes a line of snake fence: outdoor sculpture, folk art.

In Seven Mile Creek, sunk among meadow grass and thinly fringed with willows, I used to catch a lot of trout, sometimes in channels hardly more than a yard wide. It looks as if one still - could. I am grateful to the Forest Service for having kept this part of the plateau without visible deterioration or change. But the future is being prepared. Trees have been cut in preparation for the widening of the road, and as we come down past Johnson Reservoir, into which Fish Lake flows and in which the Frémont River begins, graders are tearing up stumps and moving dirt.

I look across the reservoir somewhat bemusedly. Somewhere in the mud of its bottom are two pairs of hip boots well on the way to becoming fossils. Fifty years ago, in the company of a boy who later became a U.S.C. quarterback, I tried to walk across the reservoir bottom in a time of deep drawdown. Slime and quicksand welcomed us in to the tops of our boots, and it was all we could do to work out of the boots and half crawl, half swim to solid ground. I still remember that long stocking-footed walk up the rocky road to the lake.

Now it seems almost as long, driving, as it did then walking, for everything is being butchered and improved. When we stop to take pictures of the golden slopes perfectly reflected in the still waters of Widgeon Bay, we find the shore littered with dead fish. The girl in the store at the public boat ramp, a structure new since my time, says that Fish and Game has just poisoned the reservoir to kill off the junk fish, the product of dumped bait buckets, and that some of the poison seeped back into the foot of the main lake. But next year, she says happily, the trout fishing will be super.

Maybe. I remember when it was *really* super, when Johnson Reservoir gave up big natives and native-rainbow crosses, and when I could wade into the main lake off our dock just at dusk and, fishing a wet fly, white miller or silver doctor, hook big rainbows coming in close to feed. I remember history, too, especially the account written by Lieutenant Brewerton, who came east along this variant of the Spanish Trail with Kit Carson in June 1848. Carson was carrying dispatches from California to Washington, and he had in his saddlebags, like a time bomb, the April 1 issue of the California *Star,* reporting the discovery of gold at Sutter's mill. That was the news story that set off the Gold Rush, but it is not the reason I remember Brewerton's narrative. Something else: the big lake trout were spawning in Twin Creeks, as I have seen them spawning, and the Utes camped there were shooting them with arrows. They sold a good many to the Carson-Brewerton party before the whites discovered that they could go down to the creeks and kill their own with clubs.

I drive slowly along the shore, looking for our old cottage, but somehow miss it. They must have changed the alignment of the road. It should be in plain sight, for it stood in the edge of the aspens within a hundred feet of the water. I drive back, taking a diversion through a new campground, but still can't find our place. Not until we stop at Fish Lake Lodge, once called Skogaard's, do I get an explanation. All the cottages along there were bulldozed out some years ago to clear the way for the sewer system. The man who tells me this tells me also, with a commiseration that seems half pride, what that cottage would be worth now if we still owned it.

I doubt that I would want to own it now. Nor do I covet any of the expensive-looking summer homes that have replaced the old shacks along Twin Creeks. I like this place better when it was limited, simple, and austere, without sewers, running water, or fishing that had been improved by poison. I liked it when muskrats still dug in the bank by our dock, and when, once or twice a summer, a mountain lion would come down and steal the fish hanging on nails in the unscreened porch where I slept.

Any return is a journey across both space and time. Driving along the top of the low, treeless Awapa Plateau, aiming for the gap between Thousand Lake and the Aquarius, I find my memory as busy as a squirrel digging up acorns. My first trip into this country was in 1924, pretty primitive times, in the company of my scoutmaster and his son. The scoutmaster, an Episcopal missionary to the Mormons, died a disillusioned man, without converts, but in the back country he was an enthusiast. Also he was a pipe smoker. Coming around the corner of Thousand Lake Mountain, as we are coming now, with the Red Gate cliffs on the left and Rabbit Valley around us and the white domes of Capitol Reef showing ahead and the profile of the Aquarius high and dark on the right, he made a sudden, excited gesture with the pipe in his left hand. The wind blew the coal out of the pipe and up his sleeve, setting his armpit afire. His son and I died laughing and were buried just here, where the road dips down toward the canyon on the Frémont and the lost village of Fruita, now absorbed in Capitol Reef National Park.

Fruita used to be one of our favorite places—a sudden, intensely green little valley among the cliffs of the Waterpocket Fold, opulent with cherries, peaches, and apples in season, inhabited by a few families who were about equally good Mormons and good frontiersmen and good farmers. Over the years it has also been sanctuary for a number of enthusiasts with the atavistic compulsion to hole up in Paradise, people who like Zane Grey's Lassiter put a bloody hand to the balancing rock and rolled it down to block away the world.

One was Doc Inglesby, who at the beginning of the 1930s sold out his business, the Salt Lake–Bingham stage line, and came down here to be a rockhound, run a little motel, and listen to the singing of the cliffs. He was a little round gnome with a little round belly and a little round cocker spaniel that he used to carry on the pommel of his saddle when he rode around exploring undiscovered canyons, measuring unnamed natural bridges, and hunting jasper geodes. His passion for the country

was as explosive as gasoline: he could scare you to death calling your attention to a sunset or the light on a cliff. I hope the
sunsets are good where he is now, and the ledges red.

Another was Charlie Kelly, a considerable Mormon-eater, the
author of several basic books on Utah's frontier history, especially its outlaws, and the first superintendent of the Capitol Reef
National Monument. He was a good historian and a good com-
panion. *Requiescat.* He too deserves an Eternity of red ledges.

A third was Dean Brimhall, whose father had been president
of Brigham Young University and who had spent much of his
mature life in the Department of Commerce in Washington.
Related by blood to half the Mormon hierarchy and by marriage to the other half, he was a sadly lapsed Saint, as antagonistic to the Church as he was devoted to the geology and
ethnology of the plateau country. In the early 1940s, when he
and his wife Lila were visiting us in Vermont, he wished aloud
that he knew of some place in Utah as quiet, remote, and
peaceful as our Vermont farm. I suggested Fruita, and the next
I knew he had gone down there, fallen in love, and bought a
piece of land, with a log cabin, a grove of big Fremont poplars,
and an orchard. Before long he built a house, before much
longer he was living in it most of the year.

By the time of his death in 1974, Dean had become the greatest student of the plateau region since the Powell Survey quit
working there. He knew every crack and canyon, every arch
and natural bridge, every petroglyph and pictograph, within a
hundred and fifty miles of the Capitol Reef. With great labor he
brought in scaffolding and set it up in remote canyons to photograph cliff murals that constitute the finest body of native
American art north of Mexico. Some of these Mary and I have
seen *in situ;* most of them we know from studying color trans-
parencies in Dean's Fruita house—deer, elk, bighorn sheep,
square-headed men, hands, the records of how the people who
lived in these canyons a thousand years ago responded to their
surroundings. One pictograph in particular seemed to all of us
the quintessential statement of life among the Anasazi. Life
size, painted in ocher on a clean pink cliff, it shows a man
standing stiffly with his hand outstretched. Growing from the

hand is a tree. In the tree, unmistakable, done with love, is a hummingbird.

Whenever we were within three hundred miles of Fruita, we used to stop. At first we stayed with Doc, later with Dean. If Dean happened to be away, we camped in his orchard. Now, we know, Doc's old motel under the big poplars, fenced with slabs of ripple-marked sandstone, has been cleared away and the land leveled to make the park's picnic ground. Dean's house is now the house of the superintendent. Not even Lurt Knee's Sleeping Rainbow Lodge is open, for the National Park Service has bought up all the in-holdings, as it should have. So we will have to stay outside the park at the Rimrock, spectacularly perched on a stone ridge between the Reef and the Aquarius, with three hundred and sixty degrees of view. Mary, who is tired, is content to sit and look at it. I go in and spend a couple of hours talking to Eugene Blackburn.

Much can be learned from a man like Blackburn, whose memory goes back almost as far as mine, and who has watched all the changes. Though he still has a farm in Bicknell, he has worked for the Park Service for nine years, managing the camp and picnic grounds and running the water treatment plant, and his native attitudes have been tempered by friendly contact with the feds. In his relaxed local voice, without a flat *a* in it—he says "squar" and "thar" like a character out of the Leather-stocking Tales—he fills me in on what has been happening since the Reef was upgraded to a National Park in 1971.

I am an interested listener, for I was involved in that upgrad-ing. In 1961, when I was working as a special assistant to the Secretary of the Interior Stewart Udall, I came through here with Joe Carithers, from the Secretary's office, and Bates Wilson, then superintendent of Arches National Monument, later superintendent at Canyonlands National Park. We picked up Dean Brimhall and the then superintendent of the Capitol Reef National Monument, Bill Kruger, and spent a good many days running up and down the Waterpocket Fold and through Cathedral Valley and the South Desert, looking at areas that might go into an enlarged and enhanced park. We anticipated local objections, because the feds are often looked upon as ab-

sentee landlords in Utah, and because one cattleman whom
Dean and I encountered in the state liquor store in Torrey took
one look at us and puckered up his mouth as if he had tasted
something nasty. "Washington men," he said. "I think I'll go
over and get me two boxes of shells, one for the elk and one for
the Goddamn Washington men."

But that attitude, according to the Blackburn, was not widespread and did not last. Most cattlemen had already overgrazed their publicly owned range and were going broke. The
national park seemed then, and seems now, a reasonable com-
promise with Progress. Living up to its obligation to provide
for "use without impairment," it protects country that the local people find good to live in, as tourists find it good to visit.
It brings outside money into a county whose 1970 population
of less than fifteen hundred people is as many as the few irriga-
ble acres in this stone desert can support. It provides a few
steady jobs like Blackburn's. And it keeps out worse things, or
has so far.

Under much of this country, in the Green River beds, there
are strata of low-sulphur, high-BTU coal, and all over the West
there are companies eager to exploit it. The first proposal, for
a giant coal-fired power plant on the Kaiparowits Plateau
south of here, was killed in 1976, some said by Robert Red-
ford, who was hanged and burned in effigy in Kanab for his efforts. The successor to the Kaiparowits, the Intermountain
Power Project, or IPP, was sited for the Escalante Basin within
eight miles of the boundary of the Capitol Reef National Park.
Secretary of the Interior Cecil Andrus forced a resiting of that
because it would inevitably have polluted the air of the park,
which under the terms of the Clean Air Act should be protected
Class One air. Now the IPP, which will be the largest coal-fired
generating plant in the United States, is scheduled to be built at
Lynndyl, on the Union Pacific at the edges of the Sevier Desert
in central Utah, where presumably there is less for it to spoil.

But the IPP is not all. The Union Pacific and thirteen other
companies want to mine the coal seams on the Kaiparowits—
the largest unexploited coalfield in the nation, and surrounded
by national parks. A group of utilities wants to open a huge

strip mine at Alton, four miles from Bryce Canyon National Park. The same plan includes a 500-megawatt coal-fired plant in Warner Valley, seventeen miles from Zion, a 2,000-megawatt plant north of Las Vegas, and two slurry pipelines to serve them—pipelines that would mine the water table as ruthlessly as the draglines mine the coal. The long-range projections for the plateau area foresee 21,300 megawatts of electric generation, six coal gasification plants, a strip mine in the Henry Mountains four miles from the boundaries of Capitol Reef, and another large coal mine in the Paria Amphitheater very close to Bryce.

It is quite possible that in the tradeoffs between energy and environmental health the local people will have little to say. Nevertheless I am curious to know how they feel about the progress that prowls around their doors. Blackburn says, and the people who wander into his office and join the conversation corroborate, that they are changing their minds. At first they wanted the jobs and the tax base and the economic boost. This is a dirt-poor country whose young people have always had to go away to find jobs. But as the argument about successive proposals went on, people have discovered that the proposed generating plants would pay no local taxes whatever, being on federal (BLM) land; and that the jobs would go mainly to migrant construction workers in the first phase, and to outside technicians in the second. As for the power itself, that is for export to more populous places. Blackburn says that people have begun to ask why they should tear up the country and bring in a lot of beer parlors and roughnecks and whores, and disrupt the towns and run down the water table and dirty the air, just to light Las Vegas.

He thinks they are better off as they are. With pipe irrigation, water goes farther than it used to. Young people still go away to school and stay away to work, but that is nothing new, and at least now the towns are not losing population as they did for many years. The park is a steady engine pumping life into the local economy. Visitation goes steadily up. The latest wrinkle is foreign tourists, in buses or rented RVs, who make the "Golden Circle" from Arches and Canyonlands through

Capitol Reef, Bryce, Zion, and Grand Canyon. He saw one the
other day with a banner on it: "We Are French. Please Help Us
to See America."

All in all, Blackburn gives the Park Service good marks.
Pressed, he would probably say it is the best thing that could
have happened to large areas of southern Utah. He has only
one complaint: he wishes they hadn't torn down the old Chesnutt store in Fruita when they started to face-lift the place. Old
store like that, with a hand-cranked gas pump out in front,
that's practically archaeology, that would interest tourists, especially foreigners. The old days were sort of wrapped up in
the Chesnutt place. He speaks with feeling; it is clear that his
affections are wrapped up in it, too.

I agree. Capitol Reef would be richer if the Chesnutt store
had been kept. The land is not complete without its human history and associations. Scenery by itself is pretty sterile. The
Chesnutts were living folklore, survivors of the frontier. I
would go a good way to have one of Mother Chesnutt's break-
fasts again, with peaches and cream, hot biscuits, corned elk,
and eggs baked in the oven in a muffin tin. A menu like that
might be as good a souvenir for a French tourist as a Ko-
dachrome slide of Cohab Canyon, named for the polygamists
who hid out here in the 1880s from U.S. marshals trying to
serve warrants for unlawful cohabitation.

We have looked forward to the Aquarius, whose top is richly
forested, watered by swift streams, and dotted with lakes, and
whose southeastern salient commands one of the grandest and
most colorful views anywhere—a view even more colorful and far
more expansive than, say, the Grand Canyon from Point Sublime.

From up on top one does not see the cliffs by which the
Aquarius breaks down upon the Waterpocket Fold and the Escalante Basin. One looks over them, catching only glimpses of
red in angle and buttress. But what one sees beyond! Northward, Thousand Lake Mountain lifts in tiered red cliffs to its
high, level, timbered crest, and northeastward the colored
desert stretches its maze of canyons and mesas down the valley
of the Fremont until it hazes out somewhere about Goblin Val-

ley. Directly below us, several thousand feet below, the bloody welt of the Waterpocket Fold, crowned with calm white domes, runs nearly north-south until it too hazes out in the glowing pink Navajo sandstone through which the unseen Colorado has cut Glen Canyon. Beyond the Fold, eastward across labyrinthine mazes of stone, rise the gray-green cones of the Henry Mountains, "Gothic superimposed upon Byzantine," a sharp contrast both in color and shape to the flat crestlines and predominant red of the surrounding desert, and absolutely lyrical when capped with snow. Beyond the Henrys the level desert platform, barren, blistered, cut by cliffs and canyons, reaches almost to the edge of vision, a hundred and fifty miles out, to the rich red rim of the world which we know to be the almost impenetrable country around the junction of the Colorado and the Green, in Canyonlands National Park. But above that desert rim rises another, farther outburst of Gothic—the snowy peaks of the La Sals, laccoliths like the Henrys, high cones of snow. And then, if the light is right, you can let your eye range beyond the La Sals into the remotest edge of sky, and incredibly, far beyond those far cones, you make out other snowy crests, insubstantial as cloud: the La Plata Mountains, two hundred miles away in Colorado. Dutton, who loved the Aquarius better than any other place in the plateau country, said it should be described in blank verse.

We are disappointed. The day is not clear. Some power plant? There is none close—not yet. But this unusually obscure air gives us an idea of what a Kaiparowits or IPP would do, both to seeing and to photography. It is a lesson we have already learned, for the last time we were in Canyonlands, particulates from the Four Corners plant one hundred and fifty miles to the south had made photography chancy and at times impossible.

The old forest road to Escalante, once hardly more than a fire road and passable only by jeep, has been paved as far as Grover. I see by the map that it has been paved in from the other end, too, all the way to Boulder. That is change indeed. Until about 1930, Boulder got its mail by packhorse. And there are other changes. Every few miles, as we rock and lurch up the mountain, the Forest Service has tucked campgrounds into the shelter of the Engelmann spruce, or among groves of aspen like pooled sunlight. As on Fish Lake, trees along the trail have been felled in preparation for road-widening and I suppose paving. Improved to tourist standards, this once adventurous road will make a convenient shortcut between Capitol Reef and Bryce.

My feelings are mixed. I hate to see a lovely mountain, in which I have always had a selfish and proprietary interest, overrun; and yet because I have known it a long time, and loved it, I find myself fantasizing, instructing a carful of friends, perhaps Europeans who come to this country with no knowledge of its geology, its life zones, its history—people like the original explorers, put onto the mountain knowing only what is before their eyes, and not really knowing that. For a schoolteacher like me, a perfect audience.

Smell that air? I might ask them. That wonderful bitter tang is aspen. Bite a leaf and the taste puckers your mouth. Light a fire and you smell it in the smoke. The leaf junctures and stems are flattened contrary to the plane of the leaf, so that at every slightest breeze the leaves tremble. Father de Smet tells of hearing French mountain men guess that the wood of the Cross must have been aspen, since ever afterward the leaves have quaked. The whiteness of the trunks is a powder, and rubs off. A gang boss can tell if his crew have been sitting on a log, simply by looking at the seat of their Levi's.

This is the gentle end of the plateau, I might tell them. The north end is much higher, lava-capped, rough with the chunks that give it its local name of Boulder Mountain, and full of lakes. Only jeeps up there. This trail we are following, once an Indian trail, was the route of Major Powell's brother-in-law, Almon Thompson, when he came up from Kanab in 1871 trying to find a supply route to the mouth of the Dirty Devil, where Powell had cached his boats the autumn before. Thompson's *entrada* was the swan song of true exploration in the lower forty-eight states. His party was probably the first to see the flaming amphitheater of Bryce Canyon, though only from a distance. He saw and named Table Cliff. Mistaking the Escalante for the Dirty Devil, he tried his best to get down its side gulches, dug deep and twisty in the Navajo sandstone that is the country rock in that basin, to reach the Escalante and the Colorado. Eventually he determined that he was not on the Dirty Devil (Fremont) River, but on a totally unknown and unmapped stream. He named it and went on over the Aquarius, which he also named. From its top he got a good panoramic view of the Henry Mountains, seen earlier by Powell from the river, but never visited. Going down across the Waterpocket Fold through magical and incredibly rough country, Thompson finally found his way down to the Colorado along Trachyte Creek. His report makes a chapter in Powell's *Report on the Exploration of the Colorado River of the West*—required reading, along with Dutton's *High Plateaus of Utah* and *Tertiary History of the Grand Canyon District,* for any tourist, American or European.

Lecturing like a tour guide, I steer us down past Boulder, now part of the accessible world, and the Hell's Backbone road, now sadly tamed by pavement, and across the small, clear, shallow Escalante, and into the town of Escalante, asleep under its cliffs. The Kaiparowits stretches its blade southward fifty miles to confront the dome of Navajo Mountain across Glen Canyon. Table Cliff rears over us on the north. We catch glimpses of Bryce, miles ahead, like a fire on the side of the Paunságunt. Three oasis villages, Henrieville, Cannonville, Tropic, and we are climbing the slope toward Ruby's Inn. Up on top, we meet a flow of traffic from Panguitch, on U.S. 89, and are once again on the tourist track. The Paunságunt is relatively low—the Bryce rim is only about eight thousand feet—and the roof is pine-forested. There is a combined smell of resiny, sun-warmed pines and of automobile exhaust—the ambiguous odor of use without impairment—as we pass through the gates into the park.

Superintendent Thomas Hobbs, whom I find in his office at the Visitors' Center, has the patient courtesy of a man used to dealing with an often irrational public, and the disinterestedness of a man who is engaged in the tourist business without being engaged in it for profit. He is more like a museum director than a resort manager, and he takes seriously his double, difficult obligation of showing and interpreting his park to the public while at the same time protecting it from them.

We talk of visitation. The gas shortage of early 1979 cut it back in the spring, since a big proportion of Bryce's visitors come from California, which was hardest hit. Now the crowds are up again, and the total will be only about 12 percent below that of 1978, the record year. A renewed gas shortage would of course bring another slowdown, especially of gas-guzzling RVs. It seems to me that, saying this, Superintendent Hobbs wears a certain kind of smile. A slowdown would have an effect like moving stock off an overgrazed range, and the Park Service - could concentrate on what it likes best, preservation.

We talk of foreign tourists. Increasing numbers of them, mostly French, German, and Japanese. With the dollar where it is, America is the biggest bargain in the world; and of all the possibilities in America, it is the national parks that many foreign tourists seem most interested in. Cities, monuments, and museums they have plenty of, alpine mountains they know. But places like this desert of warmly colored stone they have never seen and can hardly conceive. At least in this back corner, America still shows itself to European eyes as open, empty, strange, full of wonder and possibility.

Language problems? Nothing serious. Nature walks and ranger talks are now conducted in French and German as well as English, and there are times when Hobbs wishes he had a ranger who spoke Japanese. We will probably run into one of those foreign-language hikes while we're in the park.

Sure enough, a bus pulls in behind us in the parking lot of Bryce Canyon Lodge. It is the same that Blackburn saw in Capitol Reef, apparently, for it wears a banner asking help in seeing America. Forty or fifty men and women pile out, and within minutes are on the crumbling brink of the Pink Cliffs, screaming, pointing, crying "Voilà!" and "Regardez!" They need no help in seeing America. Some run down to the first turn of the Navajo Loop Trail, and from there photograph their companions on the rim, who are in turn aiming cameras down at the trail. They are at least as noisy as the French used to say American tourists were, but nobody ever got more enjoy-

ment out of sightseeing. Table Cliff, that noble facade cut out of
the same Pink Cliffs as Bryce, but lifted two thousand feet
higher in the air, never had a more appreciative audience for its
afternoon glorification. The red, white, yellow, violet, and purple statuary that crowds Bryce amphitheater never stirred more
excited comment. I even find these folks somewhat excessive
and uncritical. Bryce always seemed to me a trifle gaudy, and
its names—the Gossips, the Palace of the Fairy Princess, the
Peekaboo Trail—over-cute. These people respond as gushily as
Sunday Austrians on the Raxalp: Ah, wie schön! By now most
of them have started down the trails and are lost down among
the passageways and colonades and lines of hoodoos. Their
voices float back like the talk of traveling geese, perhaps asking
one another What signifies Peekaboo? What is meant, Alley
Oop and Dinny?

It is something we never expected to hear in the stone wilderness of southern Utah. And after we have spent a couple of
hours walking the rim and the trails, and sitting for long minutes watching the changing afternoon light throw gargoyle and
curtain wall into deep relief, and play like a color organ on the
brilliant cliffs, we go back to the Lodge to arrange a bed, and
encounter a consequence of the European invasion: No room
at the inn. We suspect that TWA, which has the concession in
this park, has been offering package deals through European
travel agencies, selling air tickets along with park tours, and
block-booking the rooms.

Well, outside the boundaries then, where our environmental
conscience tells us accommodations should be located anyway.
Same story. Ruby's Inn and two other motels outside the park
are also full. We have to go clear to Panguitch, twenty miles, to
find a motel with a vacant room.

Business is good, obviously, and if it is good here at Bryce it
is good all the way around the Golden Circle, four of whose
five national parks are in Utah. The worth of that business is
something for the people of Utah to bear in mind when they
hear proposals for a power plant within plain sight of the Bryce
rim, or when they hear their senators argue for the Sagebrush
Rebellion, whose proponents would take all that desert land

out of federal hands and put it into hands that would know what to do with it. It is a question whether there would be so many cameras pointing up from and down on the trails, or so many rolls of film sold in the park store, if the air, now dry and brilliant and made for color photography, were clouded with particulates. It is a question whether even so well placed a conglomerate as TWA would sell many package tours to watch evening cast the shadow of a smoke plume on Table Cliff.

And if high prices and short supplies of gasoline inhibit the RVs and family cars, and the visitation drops, and the parks lie nearly empty, then what? Should we acknowledge that a country whose resident population is hardly one to the square mile is a reasonable sacrifice area, and remove all restrictions on the mining of coal and the production of power from it? Sacrifice a few Mormon irrigators to benefit a lot of Las Vegas gamblers? Is a national park justified only by the numbers of visitors it draws? Arguments before appropriations committees sometimes sound that way, but we think not. We think these crown jewels of the American land are their own justification, and we would think so if we knew that we were ourselves never going to be able to visit them again.

As a matter of fact, this trip has had from the beginning the feel of a final one, a last visit. We are getting beyond the age when we can unroll our sleeping bags under a pine or in a sandy wash; and the gasoline situation throws the future of automobile touring, especially touring in places as far as this from great centers of population, into doubt. I would hate to have missed the period of extravagant personal liberty that wheels and cheap gasoline gave us, but I will not mourn its passing. It was part of our time of wastefulness and excess. Somehow, - people will continue to get out to see country like this. They will come by public transportation and tour bus, as tourists once came to Yellowstone and as our French party came to Bryce. Or they will discover the high plateau as horseback and backpack country—get to them by whatever means is available and then go by shanks' mare instead of racing around covering miles as we have been doing. Looking a long way, for a long time, may be more salutary than traveling maximum miles in the shortest possible period. And if few people come, their benefits will be qualitatively greater, for what most recommends the plateaus and their intervening valleys and deserts is space, emptiness, silence, awe.

I could make a suggestion to the road-builders, too: the experience of driving both ends of the Aquarius road on pavement is nothing like so satisfying as that of driving the roof on rocky, chuck-holed, ten-mile-an-hour dirt. The road will be a lesser thing when it is paved all the way, and so will be the road over the Fishlake Hightop, and the road over the Wasatch Plateau, and the steep road over the Tushar, the highest of the plateaus, that we will travel tomorrow. To substitute comfort and ease for real experience is too American a habit to last. It is when we feel the earth rough to all our length, as in Robert Frost's poem, that we know the earth as creatures ought to know it.

THE NEW RIDERS
OF THE PURPLE SAGE

*There must be in this province [New Mexico Territory], to make
a conservative estimate,* seventy thousand Indians, settled after
our custom, house adjoining house, with square plazas. They
have no streets, and in the pueblos, which contain many plazas
or wards, one goes from one plaza to the other through alleys.
They are of two or three stories; and some houses are of four,
five, six, and seven stories. Even whole pueblos dress in very
highly colored cotton* mantas, *white or black, and some of
thread—very good clothes. Others wear buffalo hides, of which
there is a great abundance. They have most excellent wool, of
whose value I am sending a small example.*

*It is a land abounding in flesh of buffalo, goats with hideous
horns, and turkeys; and in Mohoce there is game of all kinds.
There are many wild and ferocious beasts, lions, bears, wolves,
tigers,* penicas, *ferrets, porcupines, and other animals, whose
hides they tan and use. Towards the west there are bees and very
white honey, of which I am sending a sample. Besides, there are
vegetables, a great abundance of the best and greatest salines in
the world, and a very great many kinds of very rich ores, as I
stated above. Some discovered near here do not appear so, although we have hardly begun to see anything of the much there
is to be seen. There are very fine grape vines, rivers, forests of
many oaks, and some cork trees, fruits, melons, grapes, watermelons, Castilian plums,* capuli, *pine-nuts, acorns, ground-nuts,
and* coralejo, *which is a delicious fruit, and other wild fruits.*

---

*By all accounts an exaggerated figure. Ed.

There are many and very good fish in this Rio del Norte, and in others. From the ores here are made all the colors which we use, and they are very fine.

The people are in general very comely; their color is like those of that land, and they are much like them in manner and dress, in their grinding, in their food, dancing, singing, and many other things, except in their languages, which are many, and different from those there. Their religion consists in worshipping idols, of which they have many; and in their temples, after their own manner, they worship them with fire, painted reeds, feathers, and universal offering of almost everything they get, such as small animals, birds, vegetables, etc. In their government they are free, for although they have some petty captains, they obey them badly and in very few things.

We have seen other nations such as the Querechos or herdsmen, who live in tents of tanned hides, among the buffalo. The Apaches, of whom we have also seen some, are innumerable, and although I heard that they lived in rancherias, a few days ago I ascertained that they live like these in pueblos, one of which, eighteen leagues from here, contains fifteen plazas. They are a people whom I have compelled to render obedience to His Majesty, although not by means of legal instruments like the rest of the provinces. This has caused me much labor, diligence, and care, long journeys, with arms on the shoulders, and not a little watching and circumspection; indeed, because my maese de campo was not as cautious as he should have been, they killed him with twelve companions in a great pueblo and fortress called Acóma, which must contain about three thousand Indians. As punishment for its crime and its treason against his Majesty, to whom it had already rendered submission by a public instrument, and as a warning to the rest, I razed and burned it completely, in the way in which your Lordship will see by the process of this cause. All these provinces, pueblos, and peoples, I have seen with my own eyes.

Don Juan de Oñate (1599)

I have a recurring dream from the Pliocene period of my life in which a skinny kid of about thirteen, lank haired, with a swamp of pimples on his chin, sits perched on a narrow lip of redrock that has split away from its mother cliff, legs dangling over the edge, Keds bouncing arhythmically against the crumbling sandstone. Smoke curls from a Lucky Strike cupped in the left hand (the fourth on the hour); the right flips pebbles like a marble shooter out into the void. He listens intently for the tiny pock as they hit the scree pile far below and bounce into the wash. If his usual luck holds, he thinks, the ledge to which he clings more or less by imagination and a tight sphincter will give way and he'll join his pebbles down there among the cholla and collared lizards and jack rabbit dung. Can this kid be *me*? Unfortunately.

The dream, dull as it is, features the best and worst from my memory-bank of that distant time—the beginning of a thirty-year bad habit, and the beginning of a symbiotic relationship with solitude manifested in empty, open country. The key word is "open." The kid is not happy with the specifics of his situation. How he is going to inch his way back over the rim above is as mysterious to him as it is to the jay bird inspecting him from an insane bush growing out of a crack in the solid rock below. But he is intensely moved by the landscape around him—the flaming buttes, the pale olive chaparral, the cobalt sky with those thunderheads piling up over the western margin. So that salvation becomes, finally, irrelevant. He is as indifferent to it as that mouse down there under the agave is not, its normally frantic EKG going berserk every time the shadow of a cruising hawk slides overhead. If there is anything that - really concerns this solemn child, it is whether his supply of butts will last until the next town trip.

Sedona, Arizona. Admittedly, memory stretches nearly three decades here, but if there was anything more to Sedona, Arizona, in 1951 than a combined grocery, garage, and post office, then time has erased its image just as surely as it has transformed the skinny kid into a sweet-smelling non-smoker with just a pinch between his cheek and gum. Sedona was where they coined the phrase "if you blink you'll miss it." Town trip was something of a joke played on the asthmatics, miscreants, and discards who constituted the student body of a boarding school I attended for a time just outside that gas and cigs quick-stop.

I admit that my intellectual lordosis as a teenager ensured an unhappy relationship with books and classrooms, and that I spent most of my time looking for ways to escape. No doubt that accounts in some part for my attraction to anything that lay beyond the perimeters of the school. I fled whenever I could, tramping the brush-choked washes, climbing those fabulous parapets of siltstone, sandstone, limestone, clawing my way up narrow chimneys of crumbling rock to stand at the top of some eroded column and look across a plain of juniper-piñon to the dark, contrasting line of sycamore and cottonwood that marked the passage of Oak Creek through the valley.

Relatively speaking, it did not seem as if there had been many people there before me. Around A.D. 700 the Hohokam Indians settled along the Verde River and pursued an agricultural life. Around 1125 they were joined by the Sinagua from the Flagstaff area. The two tribes were either replaced by or transmogrified into a nomadic group called the Yavapai-Apache around 1582, and at about the same time a Spanish explorer, Antonio de Espejo, came down through the Verde Valley in search of that elusive prize that galvanized all Spanish explorers. All he could turn up was some copper and he left in disgust. And then in 1863 Captain Joseph R. Walker, trapper and trail-breaker for Captain Benjamin Louis Eulalie de Bonneville (leader of the first wagon train across South Pass and inventor of the salt flat), began prospecting for gold in Yavapai County. He is generally regarded as the first American in the Oak Creek region, though there were undoubtedly anonymous prospectors and hunters who passed through before him. Without the advantage of plastic and aluminum they were unable, however, to leave behind any non-biodegradable spoor. I found no trace of my spiritual ancestors during my rambles.

But the first homesteaders in the area didn't come until the 1870s and 1880s, and Sedona didn't get a post office permit (and hence a name) until 1902, when T. C. Schnebly and family, pioneers from Missouri, settled eighty acres on the banks of Oak Creek and applied for that permit under the name Oak Creek Station. Some bureaucrat objected that the name was too long, so T. C. called it after his wife instead. I have an 1897 portrait of dark-haired, doe-eyed, mustached Sedona Schnebly. She reminds me more of Marcello Mastroianni's rejected wife in *Divorce Italian Style* than of the fair-skinned, high-bosomed trail queens who helped Randolph Scott and Rod Cameron win the West. But T. C., who is in the portrait also, looks properly stolid, square-jawed, and wet-combed. Like the founding father of a gas and cigs quick-stop.

Sedona was (and is) nestled right at the mouth of the Oak Creek Canyon where it plunges, ten miles south of Flagstaff, down a four-thousand-foot gorge, from the Mogollon Rim of the Colorado Plateau to the sloping mesa of the Verde Valley. The road from the top corkscrews through pine and Douglas fir, lower and lower, until it bottoms out in the pygmy forest of juniper-piñon that flows around the weather-battled architectonics of Coconino and Yavapai counties, the buttes, spires, columns, domes, arches of the redrock country. I learned in my regional geology class (required) that the Mogollon Rim is formed of varying layers of Redwall limestone, Supai sandstones, Fort Apache limestone, Coconino sandstone, Toroweap formation, Kaibab limestone, Moenkopi sandstone, gravel, and a frosting of basalt. But, they said, the red cliffs and rock formations for which this area is justly famous are composed mainly of Supai sandstones, about fifteen hundred feet thick and varying in color (according to time of deposit and iron oxide content, substantial penalty for early withdrawal) from pink to reddish brown to brownish orange. I remember a promise of more, equally dusty, information about Permian ages and Triassic periods and Pliocene times, but I left the school under a cumulonimbus cloud before we got to that section.

Tedious data anyway. I prefer to remember that country by the title and content of all those Saturday matinees shot beneath its towering buttes: *The Cowboy and the Redhead, Johnny Guitar, 3:10 to Yuma, Riders of the Purple Sage*. I like to think about Randolph and Rod protecting some hapless nester with a bevy of stunning daughters from that blood-sucker Cochise and his repulsive rabble. Never mind that Cochise (generally outfitted in a Sioux war bonnet and waving a Winchester repeating rifle barely invented by the time of his death) was a Chiricahua Apache and probably never got within two hundred miles of the Verde Valley. Never mind that he was a man of considerable courage, skill, and integrity. He was no match for Randolph Scott.

Better yet, I like to remember it by the way it smells when a sudden afternoon shower sweeps by and leaves just enough of itself to clean the dust off the chaparral and darkly stain the rocks. And the way the sky looks as that little storm approaches, one low, isolated cloud framed on the horizon by two silhouetted mesas, rain shot, its underside tattered like the fringe of an old lady's shawl. I like to remember it by the way the light changes from moment to moment on the face of its redwall cliffs as evening comes down and plunges the canyons in cold shadow while the ramparts above still blaze in the setting sun.

At Sedona, where the end of town used to be, the highway climbs a low rise and slides off to the southwest toward Cottonwood and Jerome. A U.S. Forest Service road splits off just before an inflated hill called Schuerman Mountain. This road is well graded and much used now, but when I first saw it, it was nothing more than a wagon track that snaked through a stunted forest of juniper-piñon, crossed Oak Creek at a spot where a slab of sandstone provided a solid ford, then climbed - gently through the buckbrush, scrub oak, and yucca to the dozen or so buildings that comprised the school. A mile or so to the east the colonnades and flying buttresses of Courthouse Butte (misnamed Cathedral Rock on Geological Survey maps) rose up a thousand feet above the valley floor, looking like a sort of confectionery Pantheon half melted by the sun. Behind the school the rim of House Mountain formed a box canyon where I once saw, from my perch in the smoking section, a mountain lion picking its way through the boulders below the northern escarpment.

As much as anything about this region I remember Oak Creek itself, a clear, swift stream, thirty to forty feet wide at the

ford, bordered along its passage through the valley by sycamore, cottonwood, and occasional stands of New Mexico alder.
The banks were covered by river sedge, Virginia creeper, mes-
quite, and thickets of willow. On days when the sun would
bake the valley to a brick yard, and the red dust would powder
so fine that it clogged the pores and formed a little nosebleed
rime around the nostrils, I'd scuttle down through the washes
like a scorpion shaken out of a hot boot, fling myself into one
of the sandstone pools upstream from the ford, and cling there
to a root snaggle below the surface until my head would ache
behind the eyes from the cold.

I don't wish to portray myself as a complete loner. Occasionally at night I would join other young gentlemen of comparable breeding and station in sneaking out of the dorm to
meet with the more adventurous (or desperate) of the young
ladies in attendance, and we would all slip off to a place where
the creek divided for several hundred yards and formed a sandy
island of willow and cottonwood. We would build a fire from
the driftwood that littered the banks, sprawl about watching a
fat, white moon swarm up over Courthouse Butte and flood
the river bottom with etiolated light, and then, well, by God,
we'd just have at it hammer and tongs. We'd sing "Red River
Valley" and "Strawberry Roan," "When My Blue Moon Turns
to Gold Again," "Down by the Old Mill Stream," "Ninety-
nine Bottles of Beer on the Wall" (which easily took an hour),
and all of the fifty greatest hits from the golden forties that anybody could remember. Did we fumble, smooch, and carry on?
We did not. At least, not so as anyone would notice.

However catalytic Sedona and the Oak Creek Canyon may have
been in awakening my meager sensitivity to natural surroundings, and however defective my memory of a somewhat simpler
time, even middle-aged cynicism doesn't save me from gape-
mouthed stupefaction as I drive down from Flagstaff into the
Verde Valley one not so fine March day thirty years later to see
what, if anything, has happened in my absence. The trip is not
entirely whimsical. For some time I have been listening to both
students and non-transient acquaintances talk about pulling up

stakes, moving out of Santa Cruz, California, the coastal amusement park and all-round Mecca of Mellow where I reside. Their reasons are sundry and conventional enough (population growth, limited and expensive housing, a growing awareness that their skills are becoming devalued by duplication), but what interests me is the places they talk about going to. There seems to exist a kind of underground guide to the outposts of Eden, and one of the regularly featured possibilities I hear mentioned is Sedona. Sedona? Cold pop, gas, cigs?

There is a broader base than mere curiosity that motivates me to climb into my gas-guzzling, four by four, three-quarter-ton GMC, which came to me equipped with Jackman rims, meats, eight-track stereo, and gun rack. I suspect that this may be about the last time I'm ever going to be able to do such a thing. I suspect that even if I could afford to tool around the vast western outback in a vehicle that gets somewhere around twelve miles to the gallon, my conscience might nag me into practicing what a number of people I admire preach. "We have used up the possibilities inherent in the youth of our nation," Wendell Berry says, and I suppose more and more evidently this includes the cheap and unlimited use of oil.

Also, I have some vague theories about population migration, changing economic aspirations at various levels of the society, revisionist thinking about one's "life style." I am persuaded by those wiser analysts than I that we have, as a nation, just about consumed ourselves into a state of narcolepsy, suffering the boredom of acquisition while at the same time enduring the frustration of increasing incompetence (our own). Why else do we canonize folks like the Waltons, now in their eighth year as one of television's most popular families, unless because they know how to do all the things we've forgotten, or never learned?

In any case, I want to see what is going on in some of these out-of-the-way hamlets when they begin to be infiltrated by those in search of an "alternative" way—places like Sedona, and Eureka and Arcata up in the redwood country near the Oregon border, and Bishop and Lone Pine in the Owens Valley on the eastern slope of the Sierra. I have a month or so to kill before I meet an old friend up on the upper Missouri at Fort Benton, Montana, and I don't want to be in the Northwest until after the tourist season subsides—I've been to that festival. The north coast of California is a three-hundred-mile vestibule train of Winnebago campers grinding along bumper to bumper on a conveyor belt that does not stop until late fall, and in any case my brother-in-law who lives there works until the rains bring logging to a halt in Humboldt County. He isn't available to play until the networks start broadcasting football games. So for a while my residence is going to be where I park it.

But right now I'm already lost. I've taken the wrong exit off Interstate 40 and wound up in downtown Flagstaff. And also, in spite of the fact that it's nearly the first of May, I'm engulfed in a furious snowstorm. The Navajo and Hopi have warned— from their sacred home of Old Oraibi at Second Mesa—that a disrespect for the San Francisco Peaks, home of the Kachinas, will release forces of destruction on the land. A local newscast on my radio informs me that the Forest Service has granted the Arizona Snow Bowl a permit to expand its skiing facilities in the Coconino National Forest, and clearly this spring blizzard is the fulfillment of prophecy. A pox on the sunny Southwest and the hell with that sign that says "Chains Required." I have no chains.

When I finally find it, Route 89-A is a foot deep in snow, and I drive slowly south, thankful for the off-road tires that back home make me feel somewhat red under the collar. At Canyon View Point I pull into the parking lot with the absurd notion that maybe I'll be able to see *down* if not up, but there is no place to park because the spaces are filled by pickups with Indian women waiting to sell Hong Kong turquoise to white tourists. They do not appear to be doing a brisk business this day.

I wind down through a Christmas forest of Ponderosa pine, Douglas and white fir. Visibility zero. The weather is no better twenty-five hundred feet below the rim, and I find myself in . . . *Switzerland?* Well, no, that Matterhorn there is a motel. Which is right next to another motel. Which is across the road from another motel. In front of which there seem to be a dozen tour buses, all of them idling on an apron of asphalt as their cargo mills about, spilling out onto the highway, crowding around a little cluster of outdoor trinket vendors who seem oblivious to the snow. Where am I? I creep along for about a mile, past a continuous strip of gift shops, real estate offices, motels, restaurants, cocktail lounges, craft centers, art galleries, boutiques, Indian pottery, baskets, jewelry, kachinas, sand paintings, pawn, handcrafted this, authentic that, unusual, exclusive, unique. It suddenly occurs to me that I am here. Sedona. My town trip.

Numbly I stop at the Chamber of Commerce to inquire after the one commercial enterprise I have not observed after four passes up and down the strip—a grocery store. "Your best bet is in West Sedona," I'm told by a bolo-tied young man made out of, apparently, polystyrene. "Let me give you some of our pamphlets." He manages somehow to speak without using any muscles in his face. West Sedona? "It's just a mile or so over the hill." The map he gives me shows 89-A running through something called Grasshopper Flat and then a parade route of little developments—Sedona West, Coffee Pot Subdivision, Sedona Meadows, Harmony Hills, Road Runner Rancho, Juniper Knolls. I stumble out and drive to the Bayless (sic) Shopping Center, pick up something for my dinner, and head south out of town to find a place to camp. I am not tempted by the six-foot Giant Submarine Sandwich offered by Appetito's. Nor do I think Sri Darwin Gross, the living ECK master of ECKANKAR (West Sedona's Satsang spiritual center), can tell me much at this point about getting in touch with myself that I do not already know. I don't want a hot tub or a spa or a tennis lesson at the Racquet Club. I don't want any moccasins or western belts or Mexican souvenirs. I just want to get out of this metastasized tourist trap and into the desert where I can watch the snow drift into the chaparral. What ever became of that little trading post and gas station with its cold pop and cigs?

I find the old Forest Service road (now called Red Rock Loop), and follow my nose around the side of Schuerman Mountain, down toward Oak Creek and the crossing where I used to swim in the shadow of Courthouse Butte. It has stopped snowing. Light slants through the low clouds in tabernacular shafts. The red cliffs with their cold mantles of snow

appear in a burst of celestial chicanery, then vanish just as suddenly in a swirling mist. I will stop at the creek, climb in the
camper shell, and fire up my Coleman stove, have a toot of
Beam's Choice while I cook up these here pork chops and a
mess of fried potatoes, toss a little green salad with oil and
vinegar, open that bottle of Ridge Zinfandel I tucked away for
just this occasion. Then, if the ford is passable, maybe I'll drive
up into the juniper forest on the other side and camp for the
night.

I'm in such a dither just thinking about the gratification of
my palate that I do a quadruple take of the trailer park sitting
smack dab in the middle of my illusion, and even then I'm not
sure I believe it. Red Rock Crossing Mobile Village. *Mobile* Village? So why are they imbedded in concrete foundations with
little porchlets and awnings and crushed rock lawns and plaster
geese? Why are they here at all? I found this place first. In fact,
I invented it. I gave nobody permission to erect a God-damn tin-
foil tenement in my private preserve. Constable, I want this
abomination removed. I want it out of town by sunrise.

The ford is closed, a steel cable strung across the opening
and padlocked to two iron posts. I park and walk upstream until I find a fallen cottonwood, cross the deepest part of the
stream on its massive trunk, then walk through the shallows
onto the island where we used to court the ladies and howl at
the moon. The water is icy on my bare feet, the stones of the
creek bed smooth and slippery. Holding my arms out for balance, my heavy boots in one hand and my pants in the other, I
look like a cartoon drunk staggering home on Saturday night.

The news is not good, alas. My hideaway is obviously no
longer a secret. In the willows along the bank, shards of plastic
wrap, napkins, and newspaper flap a forlorn greeting as I cake-
walk ashore. The top of a woman's bathing suit lies half-buried
in the gravel; farther up, I find a tennis shoe and a rusty cap
gun with the grips missing. I judge from the rubbish strewn
everywhere about—the bottles and cans and cigarette butts,
the pull tabs and pop tops and half-burned picnic garbage, the
Styrofoam cups and broken glass—that the area has either
been designated the town dump or specially arranged for a

documentary film on the desecration of the American wilderness. I don't see any cameras around, however. I take out my notebook to make a trash list but return it to my pocket unmarked. Not an original idea.

Barricaded in my camper shell with my Jim Beam, my pork chops simmering in the frying pan, I sort through the booster's club pamphlets and what-all given me by the polyurethane man. In the *Red Rock News*, "the voice of Sedona and Oak Creek Canyon," I find articles on how to watch a St. Patrick's Day parade, a regional profile that tells me "bus transportation is furnished by Continental Trailways and freight is handled by Consolidated Copper State Freight Lines and Western Gillette," an essay that announces "many seasoned travelers contend . . . Sedona-Oak Creek Canyon Red Rock Country 'most impressive'"; nothing, however, that gives me an insight into the cultural values of this settlement except twenty-one advertisements (many of them half and full page) for real estate offices, land companies, development property investments, home sites, lots, parcels, ranches, rentals, mobile parks, acreage. I am pretty much demoralized by this observation and begin to seriously reconsider my expected time of departure. The chops, on the other hand, with just a sprinkle of sage and lemon pepper, are outrageous.

Where are the forces of salvation, I wonder as I wander around town the following night looking for the action. Where are the environmentalists, preservationists, alternative-life-stylers, the young, the hip, the people who *care*? Where are all those ex-Santa Cruzians who went forth into the boondocks to reinvest in social utopia and pursue a simple, more natural life? I had expected to find a thriving congregation of whole-grain, vegetarian, Sierra Club, Save-the-Whale, Zen fugitives from the great consumer society, all of them fighting for the remnants of their national inheritance, but I have not seen much of that cultural stratum in evidence around Sedona. Maybe I haven't been here long enough, haven't looked in the right places.

So a saloon in the old town perks me up. It is full of funky-looking guys with hair of the requisite length. Everybody has a buck knife and a mustache, and boots are still the style in manly footwear. The ladies' bosoms jiggle and jounce, properly unconfined—all four bosoms. The ratio of men to women in this joint seems to be about thirty to one. Odd, but at least I know where I am. I order up a Coors, and alternately watch a fight on the color TV above the bar and an enthusiastic but not so skillful pool game at the end of the room, right there under the arrested charge of an enormous, snarling, stuffed polar bear. Not indigenous to the region.

My conversations are various, but everybody I talk to is in some form of construction, from building spec homes to installing molded plastic spas. One gent I shoot a game of nine-ball with, a carpenter with a growth on his face so luxuriant and so sculpted into his perm that he reminds me of a hydrangea, is doing finish work on a forty-five-hundred-square-foot house for one of the estimated two hundred millionaires who live in the area. "Man, you wouldn't believe this guy's casa," he says. "Gold-plated fixtures, gold-plated *toilet* paper dispensers. The wife's bath has a full wall mood screen with seven different panoramas she can call up with the push of a button. Quadraphonic musical motifs coordinated with each scene. You believe that?"

With difficulty. But I also have difficulty accepting the rather casual indifference all these gentlemen exhibit toward their *contribution* to the demise of this outpost of Eden. I assume they came here because it represented an alternative to the high-priced, clogged-up, bogged-down, progress-oriented rat race they started out in, but I find out I'm wrong. "Oh yeah, a lot of people come through here thinking they're going to get away from it all, but the only ones that stay *now* are retired with bucks. You know what land costs?"

"Well, what about you? What about everybody in this room?"

"Oh, man, I'm just here making a stake. When I get it together I'm going back to Pennsylvania where my folks still got some property."

In the morning, sprinkling a bit of parsley on my mushroom and cheese omelette and waiting for last night's coffee to boil, I decide that a little is already too much. I could hang around and gather statistics to bolster my despair, but to what end? What chance does (did) a little town with a population of six thousand (fifty-five hundred more than when I first saw it) stand against a tourist influx of over two million people a year? When one out of every twenty residents is a real estate agent, what else is going to proliferate except real estate development? How can an environment possibly survive when nothing will grow in it much higher than a man's head? You can't even hide from Randolph Scott and the posse out here; how can you disguise the shake roof on your split-level, green stucco, California ranch style house? Particularly when you build it out there in the middle of the chaparral like the Village of Oak Creek, or Oak Creek Valley, or any of a dozen other "developments"?

Well, I tell myself, wheeling my guzzler back up the road to Flagstaff, back into the conifers and the scarf of melting snow, back into the home of the Kachina and the Arizona Snow Bowl, I suppose you could restrict the places that people can build. You could limit density and pass zoning laws. I guess in those areas where construction *is* allowed you could build more in keeping with the terrain, and out of local, natural materials (there is, after all, a pretty good tradition of southwestern architecture), and you could resist the temptation to paint it canary yellow. There are ways for people to exist in *some* measure of harmony with their natural surroundings, even though you might rather there were no people at all. But these ways require that we exhibit forethought and planning and aesthetic sensitivity, and they also require, particularly in this day and age, that we abandon the notion that a property owner can do anything he pleases with his property simply because he owns it and because that's the way it has always been. On occasion communities have managed to figure this out before it is too late. But Sedona is, sadly, not among them.

THE REDWOOD CURTAIN

Out there to the west of an old logging road that runs along the ridge above the Humboldt Bay, the horizon is an all but invisible line, the finest of pencil strokes drawn straight, as if with a carpenter's rule, down the seaward seam of the earth. The cloud cover lies in a sullen blanket over my head, tattered occasionally where it has snagged the tops of the highest stands of redwoods and torn its otherwise immutable mat. It rains steadily and without enthusiasm.

In the cab of the pickup I'm sitting with my brother-in-law, John Shelton, drinking a Molson's Ale, eating peanuts, and trying to get him to tell me why a young man with talent, energy, and unlimited options would choose to live in Eureka, California, the world's soggiest outpost of progress, when he could just as well be wasting away in some Margaritaville to the south, some laid-back, mellowed-out California of the mind where one doesn't have to wear waders to step out to the privy. Like Sedona.

Below us, running along the inland side of the bay, a shaft of pale sunlight slants down on the main road, glints for a moment off the windshields of logging trucks grinding south - toward the mills at Scotia; then the fog swirls in again to close this embarrassing breach in its defensive line. No favoritism for a road, not even this one, the Redwood Highway, U.S. 101. Until they built an Interstate through the broad, rich farmlands of the San Joaquin and Sacramento valleys, between the Cascade and Salmon ranges, and up through Medford, Eugene, Portland, Tacoma, Seattle, and on to the Canadian border, 101 was the major north-south route along the Pacific Coast. Now, in this remote upper-left-hand corner of the state, it services mainly the timber industry, the local population, and an endless summer procession of RVs touring the redwood country. Or what's left of it. What's left of it is mostly right here, 180 miles north of San Francisco, 60 miles south of the Oregon border, on a little eruption of land that looks on a map like a blemish on the skin of the California coast, but which looks in the cold light of morning like high alpine country; tall trees, mountains, deep canyons and river valleys, everything green and lush and . . . *damp*. If it weren't for that gray slab of ocean out there I'd swear I was somewhere in the Sierra.

A hundred and thirty years ago, before a Dane named Henry Buhne crossed the Humboldt Bar in one of his ship's longboats and "discovered" the region, there was nothing much here but some Indians and a twenty-mile-wide belt of virgin redwoods, a belt that extended along the coast for 450 miles from above Crescent City to the Santa Lucia Mountains below Monterey. A hundred and thirty-five billion board feet of studs, siding, and sauna panel. One and a half million acres of the tallest, most majestic, and (except for the bristlecone pine) oldest trees on the planet. Forest Service estimates in 1953 guessed that of the original 135 billion board feet only 35 billion remained, and what is left of that, for the most part, lies within thirty miles of where John and I sit eating peanuts and looking down over two-thousand-year-old stumps, Eureka, Humboldt Bay, and the Louisiana-Pacific pulp mills sitting on the broad spit of sand that forms a natural breakwater between bay and ocean. The high stacks of the mills, and the white plumes of steam that unfurl ceaselessly from their cones, are like fairground banners announcing the major business of this land, the *only* business of this land worthy of the name—lumber.

Henry Buhne's original intention was to establish a supply outpost on Humboldt Bay to service the mines up in Trinity County to the east; but the timber value of the area became so quickly obvious that the first white settlers who followed him forgot about mining, and went into the lumber business. In 1851 two entrepreneurs, James Ryan and James Duff, bought an old sidewheeler down in San Francisco, brought it into the bay, and ran it hard aground on the mud flats at the edge of what is now Eureka. They built mill machinery on either side, removed the paddlewheels and fitted them with pulleys, used the steam engines to provide power for the milling operation . . . *Eureka*, 85,000 board feet a day. Not a great deal by modern standards, but it was a start. And for 125 years the cutting and milling of timber so dominated the business of California's northwest that today, with very little redwood left to cut, and legions of crazed young environmentalists helping the Sierra Club and the Department of the Interior protect that little, much of it in park lands, the region is in economic trouble.

Or so John, who is a log-scaler, tells me. When he puts on his hard hat and forgets that the real reason he's a scaler is that it's a seasonal occupation that gives him six months off on unemployment compensation to watch football games, he can argue the Chamber of Commerce line with the best of them. The expansion of the Redwood National Park, signed into law in 1978, will result in the loss of from 1.3 to 1.6 billion board feet of prime redwood to the industry. Anywhere from twelve hundred to two thousand jobs will be lost. Timber-yield tax revenues will drop a million dollars a year. Sales tax revenues will fall off nobody knows how much. To hear John tell it when he gets cranked up, every social, political, and economic evil imaginable will result from the inclusion of more acreage into the park—has *already* resulted. "Thanks to the God-damn park two hundred men got laid off at the Louisiana-Pacific plywood division at Samoa."

But then John takes his hard hat off and uncaps another Molson's. He smiles slyly at me in the windshield's reflection. "Of course L&P didn't bother to mention, when they were blasting the park, that they don't *make* plywood out of redwood. And your hard-core logger type tends to ignore the fact that of the 48,000 acres that have been added, 36,000 have *already* been logged, and 3,000 more are grasslands. Wouldn't do to look too closely at some of their statistics. The lines get drawn pretty fine up here. Either you're *for* parks or you're against them."

Right now I'm for movement, anything to get the heater going in the truck. Also, I want to see some country. We leave the ridge and drive down toward the coast through a forest of Douglas fir so darkly green as to appear black, down along open clear-cut country turned into pastures that drops steeply into canyons choked with brush and the beginnings of second-growth redwood, across flatter land to Highway 101 where the Elk River runs into the bay. From there we turn south, past Field's Landing and Lolita to the Fern Bridge, and across the Eel River and its broad delta to the town of Ferndale. The country here is open bottomland, a flood plain for the Eel, and dotted with dairy farms, thick pastures, and double-pitched roofs of traditional California barns. Ferndale, John remarks, has been transforming itself over the past ten years (actually since the 1950s when bohemia first discovered it) from a farming community to an artsy-craftsy hamlet like Mendocino or Sausalito, but it seems to me not so bad as some of its prototypes—perhaps because it's somewhat off the main RV route and not obviously overburdened with tourists.

We drive past a number of restored Victorians, New England saltboxes with neat yards and rhododendrons blooming everywhere, down the town's main street with its galleries, craft shops, "studios," and the Ferndale Playhouse where *Fiddler on the Roof* is the bill of fare, then begin to wind up out of town over the coastal mountains that protect the delta from the sea. At the lower elevations the narrow, unpaved road is choked along the bank with thimbleberry, wild currant, Oregon grape, and wild strawberry. The trees here are mostly alder, delicate and lacy in their first spring foliage, and a pale, apple-green color that is almost luminescent against the dark backdrop of Douglas fir and heavy-limbed Sitka spruce. Grouse ladder, John calls these many-branched, heavily knotted trees. Good for birds, not for mills. Which is, no doubt, why there are still standing.

"Gyppo loggers went through here during the fifties and clear-cut everything of value," John says. "Left the grouse ladder and piss fir [white fir]. When we get down the other side into the Mattole Valley you think you're in God's little acre until you look up from the river bottom to the slopes. Then you think maybe it's Pork Chop Hill."

We wind up the narrow road through more stands of white fir (its more colorful name arises from its smell when freshly cut), then break out into high pasture land, ridge tops, and precipitous slopes of wind-swept grass sprinkled with lupine and tiny purple iris. We're completely engulfed in clouds now, though whenever the road dips below the summit we can see across to the opposing ridges and occasionally down the narrow valley to the sea, gray and featureless, distinguishable from the gloom above it only by a kind of slickness.

The terrain here is like Andean *paramo*, useful mainly for grazing sheep—and indeed sheep are everywhere, dotting the slopes like dandruff on a dark sportcoat. At a turnout where the road reaches a crest and begins to descend the western escarpment we stop and get out to water the roadbed and to watch a bunch of spring lambs scamper away from the truck on stiff legs, back to the protecting flanks of their mothers. Parody sheep, these corpulent ewes, somebody's cartoon drawings. If it weren't for their little lips nibbling away under those black muzzles you'd take them for piles of soggy old rock wool dumped in the grass behind a construction site.

"John," I say, "this is all very pastoral and redolent of *Lassie Come Home* movies, but . . . why does anybody want to live where it's always *raining*?"

"Because where it's always raining, the rest of the world - doesn't want to live."

For John, as for many others I've met on my excursions through Colorado, Montana, New Mexico, Oregon, Washington, California, that simple statement is almost enough. I remember asking a couple in Lander, Wyoming, why they had migrated from Connecticut to that particular frozen spot, and they said, in essence, the same thing—fed up with air, water, and noise pollution, fed up with crowding, toll roads, taxes, crummy schools, rising crime, fed up with a lockstep "get ahead" mentality when it was increasingly clear that what they were getting ahead *to* was nowhere. "You remember that scene in *The Graduate*?" the husband said to me. "The one where Dustin Hoffman is taken aside during a party at his parents' house by some polyester, Grecian formula creep . . . maybe it was his father, I don't remember, and the older guy says, 'I just want to say one thing to you, son. Just one thing. Plastics! You think about that. Plastics!' So I thought about it. Then I moved to Lander."

I ask John if this seems like a reasonable amplification to his remark about rain. He thinks so, though a lot of his friends were less calculating, more interested initially in escape than discovery. They dropped out for a long time before they dropped back in. He squints through the Scotch mist that is now streaming down our cheeks. "But then, you know, you get a little older, you old lady begins to grumble about the limits, she wants to have kids, you want to watch the ball game in color instead of black and white. Before you know it you're part of the work force again, and if you like where you live because it's the kind of place that allows you to listen to your own head now and then, you get uptight about all those people, most of them 'natives,' who are always clamoring for growth. They don't want change, but they sure want *growth*." He looks at me and laughs. "The only growth most of the people I know around here want to see is the kind you sprout in a peatsy potsy in your closet with the light on."

Back in the truck I turn on the defroster to clear the windshield. There are golden poppies scattered through the fields, and along the fence line that holds the sheep a profusion of banded weed called horsetail. At this stage of its growth it looks more like zebratail. The ridge drops away to our left in a sudden plunge to the Bear River valley, maybe a thousand feet below, and there is a little dream ranch tucked back along the bank about a mile inland from the river mouth. Again I am reminded of old movies—John Wayne, "the quiet man," striding up the path, with cudgel and cap, beautiful girl silhouetted against the sky in billowing skirts and peasant's blouse, stone cottage below with thatch roof, border collie yapping at approaching stranger.

We descend to the Pacific less than a mile south of Cape Mendocino, farthest point west (except for Alaska) on the North American continent, then follow along the beach. The road is pocked and eroded by fierce winter storms. An immense heap of driftwood, much of it full-sized logs bucked into mill lengths and barked by the surf, stretches as far as I can see, piled up on itself in tangled layers and covering the sand from the high-tide mark almost to the road. The wind blows incessantly and hard, sculpting the low vegetation along the base of the mountains into swept shapes that might have been cut with hedge-trimmers. Even though it has stopped raining, the mist thrown up by the breakers is so heavy we need the wipers to keep the windshield clear. No Pepsi generation, beach-blanket bongo parties here. No weenies, no bikinis. This is as wild and desolate a coast as I have seen anywhere along the Pacific.

"I understand from impeccable sources that Humboldt County is the dope-growing center of the North American continent," I say to John, the real pastime of the Pepsi generation suddenly popping to mind.

"Now that old slur (more or less true, by the way) is more interesting for what it suggests about rural economics in the modern world," he says. "I mean that a lot of people who came in the sixties found the scene up here suited them perfectly but there wasn't much to do in the way of making the payments. They found they could grow a little weed along with their corn and beans, and when that worked out so nicely the first time or two they began to cultivate larger, more isolated plots.

"The word got out. Quality stuff could be had in significant quantity up in Humboldt. A new industry was born. Of course, the same word got out locally and the natives got indignant and a little civil war broke out around places like Garberville between the hippies and the rednecks. In fact, it got pretty nasty.

"But then the rednecks began to notice that there was a lot of new money floating around, the local economy took an upswing that went off the charts, and they began to figure that maybe busting freaks could be left to the man. And since that generally meant some savvy sheriff who wasn't in a hurry to get mistaken for a deer out in somebody's back forty, everybody prospered. You'd be absolutely amazed at the number of small businesses in Eureka and Arcata that were, in fact, financed out of dope money—one-timers who found themselves with a bundle of cash and needed to do something with it. All of a sudden they became *merchants*, pillars of society, the new burghers of the town. They get stoned now and then, but they stay straight for the city council meetings. Sort of."

The road turns inland and we begin to wind through the hills again toward the little town of Petrolia. "Town" is an exaggeration. A general store and a post office, a school. Otherwise Petrolia is notable only because it contained the first producing oil wells in California, though the most successful of these (owned by Leland Stanford and the Mattole Petroleum Company) produced only a hundred barrels in all, at a rate of one barrel a day. Now it's a bend in the road, shingles painted white, a low fence of tilting grapestakes, a rusting tractor, a burst of pink rhododendron, and two narrow lanes of asphalt heading south.

The country has changed on us. By crossing a few hills we have moved into a completely different climate zone. All the way down through the Mattole River valley there are apple orchards in early blossom. The ranches are more numerous (or simply more visible), but we have yet to pass another car since we left Ferndale two hours ago. Broadleaf and vine maples line the road, and the hillsides, which still show the ugly scars of clearcut logging, are scattered with madroña and bay and flowering dogwood. These are not trees that thrive in cold, fog-shrouded forests, and yet we are only two or three miles in from the coast.

The Mattole River flows broad and muddy through the valley, swollen with spring rains and probably still running with the steelhead and salmon which spawn in it. I suspect that this river is *always* swollen with spring rains. When we stop at a one-horse hamlet called Honeydew I see a rainfall chart on the bulletin board inside the general store that claims the record for the year 1958: 174 inches. I think about that for a while. In 1958 I was in Denver, Colorado. It rained fourteen inches that year in Denver.

Late afternoon is suddenly upon us, and since John has decided that the best way to illustrate the cultural contrast that defines Humboldt County is to take me to the E & O Club in

Blue Lake, and then to a place called the Jambalaya in Arcata, we leave the Mattole Valley at Honeydew, climb steeply out over a pass called Nigger Hill, and descend the eastern slope of the mountains through Humboldt State Park. Back on Highway 101, where we are once again flanked on both sides by giant stands of redwood, there is so little evidence of the effects of 125 years of logging that it's hardly surprising if the casual traveler wonders what all the fuss from environmentalist groups is about. "The lumber companies aren't stupid, you know," John says. "Where the public can see it, they don't cut it. Get in from the road and you'll see the same ruin we saw along the Mattole, but not out here. In fact, my boy, that's why they call it the redwood curtain."

There is absolutely nothing unusual or memorable about the E & O Club. It's growing dark when we pull in, but I have the impression that it is a temporary building set back off the road to Blue Lake: metal, maybe twenty by forty feet, painted mauve or pink. No windows. The parking lot outside is filled with pickups and the bar stools inside with their owners—all of them, judging from the dress, hair style, and muscle gut that comes from hard work and hard drinking, involved in the profession of logging. The preferred cocktail in this establishment is whiskey with a beer back. Or simply beer. Beer is drunk from the can or bottle, not from a glass. I don't see any Heinekens or Dos Equis or Guinness in the ham fists of the E & O patrons. It's Bud and Oly at the E & O.

Conversation is perfunctory, even between men who have obviously come in together or who regularly see each other after work in the same spot. Newcomers are checked out in a slow, sideward glance that slides by and sizes up but does not reveal a conclusion. One understands there is a delicate line over which one does not cross in this perusal business. To extend a visual contract is to offer challenge, and *that* particular gambit does not come into play until later in the evening.

We order our whiskey and beer back and hunch over our elbows to consider the simulated grain in the eighteen inches of Formica bar directly before us. Territorial imperative. Our private preserve. Now and then I glance in the mirror behind the rows of bottles and observe my compatriots in similar repose. John offers laconic greetings and nods to those he knows. Since I don't have long hair, and I'm not wearing any machismo badges like a cowboy hat, and I don't have my cigarettes rolled up in my T-shirt sleeve, I'm not particularly threatened. Besides, it's early. I'm minding my own business. I think I'll get out of here alive. I watch the bartender roll dice for a drink with a guy at the end of the bar in a baseball cap that says "Cat" on the forepeak. In the mirror in front of me the barmaid attends to a few booths and tables and periodically feeds quarters into the juke box. Willie Nelson, Waylon Jennings, Dolly Parton, Crystal Gayle, Hank Williams, Jr., George and Tammy, Loretta and Conway. The musical fare is a statement of community attitude. Tom T. Hall sings "younger women, older whiskey, faster horses, more mon-eey."

Two truck drivers John knows ease onto the stools next to us and a brief conversation flares up.

"Where you working?"

"Willow Creek."

"Scaling?"

"Yeah. You still driving for L&P?"

"Yeah. You hear about those hippies up by you that got their dope crop ripped off by the Indians?"

"Hoopas?"

"Yeah. Yuroks or Hoopas, I don't know. Guess they'd been watching the freaks all along, waiting till they got it all cut down and dried; then they went in and took it."

"What'd the freaks do?"

"Went into Redding and tried to press charges. Dumb? Jeesus! Must of thought with the evidence all gone they couldn't get busted themselves, but they surely fucked up."

"I guess."

I make some small remark about the irony of the white man's victimization, but neither driver seems particularly amused. They are weekend fishermen and they are sore at the Indians who live along the Klamath River because they have been claiming exclusive fishing rights granted to them back in the late 1800s when the reservations were established, and they've been taking pot shots at intruders. Also they've been netting fish on the way to the spawning grounds and upsetting the ecology of the river. I do *not* make a small remark about the irony in this outburst of environmental consciousness. I finish my beer instead, and John suggests we move on.

"Hey, John," one of the truck drivers says, as we slide off the Naugahyde. "I hear redwood's going to four-fifty a thousand, on the stump."

"Is that right?"

"Well, Christ, you're a scaler, aren't you?"

"I scale 'em, I don't price 'em."

"Four-fifty a thousand. And I hear it's going to six hundred."

The other driver leans back to talk to John across his buddy's back. "You know what they're doing, don't you? Now that the feds have taken all that land for the park, the big companies are jacking up the price of lumber just to increase the value of the acreage that my God-damn tax dollar is going to buy so that I won't have a job to go to work to no more. Son of a bitch!"

"You can take a nice picnic in it, Bernie."

"And I'll tell you something else. A lot of small mills are gonna go out of business in the next few years because these big companies are gonna stop selling off their pine and fir and start processing it themselves. They're not gonna be able to do it just on redwood any more."

"They sell half of it to the Japs right now. The slopes process it right on a ship and by the time they get over there to Tokyo - they're unloading milled boards."

"I'd like to know why the hell we let 'em do that."

John and the drivers shake their heads in commiseration. It's just too much to think about at seven-thirty on a Wednesday evening after three boilermakers and a pepperoni stick. Anyway, the barmaid has just put a house quarter in the juke box and serious drinking can commence again. As we're heading out the door I catch the chorus of the new and revised national anthem, "You can take this job and shove it/I ain't working here no more."

Arcata isn't more than a few miles from Blue Lake and the E & O Club, but it might as well be down in Marin County for all the two are alike. For one thing, Humboldt State University is located there and the town caters to a considerable extent to a clientele that is young, hip, and transient. In the past ten years more and more of those transients, mainly students, liked where they found themselves and stayed, bought property when it was still cheap, found jobs or started small businesses, opted for a life style that had fewer economic rewards, perhaps, but a lot more in plain old good living. I meet a number of them at the Jambalaya, a relatively new place in town, at least under its current guise, and one which is about as close to the E & O Club in ambience as Antoine's is to a White Castle Dixieburger.

Not exactly one of those fern bars with its boring display of stained glass, pull-chain toilets, neo-Victorian woodwork, and gas-lamp romance (for that you go across the street to Youngberg's). You can nevertheless get an imported beer here and drink it from a chilled glass. The music is live and is folk, not country. The clientele in Jambalaya would not survive an evening at the E & O. The would *not* get out alive. There is a faint aroma in the air that might be the patchouli oil behind the ears of the girl at the next table, or might, on the other hand, be the burning of the organic substance for which Humboldt has become justly famous. But however familiar the place may seem to my jaded taste, it is lively with conversation and the rules of social intercourse are less proscribed than in Blue Lake—though I probably understand them less well. People come and go, sit down at the table to chat with John and meet the brother-in-law. I talk for a while with a young couple who have recently opened a boutique/gallery in Eureka's new "old town" (what else), and who are very enthusiastic about urban renewal down on Second and Third streets; a lawyer who works with Indian Legal Services and who is currently involved with an environmental group fighting the city's proposed new sewer system (a system that will promote urban expansion but threaten the ecology of the bay, he says); a lady who works for Planned Parenthood, and the man she lives with who is a substitute teacher in the Arcata school district. Both were instrumental in the fight, a few years back, to prevent a bunch of Eureka businessmen from buying up a ranch in Butler Valley and damming the Mad River to flood several thousand acres and turn it into a "recreation" area. For water skiers. It was about the first victory for the environmentalists in Humboldt County, it marked the beginning of a new era, and they are very proud of their participation.

I meet others, all of them very much involved in various community action projects and "alternative" structures, everything from day-care centers to cooperative food stores to preservation of historical buildings to midwifery. To be sure, they threaten existing institutions and give fits to those who have not had their advantages and who do not, or cannot, share their fundamental indifference to lunch-bucket issues. It's pretty hard to convince Bernie and Mr. Cat that they need a park to have a picnic in when they don't have the price of the ham to put in their sandwich.

On the other hand, if Bernie and Mr. Cat have their way these mountains will all look the way they do up behind Willow Creek, like a scrofulous old hound with mange, eight hairs to the inch, wrecked, dying. My companions at Jambalaya understand (as Bernie and Mr. Cat and their employers do not and never will) that growth is not necessarily progress, that less is often more, that it garners a man nothing to have worked hard all his life to buy himself a plate-glass view if the scene he looks out upon is obscured in a cloud of carbon monoxide, and if his days are numbered by a lifelong ingestion of carcinogenic substances. They understand, in short, that the measures of our gross national product have for too long been severely lacking in those abstract and sometimes metaphysical areas that make life worthwhile.

On the other hand, Bernie and Mr. Cat are concerned with beans on the table and a roof over the kids' heads, not metaphysics. The belly takes precedence.

On the other hand, the motor home and speedboat and dirt bike that Bernie and Mr. Cat use 5 days a year and park 360 don't have anything to do with beans.

On the other hand, it's late, I'm awash in mind-fogging beverages, nobody asked me to solve the world's problems anyway. The folks at my table are rising, smiling farewells, preparing to wend their way. . . . Why are they going out the back door in the alley? Why is the Legal Services lawyer beckoning to me? Fresh air? I'm in that bad shape?

"You want a hit on this?" somebody says.

"What's this?"

"Humboldt County tops and flowers."

Ah yes, well, why not? Obligations of the investigative reporter. Metaphysics. Abstractions. I can now testify. It is as advertised: mild, fragrant, subtle; like driving my truck off Half Dome. It bypasses mirth, munchies, the nods; leaves me quieter than a Carmelite nun. It's straightline coma. A part of our gross national product.

THERE IT IS: TAKE IT

The master condition not only of any future developments in the West but of the maintenance and safeguarding of what exists there now, is the development and conservation of water production. Water, which is rigidly limited by the geography and climate, is incomparably more important than all other natural resources in the West put together.

Bernard de Voto

*When I came out of Mair's market in Independence, a few supplies in my arms and a new frying pan to replace the one I backed the truck over at Whitney Portal, a blanket of high cirrus clouds had drifted over the crest of the Sierra Nevada and taken what little warmth the March sun could still muster. The peaks along the boundary of Kings Canyon and Sequoia national parks and Inyo National Forest had vanished into ominous darkness below the higher scud, and there was the smell of snow in the wind blowing down from Kearsarge Pass. Until then the day had been deceptively like spring; cool, the air so bright that the abrupt wall of the mountains rising ten thousand feet out of the shadscale and sagebrush of the Great Basin, snow-covered and etched against a ceramic sky of cobalt blue, seemed more like a Bierstadt hallucination than real granite, faulted and warped, shaped by wind and water and ice. I shiv-

---

*Two sources, *Deepest Valley* by Genny Schumacher et al. (Benny Smith Books, 1978), and "The Politics of California Water," by William Kahrl (*California Historical Quarterly*, spring/summer, 1976), have been valuable background material in the preparation of this chapter.

ered in my cotton shirt and dug in the camper shell for my sheepskin.

An Inyo County Sheriff's Department van pulled in next to me, and I entertained a long, expressionless stare from its occupants as I backed out of the parking lot and proceeded at a snail's pace up the road. Maybe they thought I was the mad bomber. Yesterday in Lone Pine all the talk was about the Molotov cocktail somebody had hurled into the Independence office of the Los Angeles Department of Water and Power, and none of the good citizens I heard on the street expressed anything but deep regret that it hadn't burned the place to the ground. The authorities were edgy: it was not the first such incident. Hatred of the DWP has a seventy-year history in the Owens Valley and recent events had apparently rekindled it with such enthusiasm that department officials were even moving around the county in unmarked cars. An otherwise uncommunicative Paiute boy I gave a ride to from the Death Valley cutoff into Lone Pine told me with a shadow of a smile that he'd bet more than his boots somebody would dynamite the L.A. aqueduct before summer.

A few miles north of Independence I began looking for a place to camp. The valley floor along the west side of the highway was harsh and broken with chunks of bedrock sticking up through the alluvium; the distance between me and the upthrust of the Sierra block was only a few miles. To the east a broader, more rolling plain of sagebrush flowed monotonously to the base of the White Mountains. Nearly as high as the Sierra, they lie in its rain shadow and were never subjected to glaciation. They looked rounder, softer, more benign.

Powdery snow began to dust the windshield and I muttered about an incurable habit of driving long beyond the hour when visibility remains a factor in the selection of a camp. Along this stretch of Highway 395 there are hundreds of dirt roads that amble off through the brush, some ending at abandoned mines, some at campgrounds, some just petering out when they run into the mountain wall. As usual I made up my mind to quit at just that point when I could no longer make a roadside guess whether I'd find water and firewood, or carve up my tires in one of the many flows of basaltic lava, or wind up having to dig my way back to civilization out of axle-deep sand and soda ash.

My first mistake aborted in the front yard of somebody's ramshackle ranch. My second led me east down a set of tire tracks toward the Owens River below the Tinemaha Reservoir and ended at a padlocked gate in the middle of a barbed-wire fence. It was by now dark and the snow falling in heavy, wet flakes and I decided to forgo the amenities, heat a can of soup, and bed down in the camper shell. I had just reached for the ignition key when I heard a rifle shot. Leaving the lights on, I killed the engine, and listened. Two more, three, four, five. Not small-bore either. And then, as I sat there wondering who could be hunting elephants in the dark, hoping they wouldn't mistake my truck for an animate object, I got some arresting news. There was a man with a gun outside my window and he was telling me to step out.

"What are you doing down here?"

"I was looking for a place to camp," I said.

"This look like a campground to you?"

"Well, no . . . ," I said. "It got dark and I couldn't see much. Listen, if I've trespassed on your property . . ."

He cut my apology short. "You know Dave Walizer?"

"No."

"Jim Wickser?"

"No."

"Where are you from?"

"Santa Cruz."

"Where's that?"

"It's near San Francisco."

"Can you prove it?"

"Sure," I said, miffed but too much the coward to ask who he thought *he* was. "I've got a driver's license and the truck registration if you want to see them."

He didn't. He motioned me back into the cab. "You go on up the highway and turn north about a half mile. You'll see a sign on your left that says Goodale Creek. There's a campground about two, three miles in."

"Thanks," I said. I turned the truck around and wound up

the road, found the camp where he'd promised, and settled in for the night.

But two days later in the Inyo *Register* news office I overheard a couple of reporters talking about the DWP pump somebody had shot to pieces down along the aqueduct between Big Pine and Independence. The damage, one of them said, was increased by the use of armor-piercing shells. No wonder my man was a bit curt. Molotov cocktails? Armorpiercing shells? And windows smashed in DWP cars and trucks? Bags of concrete poured into water meters? The Owens Valley water war, cold since 1927, was obviously heating up again.

The valley lies about 225 miles north of Los Angeles between the jagged thrust of the Sierra's eastern wall and the more - gently sculpted range of the Inyo–White Mountains along the California border. It is not big (roughly 100 miles long by 15 to 20 miles wide), and the subtleties of its high-desert ecology are completely overshadowed by the Sierran escarpment that seems to rise almost vertically from the brief foothills along its western side. Oldtimers remember when nearly a quarter of its total acreage was under cultivation—apples, pears, alfalfa, corn, even watermelons the ranchers used to plant to feed their pigs—but that was before Fred Eaton and William Mulholland, in 1904, took a buckboard trip into the region and devised a plan to acquire its entire water supply and ship it by aqueduct to the city of bad dreams.

Eaton and Mulholland were not the first to recognize the potential of the Owens Valley drainage basin. In 1903 the National Reclamation Service had mapped and surveyed the area with the intention of developing a model irrigation system that would double its productive land, and the project engineer had reported to his chief of southwestern operations, J. B. Lippincott, that a simple dam at the northern end of the valley and canals running south along both sides would provide enough water to irrigate 100,000 acres of new land. Lippincott told his friend Fred Eaton (formerly superintendent of the Los Angeles Water Company and mayor of the city after that) about the

Reclamation Service study, and Eaton began to put together a complicated scheme to make himself outrageously rich. It was a long shot, but *if* he could acquire control over the water flow in the valley, and *if* he could get the federal irrigation project to a municipal water diversion project, and *if* he could find a way to fund a multimillion-dollar aqueduct to transport that water to Los Angeles, he would own something of enormous value to a growing city with almost no water resources of its own.

Eaton took a quiet trip to the headwaters of the Owens River and found that the surrounding land, about 12,000 acres, could be purchased for a half million dollars. The proposed dam site, for which the local ranchers had already signed over their water storage rights to the Reclamation Service, was on the property, and it was clear that whoever owned the point of origin would have a virtual stranglehold on all downstream users. Part one of his plan was no problem. Neither was part two. Lippincott was happy to go along (he was later discovered to have been put on the city payroll while at the same time working for the federal government), and reported to the Department of the Interior that the irrigation project no longer looked so attractive as it had at first. At the same time he made the Reclamation Service maps available to Eaton, who then felt secure enough to take an option on his headwater property.

But part three was not so easy. The cost of building a 225-mile aqueduct exceeded the resources of private capital, and in any event Mayor Eaton had won election in 1898 on a platform that called for municipal ownership of the water system—a platform that was implemented in 1902. Now he was planning to sell the city of Los Angeles what it presumably would already own once the water had been appropriated from the ranchers in Owens Valley. The aqueduct would have to be built through the sale of public bonds, and the public might be less than thrilled by the prospect of Mr. Eaton's financial aggrandizement. It was a prickly dilemma, but there was no way around it. Eaton attempted to redefine the concept of municipal ownership to include only the *system* of transportation and not the *substance* transported, but that circumscription wouldn't wash with the one figure who was absolutely essential to his success: William Mulholland, the Los Angeles superintendent of water.

Mulholland took the term "municipalization" to mean what it said, and he was vigorously opposed to any scheme that might leave the city's water supply, existing or proposed, vulnerable to the capriciousness of private ownership. But his indignation was strictly pragmatic. He was, after all, both Eaton's friend and his protégé. There was no reason why an alternative might not be worked out that would satisfy everybody. He proposed an agreement whereby Los Angeles, for an amount roughly equal to the purchase price of the 12,000 acres in question, would buy out Eaton's water rights and an easement for a reservoir, and Eaton could keep the land. Moreover, the city would immediately move to acquire key downstream water rights from valley ranchers, all of whom were still under the illusion that they were dealing with the U.S. Reclamation Service and merely aiding the development of their own irrigation system. Country girls at the fair, they could be had before they knew it. When the city diverted everything below the headwater dam on Eaton's property, they would be forced out of business and Eaton could pick up their stock for a song. He wouldn't be a water mogul, perhaps, but he would certainly be a cattle baron.

Implementation of the Eaton-Mulholland plan would have been difficult, to say the least, without the host of self-interested boosters who began to swarm around it. The most significant of these were the members of a land syndicate who bought 16,000 acres of barren, waterless land in the San Fernando Valley (for thirty-five dollars an acre), and whose names read like a register of the most influential and wealthy men in the state— Henry Huntington, E. H. Harriman, W. G. Kerchoff, Joseph Sartori, E. T. Earl, Harrison Gray Otis. The latter two owned three of the four leading papers in Los Angeles and were able initially to maintain a voluntary silence about the city's designs on the Owens Valley (while Fred Eaton, posing as a Reclamation Service agent, went about acquiring water rights for transfer), and later to exert pressure on public opinion in favor of a bond issue to build the aqueduct.

The syndicate, of course, had plans to divert the diversion: water flowing to Los Angeles could be siphoned off to irrigate their San Fernando land, and they were in a position to exert tremendous influence not only over local and state agencies, but over the federal government as well. And the final obstacle *was* the federal government, because in order to begin construction of the aqueduct, a right of way across federal land had to be obtained from Congress. Sitting on the House Public Lands Committee was the congressman from Inyo County, Sylvester Smith, and by this time the cat was out of the bag. The ranchers and farmers knew that they had been duped, and they were furious.

The right-of-way bill was introduced by Frank Flint, the Republican senator from Los Angeles. Smith proposed an amendment that would reinstate the original Reclamation Service project and make water available to the city only when there was an excess and *only* for domestic use. It was an amendment that was supported by the Secretary of the Interior and, in fact, by William Mulholland himself, but it posed an obvious threat to long-range development plans in Los Angeles, on the one hand, and disaster to Huntington, Harriman, Otis, *et al.*, on the other. The smoke in the back rooms thickened. When it thinned again, oddly enough, the head of the Forest Service and grandfather of the conservation movement, Gifford Pinchot, and his boss, champion of the little man and President of the United States, Theodore Roosevelt, had declared their opposition to the Smith amendment, and the Flint bill was voted out of committee intact. The House passed it the next day. The interest of the few, said Roosevelt, "must unfortunately be disregarded in view of the infinitely greater interest to be served by putting the water in Los Angeles." It was the final blow to the Owens Valley.

That, of course, was in 1906. The elevation of modern consciousness about the environment and the rights of the few to be protected from sacrifice to the needs (greeds) of the many would preclude a successful heist of what remains of Owens Valley's lifeblood in the 1980s. Wouldn't it? Evidently not.

———

In a Lone Pine coffee shop while I wait to pay my breakfast bill I read a xeroxed flyer taped to the bakery case urging everyone to join in the "meter strike," whatever that may be, and announcing a gathering of the Concerned Citizens of Owens Valley to discuss a plan of action against the continued deceit and malfeasance of the Los Angeles Department of Water and Power. There is a phone number to call for further information, which I scratch down on a match book and later dial from a pay booth at a gas station. Lois Wilson, local coordinator for the Concerned Citizens, invites me to stop by. She'll give me all the information I want. And then some.

Lois is a large, handsome woman somewhere in her forties. She lives in a neat modern house with all the appurtenances of solid middle-class life; the car in the drive appears to be a Pontiac or Buick; the coffee is served with cookies and in china that matches. She and her friends the Nelsons have just returned from a funeral and are therefore dressed up, but nobody in the room seems uncomfortable or unacquainted with Sunday clothes. In short, no liberal hippie activists in Red Wings and Gortex here. The Concerned Citizens of Owens Valley are not young transplants trying to defend their newly discovered outpost of Eden from corporate invasion; they are longtime residents who want to save what is left of their homes from finally and irrevocably blowing away.

"It wasn't enough," Lois tells me, "that the DWP got all of the surface rights to water in the valley, and extended its aqueduct 105 miles north into the Mono Basin so it could divert all of their water too; in 1970 they completed a second aqueduct that would increase the flow capacity to Los Angeles by 50 percent and they started a systematic program to pump all the *ground* water out of here.

"Well, in about two years you could see the results of that. All the springs dried up, a lot of vegetation in the valley that depends on subsurface water died, the dust storms got worse and worse. We've always had dust storms ever since DWP dried up Owens Lake and turned it into an alkali pit, but it got worse."

Lillian Nelson shakes her head as she remembers just a few years back, when there were pear orchards around Manzanar, the old Japanese internment camp, that survived just on ground water. Now they're dead. "There was a wonderful place up past Independence called Little Black Rock Springs," she adds, "that was probably the finest habitat around before DWP increased its pumping. And then that all died. Lois, you remember the artesian wells on Mazourka Canyon Road?"

"I sure do."

"Dry as a bone. And that dust. Lord knows what it does to your lungs. They've just started to really study the problem because we've got a lot of respiratory disease among the older - people. I don't hear anybody suggesting it does any good."

Lois ticks off a half dozen more environmental disasters and comes back to that alkaline dust. "There's a very highly respected botanist who lives in Independence named Mary DeDecker, and she's found evidence of pine forest destruction from alkali deposits five thousand feet above the lake. If it can kill a pine tree, what do you suppose it'll do to you?"

I allow that I would not want to breathe it long enough to find out. I have seen that dry lake on a windy day and it looks like smoke from a raging forest fire.

"You know what some genius from the DWP office in Los Angeles said? He said the dust problem was caused by dune buggies."

Lois shows me a Forest Service map of the Owens Valley. Land owned by the city of Los Angeles appears in yellow; it runs in an unbroken line straight up the valley floor from Lone Pine to Bishop, two to three miles wide by 105 miles long. Everything adjacent is under the jurisdiction of the Bureau of Land Management, and everything on both sides of that is part of the Inyo National Forest. In other words, except for a few small Indian reservations and a scattering of privately owned plots, everything surrounding the Los Angeles corridor belongs to the people of the United States. What happened to the safeguarding of our property under federal and state environmental protection laws? Those are *my* trees and shrubs that are dying to keep the swimming pools in Beverly Hills filled and the driveways in Santa Monica flushed.

Lois and Lillian chuckle a little grimly. "That was the basis of the first Inyo County lawsuit against Los Angeles in 1972. It didn't take a wizard to see what was happening to the environment. We wanted the DWP to file an Environmental Impact Report and asked the court to stop further pumping until levels could be set that weren't harmful, and we've been in litigation ever since; won almost every battle along the way, but we're still losing the war. The DWP doesn't care what the courts say. They go right on doing whatever they want, because they figure they can stall the legal process until finally there's nothing left for anybody to fight over. Or at least that's how I see it."

Lillian goes into the kitchen to make a new pot of coffee, and Lois sorts through a stack of legal documents looking for an injunction that dates back to 1929 ordering the DWP to stop pumping and cap wells on specified properties owned by a consolidation of plaintiffs. In those days it simply bought out troublemakers (or forced them out) and had all such injunctions dismissed.

"They have the money and the legal staff to sidetrack the court for years. Take the EIR, for example. First they argued they were exempt from having to file because their new aqueduct was completed before the California Environmental Quality Act was made law. It took our suit at least a year to work its way to a state appeals court where they were finally told they *did* have to file, because extracting ground water is an ongoing action, not a completed one, and then they fiddled around, quibbling about what had to be included and what didn't. They managed to take three years to come up with a draft *they* claimed was adequate. Fortunately the court insisted on reviewing it, which took another year, and then threw it out saying it was not only *in*adequate but deliberately misleading."

Lillian leans in from the kitchen. "And don't fool yourself. They knew perfectly well it wouldn't fly. They were very pleased to take it back to the drawing board. In the meantime, of course, they went right on pumping."

Lois nods. "I think they're on their third draft now. Isn't it astonishing that all those engineers and lawyers and experts on this and experts on that can't come up with an acceptable Environmental Impact Report in eight years? Maybe they aren't trying very hard."

One place the DWP does seem to try very hard is in thinking up punitive measures to direct against those Owens Valley communities that have seen fit to contest its authority. Nothing much has changed since the days of William Mulholland. The DWP's consciousness has not been raised very much since 1906. The reaction to this policy of intimidation that resulted in dynamite explosions punctuating the sweet summer nights back in the 1920s, and Los Angeles aqueduct water flowing into the desert sand two hundred miles north of its destination, may not turn out to be very much different either. Not unless the Owens Valley gets some measure of satisfaction. And soon.

The DWP's most recent intimidation of the valley residents began soon after Inyo County filed its 1972 suit demanding a cessation of pumping and preparation of an Environmental Impact Report. When the county asked the court to review the document eventually produced by the DWP, Los Angeles suddenly sent word that it was cutting off all water to its agricultural and recreational lessees and proceeded immediately to close valves that had remained open since the aqueduct's completion in 1913—valves apparently so rusty from lack of use they had to use dynamite to budge them. When it was loudly protested that this action was simply a punishment for Inyo's poor taste in trying to save its environment, the city engineer in charge of the aqueduct said it was not punitive, it was "educational."

Evidently the Owens Valley is full of slow learners. Their defiance continued in the court room and the DWP needed to offer a refresher course. In 1978 it declared its intention to install water meters in all residences (in spite of its own feasibility study which showed the cost of such installation to be economically impractical) and announced that it would give - people one year to put their lines in order before real billing would commence. In the interim, "mock" bills were sent so that folks could learn to readjust.

Once again valley residents were furious. They had always

been charged a flat rate for water, and they had never been careless with its use. Indeed, during the great drought of 1976-1977 they had conserved 25 percent of normal consumption, while Los Angeles refused to initiate *any* mandatory conservation measures until it was finally forced to do so by a court decision denying it increased ground water pumping levels. Only then, and grudgingly, did it join the rest of California and institute methods to save 10 percent. (Angelenos actually reduced usage 15 percent, an altruistic gesture generally lost on most of the state to the north, where 30 to 40 percent was the norm.)

The meters were installed . . . upside down, backwards, badly. Sometimes they registered water, sometimes volcanic gas, sometimes nothing. Lois Wilson gives me a demonstration by turning on her garden hose. It writhes around like a decapitated snake, hissing madly, the meter duly registering cubic feet of something per second, but whatever is coming out of the nozzle, it isn't water. Lillian Nelson tells me the same thing occurs in her lines up in Big Pine. "And that's the least of it," she says. "My husband and I are retired. We live in a single-family home. You want to guess what our 'projected' bill for forty-five days was?"

"Fifty dollars?" I say.

"Five hundred and sixty. Everybody was getting bills like that. They were trying to scare people out. I can't figure any other reason."

Whatever motivates the actions of the DWP, the installation of meters and water rate hikes from $8.50 a month to $60, $70, $100 (Lillian's real bill, when it came, was nowhere near $560) did not intimidate very many valley residents. They fought back with a meter strike, some refusing to pay anything, others refusing to pay more than the original flat rate, and when the DWP began cutting off water in the homes of nonpayers and threatening once again to cancel land leases, the effect was like throwing gasoline on a grease fire. The night riders began to strike.

Now there are negotiations. "Let's talk about this." "Let's discuss your request to purchase your own water system." "Let's not resort to violence, fellas." But it's more placatory than real and any concessions that the DWP implies it might make come with amendments demanding the dropping of existing law suits. The Concerned Citizens are willing to talk, but nobody trusts the adversary in the least. Agreements proposed by the DWP, Paul DeDecker remarks, are "only a carrot on a stick and the DWP has the stick." Tired of the endless stall, Inyo voters turned out in record numbers in November 1980 to pass an ordinance that would invest the county rather than the DWP with control of groundwater pumping levels. But the DWP does not recognize the legitimacy of the ordinance, fought its inclusion on the ballot from the outset, and is currently contesting the legality of its passage. And while the "dialogue" goes on (and this is the whole point, many would argue) Los Angeles continues to pump the Bishop Cone dry, flagrantly ignoring a 1940 superior court order prohibiting it from doing so.

This is a country of remarkable contrasts. As I drive north - toward Big Pine the clouds that have been intermittently spitting sleet for the past three days suddenly lift, and once again I find myself veering from shoulder to shoulder, unable to keep my eyes on the road in the overwhelming presence of the Sierran wall. From alluvial fans flocked with creosote brush and sage the lower canyons climb steeply, as if hacked into the fault-block by a cleaver. The mid-range is folded, bent, sheared, cusped into the cirques and moraines, cliffs and saddles that rise into peaks along its jagged crest—the whole face a towering, unbroken rampart against the Pacific, glaring in an alabaster mantle of snow.

By comparison the valley floor doesn't stand a chance. Not any more. Dry, bleak, its vegetation stunted and sparse, it looks a bit seedy to most people speeding up Highway 395 on their way to somewhere else, like Mammoth, Yosemite, Reno, Lake Tahoe. It looks, in fact, like most of the high desert country in the West—like an old chenille bedspread somebody threw out when its little green tufts bleached gray and its rich umber foundation faded dun. Not a winning combination to start with, perhaps. Its towns (only Lone Pine, Independence, Big Pine, and

Bishop are big enough to notice) seem almost marginal—overly
dependent on one-night tourists. Except at the northern end of
the valley around Bishop, there is little in the way of agriculture
except occasional grazing and a few irrigated fields of alfalfa.

But this is all deception. There is more here than meets the
gleam in a keno player's eye. The hotdogger streaking toward his
ski week at Mammoth Mountain may not know it, or care about
it, but he is passing through one of the unique natural laborato-
ries in the western United States, one which ought (according to
the botanist Mary DeDecker) to be protected and preserved in
the same way national parks, monuments, and wild and scenic
rivers are protected and preserved. I stop in Independence to ask
Mrs. DeDecker about damage caused by Los Angeles water diversion, but the conversation leads inexorably toward that one
point. She has lived in the valley for thirty years, knows it backward and forward, and she is no doubt as indignant as the rest
about water meters and punitive gestures on the part of the
DWP, but her irritation is cloaked in scientific objectivity and her
concerns primarily ecological. "If you destroy the plants that can
adapt to the Owens-Mono environment, nothing will survive,"
she says. "That's why I'm concerned about subsurface pumping.
There used to be sloughs, meadows, springs, marshes; now -
they're all gone. A whole chain of life has been destroyed, and
there will be more to follow if control is not imposed."

I mention that I've heard a proposal to introduce new varieties of plants from Australia and Israel that will tolerate almost
anything—will grow, in fact, in the alkali basin of Owens Lake.

"Well, they're studying that, but I'm very skeptical. If you
can find something that will survive in Owens Lake, you may
well have found a monster that will eventually take over the
whole valley, something that will crowd out the native grasses
and shrubs."

But what about the effects of all that blowing alkaline dust?
Respiratory problems. Those dying pine forests five thousand
feet up on the Sierran Crest. Isn't there a tradeoff?

"I've seen some evidence of limber pine damage in a place
called New York Butte. Pines are acid-loving plants, and when
alkali coats their needles and branches it clogs their pores and

will probably kill them, though I'm not sure how long it will take. The same thing is happening to the mountain mahogany, and I've heard that alfalfa ranchers east of Mono Lake where the same problem occurs have been complaining about crop damage. But I think the real reason for official concern is that military testing is being interfered with at the Naval Weapons Center south of Lone Pine and the government has probably told the city to do something. In any case, the solution is not to solve one problem by creating another. One could just put water back into Owens Lake. . . ."

The message is of course commonplace in modern ecology. When you tinker with an established system you often get results you don't want. Import fisher cats to kill the porcupines in Vermont, and when they've mopped up the porcupines, they start looking around for something else to eat, like your chickens. If your dog gives them grief, they'll eat him too. Import a creeping kudzu vine from Africa for a hearty ground cover along a freeway and it eats the state of South Carolina. Drain a lake and impede national defense. Drill a well and dry up two thousand square miles of farmland. On and on. Man is a tinkerer, and it seems rather idle to hope (much less to expect) that he will stop. Of course the snail darter will perish. Of course Montana will be strip-mined. Of course there will be genetic engineering. Of course the Owens Valley will be bled dry. Perhaps all one can do is kick and scream to slow the process down a bit. Or if one lives in Inyo County, hope that some computer at the Nellis Air Force Range and Nuclear Testing Site will run amuck and drop a big one on the corner of Sunset and Vine.

Because Los Angeles is not going to go away. It needs water and power. When the Central Arizona Project goes on line and Arizona's share of Colorado River water now used by Southern California is diverted to Phoenix, Tucson, *et al.*, then Los Angeles' problems are going to be considerably increased. The prospect makes a lot of people in northern California ecstatic. But the Owens Valley model—the dogged tenacity of the DWP to provide water and power no matter at whose expense and in spite of all attempts to curtail it through court orders and conservation methods—should be fair warning. It is idle to hope the people of Los Angeles will all find a metaphoric Jesus in the brotherhood of natural resources. And even if they did, the DWP (Devil Without Portfolio) is not directly accountable to the people of Los Angeles. It answers to its own commissioners, who answer to the mayor and the city council. In short, it operates in virtual anonymity and (if history tells us anything) regards as inherent its right to the product it sells, regardless of consequences to the environment. Anybody's environment. Teddy Roosevelt said it: ". . . the infinitely greater interest to be served . . ." Los Angeles is no more interested in the problems of the Owens Valley, or the Mono Basin, or the Sacramento delta, or Colorado's western slope (all sources, existing or proposed, of its water supply) than it is in the air quality around Page, Arizona, or the Four Corners. It needs/wants/will get more water. And to this end it is not only pumping the Owens Valley dry, it is draining Mono Lake in the next basin north along the eastern slope of the Sierra.

I drive north toward the town of Bishop and then over Wheeler Ridge into Mono County, climbing sharply to Sherwin Summit and then leveling out for thirty or forty miles through piñon-juniper woodland and forests of Jeffrey pine and red fir. Stands of aspen dot the open slopes to the west, and there are snow bush, paintbrush, corn lily, and angelica scattered through the understory. I had planned to sidetrack from Big Pine to see the bristlecone forest up in the White Mountains, 12,000 feet above sea level, but the snow was too deep and the road still closed. I'd like to take Methuselah's Walk through that wind-blasted, frozen, rock-bound area and take a look at the oldest living thing on the face of this earth, a gnarled, twisted, forked, tortured old bristlecone, 4,600 years old, that looks to me from photographs more like Grendel's ganglia than a tree. Hard to imagine something born about the time of Babylon, hitting its stride around the birth of Christ, still putting along while mankind litters the heavens with orbital junk and strives to clone itself in a petri dish. I have to assume it will be around the next time I'm through.

Thirty or forty deer bound across the road a hundred yards

in front of me, and somewhere just south of Deadman's Summit, before the highway drops down into the Mono Basin, a bobcat appears at the edge of the woods, makes an instant calculation of my approaching speed, and clears the road in two swift bounds. The wind has come up, buffeting the truck, and the familiar cloud cover has drifted over the Sierra crest.

The Mono craters appear on my left, barren volcanic cones lying like mollusks about the sand flats and pumice; then the lake itself, 40,000 acres of gray, metallic water with moonscape towers of calcium carbonate rising just beyond the banks of its sullen shore. Bubbling up over the centuries to calcify like stalagmites, this deposit lurks beneath the surface as well, waiting patiently to disembowel the water skiers who no longer come, the swimmers who no longer dive from beached docks rotting in the mud. An Ice Age lake, possibly the oldest in North America, dying. Gone to Los Angeles. Since the aqueduct was extended into the Mono Basin in 1940 it has dropped forty-three vertical feet; since diversion capacity was increased in 1970 it has receded at the rate of two feet per year, only one of the five major streams feeding into it allowed to flow. Before long it will be a chemical sump, an alkali desert surrounded by evil-smelling mud, an airborne disaster blowing mineral salts 20,000 feet into the air (already pilots have mistaken its dust storms for volcanic eruptions) and threatening the pine forests in Yosemite Park to the west, the bristlecones to the south. Before long it will be, in fact, the "solemn, silent, sailless" sea that Mark Twain described when he first saw it in 1870.

So lunar in appearance is this body of water, so unique chemically in its heavy concentration of carbonates, sulphates, and salt, that it has for years been thought of as "dead," though it is not. Its high salinity excludes fish life, but not algae, not brine shrimp, not brine flies—all that tasty invertebrate food on which gulls, grebes, and not so long ago, Paiute Indians used to thrive. It is, on the contrary, one of the most life-productive lakes in the world, a veritable Mono Hilton for aquatic birds migrating across the continent—like the 100,000 Wilson's phalaropes who stop in late summer on their way to Argentina, or the million or so eared gerbes who come in autumn and cover the water like a feathered blanket. It is the maternity ward for nearly the entire breeding population of California gulls, 50,000 of which come to nest on one of the two small islands off its northern shore.

Dead? Not hardly. Not yet. And not at all if the Save Mono Lake Committee, the Friends of the Earth, the Audubon Society, the Sierra Club, and a far-flung contingency of conservationists have their way. But their way is basically through the courts, the law, and if the Owens Valley is any example, the Los Angeles Department of Water and Power is (through circumlocution and evasion) exempt from the law. The courts move slowly. Legislation is a tedious process. And while the talk goes on, the charges and counter-charges, the lobbying, the token gestures of accommodation (DWP has volunteered, for example, to allow up to 50,000 acre feet to flow into the lake this year—because the snow pack was so heavy they can't use it all), the water level drops, the salinity increases to a point where even brine shrimp may choke, a land bridge to the islands slowly emerges from the murky water, and coyotes begin the decimation of the gull colony. This year, with the flow of surplus water, the lake is up a foot; some gulls have returned to nest. But next year? And when Arizona begins to take its share of Colorado River water?

"A country of wonderful contrasts," John Muir said, "hot deserts bounded by snow-laden mountains, cinder and ashes scattered on glacier-polished pavement, frost and fire working together in the making of beauty." Drive on, drive on. From Conway Summit, a few miles past Lee Vining, I stop to look back down two thousand feet into the Mono Valley and south over the volcanic cones to the lateral range of mountains that divide this watershed from the Owens Valley. How much would it cost to save it all? According to a recent California Department of Water Resources report, not much: installation of efficient plumbing devices, more careful irrigation of lawns and gardens, a slight reduction of water pressure, more use of dry-climate plants. One brick in every toilet in Los Angeles would be enough to save Mono Lake.

As I put the truck in gear and head north toward Carson

City, I am faintly amused by the euphemistic label we attach to that entity charged with providing our essential services—the "public utility." What public? Why does a "public utility" think its obligation to the public stops at the faucet and the power pole? Or to one segment of the public and not another? I am reminded of a letter Bernard DeVoto once wrote to the editor of the Denver *Post* on a different though not unrelated matter. "You are certainly right when you say 'us natives' can do what you like with your scenery. But the National Parks and Monuments happen not to be your scenery. They are our scenery. They do not belong to Colorado or the West, they belong to the people of the United States, including the miserable unfortunates who have to live east of the Allegheny hillocks." Most of Inyo and Mono counties fall into a similar category—BLM lands and Forest Service lands, i.e., public lands. Even land belonging to the city of Los Angeles presumably belongs to a public, not a private, corporation. To allow the life-sustaining element of an environment as biologically, ecologically, geologically, and aesthetically rich as this to flow into the Pacific Ocean through a sewer pipe is an act of criminal negligence on a national scale. If National is the magic word in preservation (as in Park and Monument) then maybe Mary DeDecker is right and we should create a new classification. Laboratory. As in National Laboratory. As in Study. Observe. Learn. Adapt. Don't tinker.

The primary questions raised by the history of the Los Angeles DWP in the Owens Valley—the legitimacy of sacrificing a small rural community for a large urban one (putting the "needs" of the many above the needs of the few), and the legitimacy of destroying a natural environment to help create an artificial one— are linked, and opponents will answer them in opposite ways. Obviously many more forces, with incomparably greater power, are on the side of the DWP than on the side of the ranchers of the Owens Valley. But the future may not be. The American Way of seizure and exploitation has a long history but a dubious future. It has produced ghost towns before this, when the resource ran out and the frenzy cooled and the fortune-hunters drifted away. Without suggesting that Los Angeles will become a ghost town, one knows that in the arid West there are many communities whose growth is strictly limited by the available water. To promote the growth of any community beyond its legitimate and predictable water resources is to risk one of two things: eventual slowdown or collapse and retrenchment to more realistic levels, or a continuing and often piratical engrossment of the water of other communities, at the expense of their prosperity and perhaps life.

Man, the great creator and destroyer of environments, is also part of what he creates or destroy, and rises and falls with it. In the West, water is life. From the very beginning, when - people killed each other with shovels over the flow of a primitive ditch, down to the present, when cities kill each other for precisely the same reasons and with the same self-justifications, water is the basis for western growth, western industry, western communities. Eventually some larger authority, state or federal, will have to play Solomon in these disputes. That, in fact, is precisely what Gifford Pinchot and Theodore Roosevelt did. Their trouble was that they made a decision which was politically sound, and environmentally and ethically wrong.

LIFE ALONG
THE FAULT LINE

The land [Monterey] is thickly populated with numberless Indians, of whom a great many came several times to our camp. They appeared to be a gentle and peaceable people. They said by signs that inland there are many settlements. The food which these Indians most commonly eat, besides fish and crustaceans, consists of acorns and another nut larger than a chestnut. . . .

It was decided that the admiral's ship should return as a messenger to the viceroy of New Spain with a copy of the records of the discoveries as far as this place [Monterey], carry back those who were the most ill, ask for further supplies of men and provisions in order to complete at this time the exploration of the remainder of the coast and of the entrance to the Californias. . . .

We ourselves remained, making the preparations necessary for our voyage to Cape Mendocino. The men worked under great difficulties in taking on wood and water because of the extreme cold, which was so intense that Wednesday, New Year's Day of 1603, dawned with all the mountains covered with snow and resembling the volcano of Mexico, and that the hole from which we were taking water was frozen over more than a palm in thickness, and the bottles, which had been left full over night, were all frozen so that even when turned upside down not a drop ran out. So urgent was our situation that necessity compelled us all to act with energy, especially the general, who aided in carrying the bottles and in the other tasks, with the good support of Ensign Alarcon and Captain Peguero, who, although ill, aided, while the pilots spared no efforts to forward our preparation, so that by Friday night, the 3d of the said month, we were all ready.

> *This day the general, with the commissary and ten arque-*
> *busiers, went inland, toward the southwest, having heard of a*
> *copious stream that ran into the sea and of another good head-*
> *land, and in order better to see the lay of the land and its people*
> *and animals. He proceeded some three leagues when he discov-*
> *ered another good port, into which entered a copious river*
> *[Carmel] descending from some high, snow-covered mountains*
> *with large pines, white and black poplars, and willows. It had an*
> *extended river bottom, and in it were many cattle as large as*
> *cows although apparently they were harts, and yet their pelts*
> *were different, for their wool dragged on the ground, and each*
> *horn was more than three yards long. An effort was made to kill*
> *some of them but they did not wait long enough. No people*
> *were found because, on account of the great cold, they were liv-*
> *ing in the interior.*
>
> Diary of Vizcaíno (1602)

Back home in Santa Cruz. Through the big window in the front of my studio I look down across a mile of gently sloping pasture land to the sea, across the wide mouth of Monterey Bay to Point Pinos and Pacific Grove, and into the low peaks of the Santa Lucia Range that rise above the Carmel fog. A dozen or so boats from the Santa Cruz Yacht Club beat north along the coast - toward Año Nuevo Island, slogging against the heavy swell to an orange buoy marker that will spell relief, the final leg of a day-long race, a beam reach southeast into the "well protected harbor" Sebastian Vizcaíno discovered 378 years ago and named in honor of the viceroy of New Spain, the Conde de Monterrey. Vizcaíno's discovery was the luck of the draw. He hit Point Pinos at sunset on December 15, 1602, a time of day at a time of year when fog is rare, and the air sparkled with a clarity that enabled him to distinguish the northern shoulder of this indentation in the coastline, ten miles across, and not so "well protected" as he thought. Cabrillo had sailed right past in 1566. Portolá's first land party, using Vizcaíno's charts, walked clear around it twice, from point to point, without ever knowing where they were. When they returned a year later, in May

1770, Portolá is reported by Father Crespí to have been some-what abusive in his comments about Vizcaíno's powers of ob-servation. The truth is that except from an elevated perspective it hardly looks like a bay at all. Ask any fisherman how much protection it affords.

The fields are bright with mustard and lupine, and the wild oatgrass stands two feet high. The swallows have returned, overshooting Capistrano by four hundred miles to build their mud-daubed houses in the eaves of my cabin and to decorate my windows while they raise their young. I have tried every way to discourage them short of staking out the cat, but deter-mination defeats ingenuity. Though I prefer less abstract forms of expressionism, I will have to learn to love action painting. The red-winged blackbirds are back too, thick for the first time since the county instituted a "weed abatement" program ten years ago and annually plowed up their nests along with the foxtails and cockleburs. God forbid we should get stickers in our socks as we walk beside the road. Since passage of Propo-sition 13 cut our property taxes in half and the county budget took a nosedive, I have seen no plows. Johnny won't learn to read, but the redwings may survive. Howard Jarvis, environ-mentalist.

Last night when I was working late the coyotes drove me to distraction with their strangulated cries out in the pasture by the studio. I turned off my lamp and watched them tumbling in the high grass, playful as puppies in the cold moonlight, fleet-ing shadows in and out of the dark lane of cypress along the road. In better days—that is to say, before the dedication on May 10, 1794, of Mision la Exaltacion de la Santa Cruz made settlement in this region a fact—there were condors, eagles, ot-ter, grizzly bear, tule elk: a profusion of wild life that vanished under Spanish, Mexican, and finally American custody. But my neighbor tells me she saw a mountain lion and her cubs down in Moore Creek early one morning last week, and I know that I have seen more skunks, more possums, more red-tailed hawks, more owls this past year than at any time since I moved here thirteen years ago. There is a coon the size of a New-foundland that knocks over the garbage can of dog biscuits on the porch every night, and stands there watching me watch it, stuffing itself on those tasteless little meat rocks, just as cool as you please. I don't understand this resurgence of critters—critters undiscouraged by a city of 30,000 people less than half a mile away—but I'm delighted to see it happen. Maybe they understand that we are less inclined to shoot at them now than we once were.

I settled here in the first place because it was still possible, in the 1960s, to entertain the illusion of living with, and off, the land. After an hour's argument with a creative writing class at the university about the "relevance of language in post-modernist society" I could go home and feed the chicken and pigs. After an endless committee meeting to discuss student demands that the doors be removed from the toilet stalls in the dormitory because they smacked of cultural elitism and social regression, and were an inhibitant to personal growth, I could go down to La Selva beach south of town, dig pismo clams on the sandbars, and watch the setting sun over the curl of the breakers. There were abalone off the ledges at Pigeon Point, mussels on the rocks below the mouth of Scott Creek, the bay profuse with cod, salmon, squid, crab. Steelhead spawned in the San Lorenzo River. Thirty miles south in the Salinas Valley, every vegetable and fruit worth eating grew in such abundance that it hardly paid to put in a garden of one's own.

There was a real sense, when I first came here, that the immediate environment provided just about everything anybody - could want—physical beauty, great plenty, entertainment of one's own making, a big dose of privacy—and few of those things that one didn't want, like industry, traffic, night life, pollution, the Oakland Raiders, the Los Angeles Dodgers, live sex acts on stage, and a lot of other people on the path. If one felt in need of some diversion not provided by an ocean, a redwood tree, or an open headland planted to artichokes and brussels sprouts, there was San Franciso an hour to the north. I went there once in five years—which says, I guess, something about me and why I live where I do. Tourists flocked to the beaches in quantity during the summer months, but the configuration of the bay spread them out and they were not yet a problem. The

university, only three years old in 1968, and consisting of about
fifteen hundred students, had not yet managed to thoroughly
alienate the town. There were a few novelists, poets, potters,
painters, metalsmiths, and leatherworkers quietly pursuing their
respective trades, but the literary scene had not yet become a
movable snack and the craftspeople had not yet multiplied like
fishes and loaves. The thumb-trippers passing through on their
way to points south had not yet discovered that Santa Cruz
would accommodate almost anything in the way of oddball behavior and was, therefore, a potential Mecca for transients.
And if one still felt hemmed in by this variation on the pastures
of heaven, there was all of the Big Sur coasts an hour to the
south—different, perhaps, but not that much different from the
description of it Jaime de Angulo repeated in a fragment, "La
Costa del Sur," back in the early forties: . . . *like a dreamland,
somewhere, not real . . . Imagine: only a trail, for a hundred
miles, bordering the ocean, but suspended above it a thousand
feet, clinging halfway up the side of the sea wall, and that wall
at an incredible angle of forty-five degrees, a green wall of
grass . . . and canyons with oaks, redwoods, pines, madroñas,
bluejays, quail, deer, and to one side the blue ocean stretching
away to China, and over all that an intense blue sky with eagles
and vultures floating about . . . and nobody, no humans there,
solitude, solitude, for miles and miles—*

Much of what made this country so attractive in the fifties and
sixties still exists, and for the most part attempts to stimulate
big growth have been consistently resisted by a majority of its
residents—particularly in Santa Cruz. A Highway Department
plan to develop an eight-lane freeway into the county to facilitate tourism and beach traffic from the San Francisco Bay Area
is defeated. So are plans for a huge convention center at Light-
house Point, and a Wilder Ranch development (the old Spanish
land grant, Rancho Refugio) proposed by Corporate Properties, Ltd., of Canada that would add 33,000 people to the population in eight "scenic villages." A limited-growth initiative is
passed that restricts the number of available building permits.
An atomic power plant a few miles up the coast is so vigorously

opposed that all further talk of it vanishes. None of these expressions of new-age ecological thinking and preservationist planning is accomplished without a fight. Development and real estate interests are strong in the county and they do their best to subvert local ordinances and legislation to their own ends. But it has been some time now since they have won on any big issues. Too many Santa Cruzians, newcomers and old-timers alike, simply want local control over their community, and want to keep it the way it was when they first arrived.

In some ways they have been reasonably successful. In others contemporary Santa Cruz no more looks like the whittle-and-spit, boats-for-hire backwater of beach cottages, funky stores, old hotels, and family restaurants owned by the Italians and Portuguese and Greeks and Chinese who settled it in the first place, than a bull looks like a banjo. I am sitting, for example, under a Cinzano umbrella at the Cooperhouse outdoor café on Pacific Avenue, Santa Cruz's main drag, now called the Mall. A local band led by a talented piano and vibes player named Don McCaslin is playing jazz at a volume that just permits conversation if one is good at filling in gaps, and the perennial street crowd pressed against the low iron railing along the sidewalk is seven or eight deep. It is hot here in the lee of the old courthouse building, three stories of sandstone brick absorbing the sun and radiating it down into the patio. A little breeze wafts among the tables, stirring the napkins and coasters, cooling the sweat around the neck of my T-shirt. I order a beer and wait for a couple of friends who may or may not show up for lunch.

Beside a magnolia tree on the corner of Cooper Street two ragamuffins looking like fugitives from a Bogotá barrio are selling puppies of indeterminate flavor out of a cardboard box—two dollars for a male, five for a bitch. A clean-shaven, short-haired man in his mid-forties, wearing a leather Dutch-boy cap and lace-up shoes that cover his ankles, is doing an "interpretive" dance, though his movements seem to have less to do with the music than with some interior vision of himself as a barnyard fowl. He holds his arms straight out from his body and flaps his hands as he twirls, pursing his lips, periodically levitating a few inches off the sidewalk in a convulsive skip-rope movement. The crowd ignores him except to give him space. There are several other dancers—women, by the look of things—in the shadow of the camera-store wall, stomping to equally private and non-musical beats and equally ignored by the gawkers and proles at the fence. A pair of bikers roar by in first gear, the baffleless pipes of their Harley choppers drowning out the band, their tattoos and sleeveless leathers and boot chains as out of place in this benign, mellow, laid-back, tripped-out joss house of cognitive centering as a horde of Mongols in the cathedral of Köln.

There is a considerable amount of flesh displayed on the street, some of it regrettable. The death of the miniskirt some years ago was a blessing to us all; the current rage for shorts that do not quite cover the buttocks seem like reincarnation with a vengeance. I am beginning to feel a slight throb in the temples from the constant swiveling of my head, and therefore respond gratefully to the young man with bright, mad eyes and a rope wig chopped off at the shoulders when he points to the chair across from me and asks if he can sit down. I nod. Of course. I see that the wig is his own hair braided to look like strands of hemp, and that his front teeth have been filed. He carries a ladies' purse out of which he takes a stack of leaflets. "I'd like to talk to you about rebirthing," he says.

"I beg your pardon?"

"Rebirthing. Rebirthing dissolves negative energy patterns that are held in your mind and body. . . ."

At which point the band drowns him out. I smile, manipulate my face in what I hope are appropriately timed expressions of surprise, agreement, amiable incredulity, concern, accept some pamphlets on "cosmic attunement" and his card (which is a little grubby around the edges, as if frequently rejected). It announces him as a "Postural Integrationist" and a practitioner of "connective tissue massage." This strikes me, on the face of it, as unrelated to rebirthing, but I am reluctant to inquire.

Later I walk down toward the bookstore through the usual panoply of drunks, junkies, lawyers, and overaged teeny-boppers outdoing each other in a spandex display of mammae and mammillae. There are a number of seedy-looking gentlemen reclining in an apparent state of sea-level narcosis in the planter boxes in front of Leask's department store, and down at United Cigar a pair of young lovers stand entwined like poor old Kawliga and his Indian maid. The pamphlets tacked to the bulletin board outside the bookstore offer a variety of information—Synergy Clearing Techniques, Fundamentals of Prosperity Training, Iridology, The Art of Sweating, Polarity Massage, Reflexology, Pyradomes, Vitamids, Portamids, Metabelief Operant Training, Postural Integration, Assertion Training, Aggression Training, and a free "cosmic tuneup" at the Getting In Touch Community in Boulder Creek. A skate-boarder in a jellaba and fez asks me for spare change. As much as I want to be right in there with the Aquarian Conspirators, I think I'll go home.

The fog creeps back from my cabin, and a drunken line of fenceposts and tattered sheep wire emerges, damp and steaming in the morning sun, circumscribing the horse pasture below. The fields across the narrow road that ends in my drive take shape; then Crazy Frank's ramshackle ranch at the edge of a deep canyon that empties into the ocean at the northernmost point of the bay. Within minutes the fog is gone, pulled far out to sea where it skulks on the horizon, biding its time. With an old pair of hunting glasses I keep on my desk I can watch the bottom fishermen's boats out on Seven Mile Reef, their windshields glinting against the sun, and a steady course of freighters moving north and south along the licking edge of the fog. Variations on an ancient theme.

In the beginning the principal business of this country was in hides and lumber, and the sailing ships, Richard Henry Dana's among them, would put into landings at China Point, Capitola, Santa Cruz, Davenport. Toward the end of the nineteenth century, Italians from the Ligurian coast began arriving, and the word went back to the old country that there were waters here so teeming with fish that anyone could prosper. The sails of the single-masted, low-sterned fishing fleet replaced the square-riggers converted to steam power. Later, when Sicilians began to dominate the fishing industry on San Francisco Bay, still more Genovesi migrated south, and it was these families, the Stagnaros, Ghios, Canepas, Bregantes, Castagnolas, Carniglias, Olivieris, Gibellis, Zelezzis, that gave this part of the coast its particular spice and flavor. I wonder what Cottardo Stagnaro, the grandaddy of them all, would think of the place where he jumped ship in the 1880s and returned to settle in 1898? I don't think we'd find him down on Pacific Avenue pretending to be a chicken.

With my glasses I can also watch the girls who now live in the old west-side dairy, sunbathing behind the farmhouse in the dappled light of bay trees and grape arbor. Students, probably, or part of a more general youth invasion that took place soon after the university opened its doors. Their number and faces seem to change with the seasons of the academic year. Only five acres and a few outbuildings remain of the dairy, and it is once again for sale, though no longer subdividable. A few years ago a horse trainer named Henry Pinkham lived there and used to train a palomino stallion where the girls now snooze, but the place was put on the market for a sum he could not begin to afford and he had to move. The asking price sent me into peals of laughter when I first heard it—$120,000, snort, guffaw. Now it's back on the block for $580,000. The figure more accurately represents its termite population than its real value.

Real value, in these parts, no longer bears any relation to market value. Market value seems to be based on how much an acre of ground would be worth if it could be cut into fifty-by-a-hundred-foot lots and two-story condominiums selling for $90,000 to $100,000 apiece could be built on them. Which, in these parts, is becoming increasingly hard to do. The speculator who ten years ago bought acreage, held it until the price went up a thousand percent, applied for a permit to develop, and got turned down at the City Council hearing is a rather common spectacle. At a meeting I attended recently (to speak in opposition to the proposed development), one such hapless soul, so hot with rage I could almost smell the acrylic melting in his plastic pants, stood up and asked the council members just what they now proposed he *do* with these apparently worthless seven acres on which he had been paying taxes for a decade? Nobody had any good ideas. Sell it to the next sucker. Donate it for a park.

The prospect of taking less than anticipated, no matter how inflated the anticipation, seemed unthinkable. To put up seven houses on those seven acres was rejected as "economically unfeasible." And what about the poor people? our man wailed. The poor people (always trotted out in defense of the high-density, cheesy construction euphemistically referred to as "low-income housing") must be given a shot at the American Dream. They couldn't afford houses on one acre. He was proposing a number of units in the $55,000 to $66,000 range for the low-income people, and that was why he was requesting a few more units than the zoning permitted in the $100,000 to $120,000 category—say ten or twenty more—to offset his losses. It did not seem to occur to this benefactor of the people that a $65,000 mortgage is about as far out of reach of the poor as one for $500,000. Or that in his fiscal ballpark the poor begin to include just about everybody who doesn't make over $30,000 a year. He left, vowing to return when the political climate had changed and "those communists from the university" (his proposed development was in an area heavily inhabited by academics) no longer controlled the council.

The University of California has indeed been an agent of social and economic change in the community, and is in some part responsible for a demographic shift that does not altogether please a lot of older residents. Town and gown very quickly clashed. When the nattering nabob of negativity parked his bicycle on the putting-green lawn of the retired Seventh Infantry Colonel from Fort Ord; when the Pepsi generation oiled its nude body on the beaches below Octogenarian Cliffs; when the dulcet tones of Guy Lombardo at the Coconut Grove were eclipsed by the Who, the Dead, and the Doors over at the Catalyst, the head-on collision of cultural values was heard for miles. The young and the scrofulous were taking over. It was obviously the university's fault.

Whether the considerable number of deadbeats and drifters who began filtering in shortly after the opening of the campus were really attracted by something like sex and drugs seems doubtful. More likely the word was just finally out that Santa Cruz County was a mellow, no-hassle place where the sun always shines and the nightsticks are made of candy. But most residents couldn't have told the players with or without a program, and, in truth, the difference between a long-haired, scraggle-faced English major ambling down to the bookstore in his surplus fatigues and flipflops, and a blown-out meth freak shuffling along in drawstring pants and a red, runny nose was not immediately apparent. Something ominous was slithering into the garden. It looked young, unhygienic, and only tenuously under control.

Sometimes it was not even that, as in the case of John Linley Frazier, a home-grown Santa Cruz product who announced the beginning of the "revolution against materialists who pollute the environment" by executing an extremely successful eye surgeon, Victor Ohta, his wife, two young sons, and secretary in the family's swimming pool and leaving a Tarot card as his signature on the windshield of Ohta's Rolls-Royce. Or the case of Edward Kemper, who over the period of a year dismembered eleven or twelve women (including his mother), and buried their parts all over the county. Or the case of a local freak named Mullins who murdered nine or ten more at approximately the same time—1971–1972. Or the case of Blue Summerhalter, who picked up two young women in nearby Rio Del Mar and left their corpses under some brush in a ravine in Felton. Or the case of . . . There are unfortunately many more. Lunatics all, one presumes. Sons of Sam. Charles Mansons. Aberrations so extreme that they become, almost, like fictional characters. Almost.

In Santa Cruz, in this oasis of tranquillity by the sea, suspension of disbelief has become uncomfortably simple. "Murder Capital of the World," *Time* magazine called it back in the early seventies. And while the remark was received indignantly by its citizens (many of whom were sleeping with loaded weapons by their beds), the ensuing years have not exactly discredited that analysis. In the past eighteen months I can recall a number of "drug-related" killings, including a marijuana farmer whose crop was being ripped off by eight high school students, and whose discovery of this event in progress left him with seven bullet holes in his chest and head; two or three small-time dealers found on the floors of their mountain cabins; a woman whose possession by the devil inspired her chemically altered "husband" to cleave her head with an ax. And, of course, we also have conventional crimes of passion, and the occasional psychopath, such as the one who not long ago killed a former student of mine as she drove from the campus to the house of some friends in Boulder Creek for Thanksgiving dinner.

It is regrettable, but I think true, that when one is unacquainted with the victim of senseless crime attention is less closely paid. When I lived in New York I took the lunatic fringe for granted. In a small community it is much harder to accept. I knew my former student, and I knew one of the women strangled by Summerhalter, and I knew Edward Kemper's mother. She was the executive secretary at the university where I teach. I had dinner with Vic and Toby Ohta a month before they were found face down at bottom of their pool. The proximity to homicidal violence over the past ten years, and the attention that must be paid, have obviously forced me to wonder, among other things, what I am doing in this place. What are my children doing here? What happened to this little outpost of Eden I regarded as home? And I wonder, sometimes, whether I am simply paranoid, or whether this is to be the shape not simply of one decade, but also of the rest of the century?

I hope neither. What I really think is that Santa Cruz has somehow become the distilled extreme of behavioral impulses, social movements, and cultural redefinitions that had their most accelerated development during the sixties, and that now, in the midst of an otherwise conventional enough community of ecologically conscious folks committed to a quality of life that places humanistic and environmental values above economic concerns, some of the chickens of the "permissive society" have come home to roost. And to dance in the streets.

I don't think Cottardo Stagnaro would be out there in a funny hat strolling down to the Mall from the old west-side colony on the hill, La Baranca, where the Rivani used to live. I don't think we'd find him here in the post office chatting about the affairs of the day with the brothers and sisters in the food-stamp line. I think the language barrier and certain cultural differences would exclude him from the conversation taking place behind me as I wait (in the wrong queue) to mail a package.

"Hey, man, what's happening?"

"No happenings, man, just hanging out. What's coming down with you?"

"Picking up my script, man, plus I also had to come in to rap with my lawyer about my bust. Some fine lady signed a complaint on me for weeny-wagging in front of the Catalyst. Like she's full of shit, man. I was coked out of my head, but I definitely never did that."

"I heard about it, man. I heard you mooned."

"Oh, man. Like this lady is on a very high voltage emotional response trip, dig? Like her security center is threatened. I went to her house to see if she'd drop the complaint, but she's *old*, you know, and her buttons are jammed, and like there's no way I could interface with her. No way."

"I hear you, man."

"I'm thinking like if I rap with her about the incident maybe she can relate to where I'm coming from, but she's not into it. It's just uptight city, right? She gets all spacey and starts yelling she's going to call a cop, get off her property, I'm a dope fiend, and anyway, I figure fuck it, I gotta get a lawyer."

"It's an ego trip, man. She's on an ego trip."

"Like I thought that too, man, but the way I see it now is more like a power trip. If you follow me."

"I can dig it. A power ego trip."

"Right on. Listen, I'm gonna be late to my lawyer's, man, I can't wait on this line any longer. I'm gonna have to split."

"Okay, that's far out, man. I'll catch you later."

"Hang in, man. Don't let the bastards get you down."

Don't let the bastards get you down. Mr. Stagnaro might well understand that. Driving back home along Mission Street I'm tempted to lean out the window and holler the same advice to the bowing Buddhist monks who are slowly making their way north from Los Angeles to Ukiah, three steps at a time and kiss the pavement, two and a half years on the road, vows of silence, the exorcism of "greed, anger, and stupidity" from their being, a pilgrimage to prevent "disasters, wars, and suffering of all kinds." Their prayers are dedicated, they say, to everyone. From what I have observed of their slow shuffle along this stretch of Highway 1, everyone is paying very little attention.

Don't let the bastards get you down. The question that occurs to me is which bastards are getting whom down? There are differing points of view around here between the haves and the have-nots—or I should say between the folks who got in the first sitting and the folks who came late. That Santa Cruz is rapidly getting out of range for most single-income, middle-class families does not make it unique in this country today. What does make it unique is that if you don't need a house (or much of one), and if you don't want a job, and if the apex of your ambition is to hang out in a mild undemanding climate and get as stoned as possible for as long as possible, and if the only responsibility you care to assume is to get yourself to the methadone center every day for your fix, and to the post office once a month for your food stamps, and to the secret little patch of ground you found back in the mountains behind town to water your weed—well, then, this is the place.

Indeed, Santa Cruz seems to many of its older residents (as well as to a number of its more recent in-migrants) to contain everything that went sour with American cultural values since the days of flower children, free-speech demonstrations, Haight-Ashbury, and the Beatles. One of the effects of the sixties, starting with the civil rights movement and culminating with Kent State, was an announcement to the burghers of the American class/caste system that a lot of people were no longer going to accept the traditional roles assigned to them. And they were not going to behave in a manner prescribed by the "oppressive" majority either. As rhetoric gave way to burning ghettos, besieged universities, bank bombings, political conventions turned to riot, and, finally, the spectacle of Ohio National Guardsmen firing on fellow citizens, the country was forced to take a long look at some of its uninspected assumptions, not only about minorities but about its sons and daughters as well. The nature of the "under-thirty" rebellion was unprecedented in manner and volume, and it demanded (generally non-negotiably) a reassessment of Establishment attitudes.

For a good many people over thirty the reviews were pretty mixed. After all, who could understand all those kids with their contempt for political institutions, law and order, materialism, industrial society, mom and pop, apple pie, the flag? Who could countenance an enthusiasm for civil disobedience that often seemed inspired more by boredom or a desire to showboat than by philosophical or ideological conviction—and that was a clear and constant threat to private property? Who could really embrace long hair, beards, beads, the unkempt appearance? In the absence of a national program of euthanasia and eugenics there seemed to be two choices to those who didn't wish to be accused of "fascism"—hope they'd grow up and go away, or join up. So vociferous a rejection of authority could only be met, it seemed, by severe repression or a gradual capitulation, and by the early 1970s it was clear to most Americans that the Gestapo tactics championed by the Nixon administration were not only morally unacceptable but weren't going to work either.

Certainly this seems to me to have been true in Santa Cruz. In a town where at one time anybody driving around in a Volkswagen bus was likely to be pulled over and have his credentials checked, constraints began to be withdrawn. Enforcement of laws for victimless crimes was relaxed. Vagrancy was ignored. So, after a time, was panhandling. Indeed, by calling a handout "spare change" the new-age bum seemed to cast begging in a different light. The state of California reduced possession of marijuana (in certain quantities) to a misdemeanor, and some people began to do in public what they had previously held to the privacy of their homes. The concept of an individual's civil rights began to eclipse the assumption of community standards of behavior.

Much of the new permissiveness was long overdue, and if it inspired people to go out and stump for everything from prison reform to nude sunbathing, the world was probably a better place for it. But for a few people it seems that public restraints were the only measure of personal restraint, and as the lid came off, some subtle, and finally not so subtle, changes began to occur. Down on the Mall a small congregation of people began to gather who were not so transient any more; in fact, who lived down in the willows along the San Lorenzo River, a few blocks from the center of town, and whose main dietary staple was opiate and hallucinogenic. They dealt a little, stole a little, and spent their days sitting on the sidewalk and in the planters along Pacific Avenue, staring with blasted, vacant eyes at the passersby. Very gradually their attitude toward the world that moved around them changed from passive indifference to lurching belligerence, and what was once, depending on your point of view, merely colorful, or distasteful, or weird, or mildly disconcerting, or vibrating with creative energy, became ominous, a danger. Women passing along the street were increasingly subjected to obscene remarks. A student who ignored a request for spare change was beaten senseless. Muggings became frequent. Merchants began to complain that business was down, thefts were up. All of a sudden (or so it seemed) things were not so savory down there on the Mall. The vector of tyranny had reversed itself. The "oppressed" had become the oppressors. All twenty-five or thirty of them. And that, at least until the present moment, is where things stand.

Few of the street people (or that element that has taken over the center of town) bear any relationship to the youth movements of the sixties—or at least not much. They are, on the contrary, the ring around the tub, a residue of human marginalia, a drug culture spinoff that exists not only on what it can bilk out of a liberal democratic society but on the tolerance that society has developed for aberrant behavior, even when it is clearly deranged. It has become increasingly uncool over the past decade to be caught in the act of passing judgments on fellow creatures, or to expect anything of them in the way of public conduct. At least in Santa Cruz, we have lost the capacity to be outraged by almost anything short of a Charles Manson, and somehow in the process our sense of helplessness to regulate social conduct has reduced us to passive observers more likely to sit around questioning the validity of our personal reaction to deviant behavior rather than the communal implications of its often savage vulgarity. We founder in the myth of mutual tolerance rather than try to determine the limits of tolerance, and we try to portray ourselves as living in an environment of vibrant, creative expression rather than a mad house. I am reminded, in this context, of my friend Tom Rickman's observation: "There are some liberal brains impervious to experience." And again, the Santa Cruz experience is not unique. Whether it is a paradigm or a peculiarity, portentous or transcendant, is anybody's guess. Maybe Ronald Reagan and Jerry Falwell know, but I don't. All I know is that as an environment it strikes me as endangered.

Because an environment is more than those fields bright with lupine and wild mustard. It is more than a view of Point Pinos and a surge of wildlife around Moore Creek and a cloud of shearwaters feeding on a dark stain of anchovies in the bay. It is more than redwoods and madroñas and coveys of quail under the glossy tangle of poison oak, more than hawks and migrating whales and sea lions breeding on the shelf of Año Nuevo Island. It is, as Steinbeck said of Cannery Row in Monterey, "a poem, a stink, a grating noise, a quality of light, a tone, a habit, a nostalgia, a dream." It is, in short, as much the ambience created by a community of human beings as it is the flora and fauna, the topography and climate. And it is as possible to destroy it with a resurgent barbarism as it is with a bulldozer's blade.

Is this the end product of our progress through the continent? Not quite. There are regions too un-hip, or with too drastic a climate, to appeal to spoilers either of the real estate or the drifter variety. The farming regions of New England, the Midwest, the South, have been largely saved because any farmer, even a one-crop tobacco or cotton or wheat farmer, is to some extent a husbander of soil, to some extent in touch with and responsive to nature, to some extent willing to share his earth with animals. There are federal and state reservations, mostly

in the public domain states of the West but with notable eastern and midwestern and southern outposts at Acadia National
Park, Voyageurs National Park, the Everglades. There are great
estates that up to now have been saved simply by private
money. There are ranching valleys in the northern Rockies
where neither the developer nor the strip miner nor the oil exploration rig has yet reached.

And there are signs of a change in American expectations, an
alteration of the free land and unregulated individualism myths
still clung to so desperately by the sagebrush rebels and "new
Federalists" of the Reagan administration. If the Reagan revolution can be interpreted in part as a reaction against the social
welfare crowd that infests places like the Santa Cruz Mall, it
should not be interpreted as a mandate for return to environmental anarchism. The environmental movement in this country
is at least as old as its first spokesman, William Bartram, but only
in the last fifteen to twenty years has it been joined by millions of
Americans who have learned a new respect for the land and acquired a new consciousness of their relationship to it. At long last
it seems that ordinary citizens have become less commonly
raiders and more commonly conservers and stewards of the only
continent they are ever going to possess.

REMNANTS

We are a remnant people in a remnant country. We have used up the possibilities inherent in the youth of our nation: the new start in a new place with new vision and new hope. . . . We have come, or are coming fast, to the end of what we were given.
　Wendell Berry

Nearly every morning a coyote works the pasture beyond our yard fence. He comes up out of the woods that fill the little canyon to the south—woods out of sight from our windows, under the roll of the hill—and quarters the field, hunting under the unpastured grass now matted by the rains. He is as pointed as an arrow; his plume, carried straight out behind his lean shape, feathers him for swift accuracy. His nose is long and sharp, his ears alert, his head is always turning while nose, ears, and eyes appraise some tenuous signal. His sonar is tuned to the slightest stir of a mouse among the grass roots, a gopher turning in its sleep underground, a cricket uncrossing its legs.

Every so often he points, stiffens, lifts one trembling front paw, quivers, flattens, and pounces. His paws hold down whatever he has caught, his nose probes under them. Generally there is nothing there, and he goes back to his restless search. Occasionally he digs, never very hopefully or very long. And even while digging, even while preparing to pounce, he is never for more than a second or two unaware of our house a hundred feet away. He gives us long stares, with his head turned from whatever a moment ago preoccupied him. He watches us to see if we have moved.

Perhaps he sees our shapes beyond the glass; perhaps he sees no more than the morning reflected there. Perhaps he hears faint murmurs of the "Today Show" or "Good Morning America" or the "CBS Morning News" that we take with our breakfast coffee. Over the years we have watched many things out these bedroom windows—pygmy nuthatches at the bird feeder, quail pecking in coveys among the grass, deer standing on their hind legs to browse the pyracantha berries, a red-tailed hawk sitting in a pasture oak getting warm enough to fly. But the coyotes are new. We have seen them only in the last year or two. Perhaps they have been driven in from the Pacific side of the Coast Range by drouth or some drastic shutting off of a food supply.

Whatever brought them, whether they came as refugees or, like most of us, in search of better economic opportunities, they are now here in numbers. On nights of big moons they hunt through the woods and pastures and close up to the houses scattered through the hills. When one catches something, or wishes he could catch something, or grows furious that he has not caught something, his yell goes up and is answered from a half dozen different directions. That chilling blood-cry makes my wife shiver and recall stories about Siberian wolves. It also starts every dog within two miles to asserting his territory. Dobermans, police dogs, Airedales, bull terriers, Basset hounds, beagles, short-haired pointers, Labradors, St. Bernards, Kerry blues, mutts big and small all declare their solidarity of domestic protectiveness and unease when they hear the wild summons from out under the moon.

Watching this morning coyote scrounge for mice and crickets in the pasture, bold at the very doors of the suburbs, I am reminded of a story Robert Frost used to tell about meeting on a train a young man who, questioned about what he did for a living, admitted that he was an exterminator. "Ha!" said the poet, interested. "Tell me. What can you exterminate?" The exterminator grew embarrassed. "Confidentially," he said, "nothing."

Wouldn't it be nice to think so! This coyote, a member of a species that has been shot, trapped, poisoned, and chased with dogs for as long as his kind and the human kind have known one another, would seem to corroborate the exterminator's pessimism. He survives; there is *modus vivendi*. Nobody is setting out poison, I hear no shooting among the hills. The professors, electronics executives, and engineers from Silicon Valley who live around here don't keep sheep or chickens. An old enemy has come to seem harmless, even attractive. We point him out to visitors, who are charmed. We crowd to the windows to watch him pounce on the matted grass. We cock our ears to his yelling in the moonlight, and smile, glad he is out there, and making it.

The coyote is to native American folklore what the fox was to the fabulists of the Old World. Trickster, demigod, he is very smart and never careless, bold but not brash. If he had an escutcheon, his motto would be *Non timeo sed caveo*. Like the wolf, he has a family and pack life that comforts and assists him in a hard world, but he can get along without it when he needs to. He is fast, shifty, good at running, good at hiding out, nocturnal when he has to be, diurnal when he chooses. Like the buzzard, he can eat anything. Content with small blessings—a lamb here, a chicken there—he will make do on mice and crickets when better is not available. And he seems to know that he is safer here among the engineers and executives in their thickening subdivisions than he used to be over on the other side of the range, where ranchers carry rifles in the racks of their pickups and the Fish and Game people, when not prevented by environmentalist outrage, drop from airplanes pieces of meat laced with 1080. The coyote finds our suburb a peach bowl, and has happily adapted himself.

But he is a special case, and in the end even he may prove to be not exempt from the consequences of sharing the earth with *Homo sapiens*. Many other local species, including some that the coyote was evolved to prey on, are already fading as my breath fades on our windowpane. In the thirty-two years we have lived in this house in these Coast Range foothills we have watched it happen. Helped it happen.

The marriage of people to a place may be close and considerate, and it may be hardly more than sanctioned rape. It may arise from choice, chance, or necessity, like human marriages. In practice, arranged marriages work out about as often as romantic elopements—a good thing, too, for not many of us can choose the place we live in. We can love a well-lived-in place even when it is essentially unlovable. I have seen a black girl, brought to a Vermont lake for the summer, grieve for the hot days in Harlem when a hydrant would be opened. If a place is a real place, shaped by human living, and not a thing created on a speculator's drawing board and stamped on a landscape like a USDA stamp on a side of beef, it will interact with the - people who live in it, and they with it. The trouble is that places work on people very slowly, but people work on places with the single-minded ruthlessness of a beaver at a cottonwood tree. Occasionally they make the desert blossom as the rose, as the Mormons are fond of saying. As often, they simply make deserts.

Europeans and their American descendants did not set out to live with this continent, learn its rules and its moods, love, honor, and obey it. They set out to "tame" or "conquer" or "break" the wilderness. They imposed their old habits on the new land, they "improved," as in homesteads, they "developed," as in towns. They replaced, destroyed, and polluted, they bent the earth and all its native forms of life to the satisfaction of their own needs. The process was dramatized in North and South America, and later in Australia, but it is not peculiarly American or Australian. I have read that in Sicily, that island which was a kind of dry run for the American melting pot, colonized by Greeks, Carthaginians, and Romans, invaded by Visigoths, Normans, and God knows who else, there is not now a single tree or shrub of the varieties that clothed the island in the sixth century B.C. People have come close to altering the whole biotic community, animals and plants alike. And though blood oranges and olives may be an improvement on some things that used to grow there, what once grew there is lost forever, and its importance simply cannot be determined now.

Changes will occur whether we intend them or not. We cannot leave one footprint in a new country, pass through it with horses or mules, careen our *Golden Hind* on its empty beach, without bringing in our luggage or our pockets, in our infested hair or clothes, in our garbage, in the dung of our animals and the sputum of our sick and the very dirt under our fingernails, things which were not there before, and whose compatibility with the native flora and fauna is utterly unknown. That is why the patriot who tucked an American flag into a moon capsule - could have spoiled everything for the exobiologists eager to determine whether any life existed on the moon. Here on earth, the conservationists who created our national wilderness system knew from the beginning that by this date, wilderness in America is an approximation only. There is not such thing as a true, pure, unmodified wilderness in the entire world. The Greenland glaciers are layered with particulate pollution, Antarctic penguins have DDT in their livers. A wind blowing across Seattle or Portland carries the taint of man into the Montana backwoods.

As naturally as ants herd aphids, we encourage the plants that feed or pleasure us, and extirpate those that don't. We cut forests, impound rivers, plow grasslands, seal millions of acres under sterile concrete, pump out fossil water, change climates to some degree. Planted crops go wild, wild crops are sprayed or crowded out, and changed plant communities encourage the ascendancy or the elimination of animal species. In mining our habitat, we destroy the habitat of whole biotic communities. We commit multiple genocide, we create population explosions. Ecology, a science hardly two generations old, has begun to teach us something about cause and consequence: that is the earth speaking, trying to state its case for survival. But experience might have taught us much sooner.

My family were homesteaders in southern Saskatchewan during World War I. In every acre we could plow, we planted wheat. One consequence, unforeseen and not understood, was that the gophers—"flickertails," Richardson's spermophiles—throve incontinently. They came from miles of bald prairie to feast on our wheat, and stayed to dig burrows and raise families. For their convenience we had dammed a coulee and created a waterhole. Lovely. A land of milk and honey.

I spent my summers trying to exterminate them. They multiplied faster than my traps, poisons, .22, and buckets for drowning them out could reduce them. By replacing buffalo grass with wheat we had touched off a population explosion beyond our containing. The creatures that preyed on gophers—the weasels, ferrets, badgers, hawks, coyotes, shrikes, and gopher snakes— multiplied too, though more slowly, and I killed them too, though in smaller numbers, not knowing they were my allies. Nothing availed. Everything gained on us. Then came a dry cycle, the wheat failed three summers in succession, and we were - driven out. The drouth that defeated us also defeated the legions of creatures we had baited into life by tampering with their environment. Once we were gone, the prairie should have settled back into something like its natural populations in their natural balances, except. Except that we had plowed up two hundred acres of buffalo grass, and had imported Russian thistle— tumbleweed—with our seed wheat. For a season or two, some wheat would volunteer in the fallow fields. Then the tumbleweed would take over, and begin to roll. We homesteaded a semi-arid steppe and left it nearly a desert.

Not deliberately. We simply didn't know what we were doing. People in new environments seldom do. Their only compulsion is to impose themselves and their needs, their old habits and old crops, upon the new earth. They don't look to see what the new earth is doing naturally; they don't listen to its voice.

Ours was short-grass prairie. Historically the tall-grass variety east of the 100th meridian did better. It is changed, but it is no desert; there is probably no more fertile farmland in the world. Nevertheless, much was lost. As white settlement advanced from the Mississippi to the Missouri and beyond, prairie flowers did not grow wilder hour by hour. They got plowed up and grazed off. Where once big bluestem and switchgrass and Indian grass grew as high as a horse, and flowers snagged in the stirrups of a rider, we have made cities, towns, shopping centers, parking lots, feedlots, highways, and fields of corn, sorghum, and soybeans. The old species are gone or only precariously hanging on. As Aldo Leopold discovered, almost the only places where the native plants could sustain and reproduce themselves were the fenced rights of way of railroads, protected from both plows and grazing animals. Those accidental preserves are now beyond price, precious to biologists trying to reconstruct the vanishing prairie biota, and more precious to all of us than we may realize.

Obviously not all human tinkering is thoughtless, nor is all of it destructive. People coming to a new world take back the new plants and animals that native peoples have domesticated. American potatoes, tomatoes, maize, turkeys, and tobacco literally revolutionized the eating and living habits of the world, and vastly increased its carrying capacity of *Homo sapiens*. A wave of green revolution rushed eastward from our shores from the sixteenth century on. Before too long, Englishmen were smoking, and were eating a bird they called a turkey, and the Italian cuisine was being enlarged by tomatoes and the maize that Italians still call *gran turco*, apparently under the impression that it came from the Near East. By the eighteenth century there were representations of corn leaves in Chinese art.

But there was a reverse process, too. Settlers brought in seeds and cuttings, and some of them had the messianic enthusiasm of Johnny Appleseed. Read in the letters between Thomas Jefferson and John Bartram the eagerness with which intelligent - people experimented with Old World plants in the New World. So far as I know, neither Jefferson nor Bartram introduced any killing pests into America, but their sort of experimentation conducted indiscriminately elsewhere has produced a history of ecological trauma, an elaborate industry of biological study and control, and the beginnings of a public concern that is sometimes sentimental but is indispensable.

Cause begets consequence, in nature as in logic. We understand that in its cruder manifestations—kill off the hawks and coyotes and you will be swamped periodically by rodents—but the subtler relationships, the web of small tensions and accommodations and standoffs that make for ecological health, we have hardly begun to appreciate.

How could the Spaniards have known (and what would they have cared, being hot for the riches of Cíbola?) that the horses they brought to the New World would find some parts of it horse heaven, and that the multiplying get of escaped studs and mares would transform the life of whole nations of Indians, and hence of the whites who fought them? How could they possibly have foreseen that after the conquest was over and the Indians crushed, the merest remnants of the wild horse herds would become a cause of contention among western ranchers who want to make dog food of them, animal lovers determined to save them, and federal land managers uncertain which course to follow?

Why didn't Captain James Cook stop to think, before he released goats in the Hawaiian Islands, that goats are very destructive and very adaptable, and that the islands contained no predators to hold them in check? Why couldn't he have predicted that the goats would defy efforts to control them, and two centuries after their release would still be peeking at tourists around the crags of Waimea Canyon?

Could the prospectors who turned burros loose in the Grand Canyon country have known that burros are as durable and tenacious as goats, and as destructive to their range? Would they have done anything if they had realized that one day the feral burros would threaten the existence of the desert bighorn and the desert range itself? And how should we respond to the tender-hearted and tender-minded people who block the National Park Service and the Bureau of Land Management from applying the only management tactics—shooting a lot of burros—that will now have any effect?

Cause and consequence occur in many combinations. It is one kind of mistake to shoot all the millions of passenger pigeons, or cut down all the sandalwood trees in Hawaii to provide incense for Chinese joss houses. It is another to import European chestnuts or Dutch elms, each carrying its endemic disease, into a continent whose native chestnuts and elms have no resistance to those diseases. Florida must find a way to deal with the water hyacinths it planted in an ill-advised hour. Virginia must somehow clear its woods of the engulfing Japanese honeysuckle that it first brought in to stabilize railroad embankments. Hawaii, a group of islands almost as much altered by exotics as Sicily, finds itself at war with plants such as lantana, a garden flower elsewhere, a weed in the islands; and with animals like the mongoose, imported to prey on rats, which has become as much a nuisance as the rats themselves.

Consideration such as these are the ABCs of our growing environmental consciousness. We are a weed species, and wherever we go we crowd our natives and carry with us domesticated species that may become weeds in the new environment. What we destroy we often do not intend to harm. What we import, we import with the best intentions. But I find myself wondering, as I watch this coyote who has survived all our direct attacks on him and our indirect attacks on his habitat, why we should have had to repeat so much dreary history on the San Francisco Peninsula in the years since World War II, why we seem to have learned so little since Segesta and Agrigento were metropolises twenty-five hundred years ago.

When we moved into them, the Peninsula foothills back of Stanford University seemed to us as untouched as New South Wales must have seemed to Captain Cook. Actually they were far from virginal. White men have been here for two hundred years, and as a consequence the pastures are a mixture of native plants and of runaways from hayfields and ranch yards. Some—shooting stars, poppies, lupines, blueeyed grass, tarweed—are surely natives. Others—wild oats, filaree, ryegrass, burclover—are just as surely Europeans naturalized. I don't know whether needlegrass, screwgrass, foxtail grass, and yellow star thistle are natives or not. They ought to be, else why are their seeds armored to withstand a climate that is rainless seven months of the year, and so cunningly equipped to attach themselves to any fur, sock, or trouser cuff that happens by? In cursing these plants for what they do to my dog's feet, ears, and tear ducts, I may be cursing intrusive weeds, but more likely I am objecting to species that have more rights here than I do. If I don't like what grows here, why did I move in? Why do I stay? And in trying to eradicate them I am being both human and futile, for they are at least as indestructible as the coyote.

The woods are more native than the pastures, for trees and shrubs must survive not simply a season, but cycles of seasons, and not many exotics have the genes to make without human help. These live oaks, blue oaks, white oaks, buckeyes, and bay laurels, with their understory of toyon and poison oak, gooseberry and blackberry and elderberry, maidenhair and lady fern, must have grown in pretty much these proportions, in these same creek bottoms and on these same north-facing slopes, since the Ohlone Indians used to gather acorns here; but I never see "wild plums" blooming in the ravines without suspecting that the rootstock of hill apricot orchards has gone wild and adapted itself.

As for the wildlife that we found—the foxes, raccoons, opossums, skunks, wood rats, jack rabbits, cottontails, gophers, skunks, wood rats, jack rabbits, cottontails, gophers, moles, voles, field mice, lizards and skinks and newts and toads and tree frogs, gopher snakes and rattlesnakes and king snakes and ring-necked snakes, hawks and owls and buzzards and quail and layered populations of songbirds, both winterers and summer dwellers—it must have been much the same, perhaps with a few mountain lions, bears, and eagles thrown in, and with native instead of immigrant coyotes, when this land was a Spanish grant. And bobcats. There had to be bobcats where there were so many gophers and mice and quail, and I know there are still bobcats because I have seen their pug tracks around a spring. But I have never seen a bobcat in the flesh in all the years we have lived here. That puts the bobcat in a special class, more durable than most of the nocturnals and small predators, perhaps as durable as the coyote.

In any case, changes that had taken place before our coming did not trouble us, and had not seriously damaged the hills. We accepted our surroundings as if they had just been smoothed and rounded and peopled by the hand of God, and we tried to keep them as we found them. Nevertheless, we disturbed them a great deal, occasionally for good, sometimes neutrally, often for ill.

We disturbed them simply because we were *Homo fabricans*. We built structures, we brought water to a dry hilltop, we planted exotic trees, shrubs, flowers, fruits, and vegetables, we brought in our domesticated animals and birds. And everything we established, even our garbage cans and our compost heap, sent out urgent messages to impoverished species that were barely holding their own in the pastures and ravines. Because we were one of only three or four houses in a wide area, we had the impact of pioneers.

Some of our installations were gestures of friendship: bird feeders and sugar-water sippers. But our inadvertent invitations were accepted as eagerly as our deliberate ones. A dozen species could have sued us for creating attractive nuisances. From every direction things converged on our island of artificial green. We brought on population explosions of several kinds, and then had to deal with them or submit to them.

Sometimes the consequences of our invasion pleased us. The linnets and Bewick's wrens that found nesting places in our carport were welcome, and we were troubled only when our cat desolated a nest. The golden-crowned sparrows that roosted by dozens in the *Eucalyptus globulus* with which I screened the watertank were even more welcome, for through the winter and spring they sweetened the air with their tremulous, plaintive, three-note call. Ditto for the mockingbirds that made our pyracantha hedge their own. Ditto for the deer that came to dine on pyracantha berries, crabapples, roses, and anything else they found. Having to choose between a garden and the deer, we would have chosen the deer, though we might have forgotten that if we had not grown the garden the deer would not be there. Because of the open pasture next to us, we did not drive away the meadowlarks, or haven't yet.

We did not much mind the raccoons, foxes, opossums, and skunks that were enticed by our garbage cans and our little clutch of bantam hens. I grumbled, but not excessively, when the coons tipped over the garbage cans and pried off the lids and left me with a lot of wilted lettuce, coffee grounds, and bloody butcher paper to clean up. As for the bantams, they - could look after themselves; they were not the soft touch that other hens would have been. They could fly like pheasants, they roosted high in the oaks, they laid their eggs in hidden places. Any coon or possum or fox that got a meal off them deserved it. One by one they disappeared, but meanwhile we had these bandit coons looking in our windows at night, and some-times, sitting in my study, I could watch a pair of foxes come up onto my deck and groom themselves, apparently unable to see or smell me where I sat, six feet away, behind the glass. Once or twice a skunk gave it to the dog cold turkey, but that was a permanent harm neither to the dog nor to us. In fact, it taught each of our dogs in turn how to behave himself, and not to rush out all bravado and teeth when something stirred in the yard.

And the frogs. Where do frogs come from on a dry hill a mile from any spring or creek, in a climate where for half the year it simply cannot rain? Nevertheless, the week we built a fish-pond, they were there, and homesteaded it happily, and filled it with their slimy eggs that turned in spring to pollywogs. Every night, in season, they conducted love concerts that could drown out conversation even inside the house. Stamp on the patio bricks and they fell silent so suddenly, from such a crescendo of noise, that the stillness rang like quinine in the ears, the sort of silence I have heard nowhere else except in the middle of the Amazon jungle.

Even a peacock moved in on us—arrived one morning by air, discovered the dog's dish with some left-over kibbles in it, and stayed. He stayed for three years, roosting ceremonially in the live oaks and making hopeless, fantastic love to the cat, and on spring nights drowning out even the frogs with his piercing call for a peahen.

Country living, the Peaceable Kingdom. But that was only one side of it. Being human, we found some forms of life more attractive than others. We believed in weeds and pests, and they found us like fulfilled prophecy.

Gophers, not the Richardson's spermophiles of my boyhood but a surlier, more underground race, *Thomomys bottae*, tun-neled in from the dry pastures to enjoy our tomatoes and tulip bulbs and gnaw on the sweet rootlets of our cherry trees. Snakes followed them. We did not mind the gopher snakes and king snakes, in fact were glad to have them, as well as the tiny ring-necked snakes that lived under damp patches of leaves and fed on angleworms. But rattlesnakes dozing on our doormat made my wife nervous, and so we applied the human remedy,

the remedy my family had found in Saskatchewan for any un-
wanted life. We killed them, as we killed gophers when we -
could catch them, and mice when they got too thick, and wood
rats when they nested in the storage cupboards. In this we had
the enthusiastic cooperation of our Siamese cat, an efficient
killer but indiscriminate. He not only kept the mice and gophers on their toes, he decimated the lizards, got his share of
linnets and sparrows and wrens, salvaged the cedar waxwings
and robins that got drunk on fermented berries and tried to fly
through the plate glass, and brought in, on special occasions,
such rarer game as squirrels, and once a jack rabbit bigger than
he was. All this in spite of our canned cat food and our pre-
cautions, our shuttings-in and our bells.

As with mammals, so with insects. We did not like to spray,
for that meant undoing friend and foe alike. So we had ants, and
with the ants, aphids. We had white flies and mealybugs and red
spiders and thrips. We had leaf miners and twig borers and oak-
leaf caterpillars. And especially we had earwigs and sowbugs. It
is not a pleasure to a husband-man to find his strawberries infested with sowbugs. They eat their way into a succulent berry
like hyenas into the body of a dead elephant. As for earwigs, they
make lace of citrus leaves, and one spring they found the clema-
tis vine over the entrance such a beautiful place to breed in that
when I shook the vine I was showered with hundreds of crawling, pincered, vicious little bodies. Shuddering, I cut off the vine
at the ground, dragged its infested tangle into the driveway,
threw gasoline on it, and set it afire. Then I went downtown and
bought snail, earwig, and sowbug poisons. Having played
Tempter, I found that I had to play God in self-defense.

We have not been alone. There have been other gods before
us and after us. In our first years here, though we had neighbors within a comfortable half mile, we could see not a single
light at night except stars and moon and the glow on the sky
above the valley conurbia. There was a great healing in that
darkness that is not present now. Now we look out on constellations of lights, nebulae spiraling up hillside roads called Way
and Lane and Drive. We see white dwarfs, but few black holes.
The security lights of some neighbors burn into our windows

all night long—perhaps to scare away the coyotes. Many yards are surrounded by chain-link fences to keep the deer out. On Saturday nights our walls and ears pound with the hard rock blasting from decks where the young are holding parties. The weeds, of whom we were among the first, have closed in.

And the life forms that we tempted, enjoyed, struggled against, loved? Alas.

It has been years since I had to go out into the moonlight, drawn by the barking of the dog, and rescue from carport or lumber pile an opossum that, lifted up onto a safe oak limb, plays possum for a while and then creeps away. I am not philosophical about cleaning up garbage spilled by a neighbor's Dalmatian, as I was when the coons used to spill it. It is years since I heard that muscular rush into the dark as the dog charged and the coon fled. No foxes have groomed themselves in the light beyond my study window for a decade, and we would have thought foxes gone for good if we had not seen, just the other day, a survivor out in the coyote's pasture hunting-ground, walking as it were in the coyote's tracks and pouncing on the same mice or insects. If I thought installing bantam hens would bring them back in force, I would call on some henhouse tomorrow.

Nowadays, few skunks come by to drink out of our fishpond and teach our dog manners. The bloom of enveloping scent now rarely spreads and lingers in our bedroom when one walks around the house. There has not been a rattlesnake on our doormat for a decade and a half, and even gopher and king snakes are getting so scarce that when I see one in the road I get out and carry it off into the grass where it will not get run over. Sometimes I bring one home and make it welcome on our turf, but so far as I can see, none has stayed. Either neighbors kill them, or they find that the neighborhood cats have so thinned out the gophers and mice that there is nothing here to live on. It is a rare spring, nowadays, when even a single gopher kicks out his piles of dirt, making his underground beeline toward our garden.

The trees are tougher, and the native species may survive all our efforts to replace them with exotics. Development has brought water mains into the hills, and except in drouth years such as 1976 and 1977, there is plenty of Sierra water for the nursery plants and trees that new householders instantly set out. For a while, at least, this semi-desert may blossom as the rose. On the other hand, what one sees around old homesteads is likely to be native, reinforced by the Monterey pines, eucalyptus, pepper trees, and oleanders that have adapted to this climate; and that may be what surrounds us all a generation from now. The genes that were evolved for these hills have a way of asserting themselves whenever a fifty-year freeze or hundred-year drouth teaches local gardeners humility. Clear away the corpses of the exotics, and you find in the duff underneath them the sturdy oak seedlings, the sprays of poison oak, the insistent coyote brush.

But also—and this should have been just as predictable—nursery escapees with the toughness to survive. Around the place where I once had a flowering peach (I cut it down because I couldn't control the peach-leaf curl) there is a stubborn patch of lippia that each season spreads a foot or two in every direction before the summer drouth slows it down. Around the basin of my new lime tree is a patch of crab grass that I know will be even more stubborn. Both those patches came from some nursery, an inadvertent bonus. Like the wild oats and the burclover, they may be part of tomorrow's pasture. If the pasture is there.

There is no reason to expect it will be. The town's policies are friendly to subdividers. In suburbs such as this, people with a tenderness for the earth seldom get elected to town councils or appointed to planning commissions. Their sentiments are seen as interfering with profits and growth. The towns are run by people who see land as a commodity. James Fenimore Cooper once described this tendency as the defeat of Principle by Interest. Whatever it is, I observe with foreboding that every individual who has held and left the post of town manager in our suburb has left it to become a developer.

So the pasture is likely to go, and with it will go much that has made our thirty years here a long delight, a continual course in earth-keeping. All around it the bulldozers are at work tearing up the hills for new houses—twelve here, thirty-one there, fifteen across the gully. That may be the reason why we see coyotes where we never used to see them, and why the one fox we have seen in years was in that same field. There may literally be no other place for them, or for the deer that in these winter months herd up in bunches of eighteen or twenty and come and go through our yard, sliding through our sagging barbed wire fences as smoothly as swallows hit a hole in a barn. What we see out of our bedroom windows may be only the remnants, deceptively numerous because concentrated in this one patch of open space.

There are, thank God, other centers—Stanford's Jasper Ridge preserve, Palo Alto's Foothill Park, various parcels held as open space by the Mid-Peninsula Regional Park District—where the wild things can keep a foothold. But all of those places are close to developed areas, all are near roads, and the creatures which live in them are regularly exposed to their greatest natural enemy, the automobile. And here is another observation that sours my ruminations: we have lived on our country road for thirty-two years. In that time, though I have seen hundreds of animals crossing the road, I never hit one. Yet the road is rarely without its flattened carcass, skunk or opossum or raccoon or snake. If I can miss these things, driving the road several times a day every day of the week, why can't other drivers? I have to assume that they try not to miss but to hit them, that they are like some trigger-happy neighbors we have had through the years—the policeman who sat on his patio in pajamas on Sunday mornings and popped off quail and towhees with a .38 revolver, the Texas lady who kept a loaded .22 in her kitchen and blazed away out the door at anything passing through.

We live among the remnants. Feral housecats, as efficient at hunting as the foxes, opossums, and raccoons, and more efficient at breeding—and constantly replenished by hit-and-run owners who drop them off in the country and drive away—have almost cleared out the gophers, and I suppose the mice as well. That means that most of the animals who depended on that food supply couldn't make a living now even if we restocked the

area with them. Even if there were enough food, the other hazards would be fatal. The last pair of great horned owls went
several years ago, both of them apparently indirect victims of
the poisoned carrots that some neighbor put out for the gophers. Both came to die in our yard. As one of them squatted in
the patio, panting with open beak in the full sun, I passed my
hand across above him to cut off the sun from his blinded eyes,
and watched the slit of pupil widen instantly in the shadow, a
miraculously controlled lens shutter, before the fierce yellow
eyes went out. It wasn't quite what Aldo Leopold saw as the
green fire went out of the eyes of a dying wolf, but it carried
something like the same message, and it shook me.

Remnants. The pair of red-tails that we have known for a
long long time still nest in the eucalyptus at the south edge of
the pasture, but I don't expect, ever again, to be sitting in the
patio talking to a visitor and see one of them come over at
thirty feet, struggling with a four-foot gopher snake and very
close to crashing. The visitor, a New York editor, accused me of
staging that episode to plug California living. If I could stage it
now, I probably would, knowing that the snake is in danger of
starving to death anyhow, or of having his head crushed by
somebody who can't see that he wears no rattles on his tail.

UNFINISHED BUSINESS

The gross national product includes air pollution and cigarette advertising and ambulances to clear our highways of carnage. It counts special locks for our doors, and jails for the people who break them. It counts the destruction of the redwoods and the death of Lake Superior. It counts napalm and nuclear warheads, and armored cars for the police to fight riots in our cities. It counts Whitman's rifle and Speck's knife, and television programs which glorify violence the better to sell goods to our children. Yet the gross national product does not allow for the health of our children, the quality of their education or the joy of their play. It does not include the beauty of our poetry or the strength of our marriages, the intelligence of our public debate or the integrity of our public officials. It measures neither our wit nor our courage, neither our compassion nor our devotion to country. It measures everything, in short, except that which makes life worthwhile. And it can tell us everything about America, except whether we are proud to be Americans.
Senator Robert Kennedy

Once, the legend goes, a squirrel could have traveled from the Green Mountains to the swamps below Jacksonville, and from Chesapeake Bay to the Mississippi, without ever setting foot to ground. A flea on that squirrel, if he got the right transfer, - could have gone on as far as the Staked Plains of Texas, or the Uinta Basin in Utah, or the upper Green River in Wyoming, or the Judith Basin in Montana, without eating anything but buffalo. If the continent's fish had decided to hold a meeting, delegates could have started from places as far apart as the West Virginia mountains and Glacier National Park, Yellowstone and the Ozarks, the Sangre de Cristos and the Minnesota height of land, and arrived unimpeded at the convention center in New Orleans.

And once, as George Stewart observed, "from eastern ocean to western ocean, the land stretched away without names." It is covered now with names we have imposed upon it, and the names contain our history as the seed contains the tree.

They are borrowed from the usage of a hundred local tribes, as in Passamaquoddy, Wichita, Walla Walla. They commemorate explorers and early settlers, as in Duluth, Cooperstown, Houston. They honor Old World origins and imperial claims—New York, New England, Virginia, Louisiana. They mark physiographic features—Detroit, Sault Sainte Marie, Rapid City—or reflect the piety of the founders—Santa Fe, San Francisco, Santa Cruz. They remind us of the aspirations toward the good life and the perfected society that their founders brought from Europe—Philadelphia, Cincinnati, Guttenberg. Sometimes a homely implement or weapon—Hayfork, Stirrup-Iron—or a battle or other incident—Wounded Knee, Quietus—has marked land and map forever, or so we say, with its human associations. Politicians usurp more than their share of sites. Sometimes the name of a place, corrupted by oral transmission or misappropriated from an Indian tongue without being understood, teases us with possibilities. What shall we make of Ticklenaked Pond?

No American needs to be told that things have changed during the time these names were being attached to places: that the forests are largely down and the grasslands largely plowed up and the rivers mostly dammed and the wildlife reduced to a few samples in refuges and zoos, so that we have to go to the Arctic or East Africa for the kind of experience that was common to Americans when the continent was being, as we say, tamed. But even yet, though our environmental conscience has been made uneasy by an increasing chorus of protest, beginning more than a century ago with George Perkins Marsh and John Wesley Powell—even yet we can be astonished by how fast it has happened, and look around us like Plains Indians wondering where the buffalo have gone. There has been some magic; they have disappeared into the ground.

It is hard to take in. The land and its rivers and forests may have been tamed, but our minds have not. Even yet there is a delusive spaciousness in our image of the continent, especially its western half where the names on the map are sparse. Free land, the arable and habitable frontier, went by 1890; the free land of the mind, the notions and assumptions that four or more centuries of spaciousness have bred into us, will last a long time. But instead of looking always forward, we more and more look back; the gilded future becomes the gilded past; indefinite expectation is transformed into the nostalgic dream of a golden age.

For complex reasons, the western half of the continent inherits the memory and assumes the dream, partly because it is newer and younger and more hopeful, partly because its open spaces create an illusion of continuing opportunity that its prevailing aridity prohibits, partly because much of it is federal land, and we have a national habit of assuming that federal land is open to our appropriation and exploitation. From the time when kings began making grants to settlement companies or to court favorites, to the latest outbreak of the Sagebrush Rebellion, America has been a country to be given away, or sold for a song, or seized by the first comer. To some extent it still is—for corporations. Not for individuals.

But there is another reason why the West assumes the American Dream. Americans have a centuries-old habit of dreaming westward.

"Eastward I go only by force; but westward I go free," Thoreau wrote in 1862. "The future lies that way to me, and the earth seems more unexhausted and richer on that side . . . I must walk toward Oregon, and not toward Europe." Actually, hope and the future had lain to the west for Europe, too. Hence Atlantis, hence the Hesperides. "Going west," the World War I euphemism for dying, could not possibly have become a catch phrase with the directions reversed. Neither Europeans nor Americans can die eastward. The unknown lies the other way.

They cannot, it seems, live or hope eastward, either. The grim history of the Golden Gate Bridge suggests to many the strength of the lemming impulse to head west when hope is pinched out in other directions; and at the end of hope, in the face of the continent's last sunsets, to jump.

In America, it used to be believed, the heavens are higher and the stars brighter, and by extension it was easy to believe, as Thoreau did, that someday American achievements in literature, the arts, and the life of the mind would also reach higher than they did in constricted Europe. "Else to what end does the world go on, and why was America discovered?"

It would be interesting to discuss that question with Thoreau now. The arts, literature, and the life of the mind have indeed done some flourishing in America since 1862; but meantime the forests have been reduced to a threatened remnant or a waste of second growth, the plains fight for their renewable life against the strip mines and power plants, the mountains are vulgarized by resorts built for the Pleasure Circuit, and the air of Denver and Salt Lake City is worse than that of Newark or Pittsburgh. One would not expect him to value the need for energy above the need for healthy land, air, and water. One would not expect his spartan spirit to celebrate the benefits of industrialization, its gadgets, its comforts, its love affair with the internal combustion engine. Nevertheless, the taming of the continent has made it a home for 220 million people, with a standard of living that until recently was the envy of the world. If that was why America was discovered, then it could be argued that discovery has justified itself.

Still, one would like to hear Thoreau on the subject of how long optimism and great expectations (and such other things as liberty, equality, private and corporate greed, and a faith in progress and human perfectibility) can survive the resource base that generated them. How long does freedom outlast riches? How long does democracy survive the shrinking of opportunity? What happens to the responsible citizen with a stake in democratic society, what happens to the Jeffersonian yeoman of our antique tradition, when the democratic society wastes its bounty, loses faith in itself, fails to deliver on its promises?

"America was promises," said Archibald MacLeish in a poem written during the Great Depression. It certainly was, for native and immigrant alike, and it still is for tens of thousands of the politically oppressed and economically deprived—Mexicans, Cubans, Vietnamese, Haitians. It has been a good while since America advertised for the world's tired and poor, but it still makes room for great numbers of them. What would Thoreau make of the fact that fewer and fewer can count on making the stake that would bring them up to full membership in this nation? Would it shake him to listen to young people, even reasonably lucky and well-trained young people, who in 1980 were looking into their future soberly, even fearfully? Would it trouble him to hear that many of them never expect to be able to afford a home or land of their own—this in the society that was made by free land—and that their life expectation is not discovery, adventure, enlargement, independence in occupation and in mind, but security? That their greatest hope is to attach themselves to some corporation, union, university, bureau, or other power cluster that pays a decent wage and has an advantageous pension plan? Would Thoreau hold still for Edwin Land's ironic suggestion that the American Dream has diminished to an eight-hour day with two martinis at its end? Would he be upset by another cluster of the young, less lucky, perhaps, less well trained, but equally fearful, whose greatest hope is for a federally subsidized handout and the legal right to alter their consciousness with drugs?

Or would Thoreau find comfort in the assurance that in 1980 his was the work most consistently read among university undergraduates, and that his message has been heard over the past two decades by a great many before them who have left the security of institutions and pension plans to find a Walden of their own? Whose man *is* the American, this new man?

It has happened so fast. Thoreau believed that the woods surrounding the Great Lakes would remain wilderness for many generations. They were leveled within forty years. The last great raft of logs from the Minnesota and Wisconsin pineries went down the Mississippi in 1915, and except in a few backwaters like the Menominee reservation there are none of the old magnificent forests left in the Middle West. Or in the East, where the broad arrow of the king's navy took the first and best of the white pine, and mills and blister rust took much of the rest; where the chestnut is wiped out, and the elms are gone from nearly every common in New England. And what would Thoreau, an expert on lakes and ponds, make of Lake Erie, which until a few years ago was so polluted that it would not support fish, and which is only being brought back to semi-health by the concerted and expensive efforts of citizens' groups and public agencies against the unreconstructed exponents of the American way? What would he think of acid rain along the Concord and Merrimack rivers?

Progress and perfectibility were concepts that rested easy on the American mind in 1862. They could be taken for granted, along with self-reliance, free enterprise, faith in the common man, and other by-products of our lavish frontier. They could be assumed so long as the ratio of population to land and resources was low—so long as, in Jefferson's words, we were poor in labor and rich in land. But as Walter Webb pointed out, by 1930 or so the population of the United States was denser, even figuring in all the open spaces of the West, than the population of Bastille Europe had been in 1500.

Thoreau could not assume progress and perfectibility as confidently now as he did in 1862. Even the progress he anticipated was of another kind than the progress we got. Now, perhaps, he would be tempted to make the Walden Pond experiment permanent, instead of the philosophical whimsy of a year. He might retreat with his latterday imitators into the Vermont or Maine woods, or to Sedona or Humboldt County. We might find him holed up close, but not too close, to Edward Abbey in Wolf Hole, Arizona, or camped just down the road from Wendell Berry in Port Royal, Kentucky. He might find sanctuary in the bypassed towns of the upper Mississippi, or in the federally managed sloughs of the flood plain.

The sort of withdrawal that became common in the 1960s, and has by no means subsided, springs from violently juxtaposed motives: disgust at industrialized living, and nostalgia for what our national life once was, or seemed to be, or had a chance of becoming. Among the unthinking, the pleasure-bent, and the technologically compromised (which means to some extent all of us) these motives are not strong enough to produce significant change. But there was in 1980 a not-so-voiceless and not-so-small body of Americans, most of them refugees from the middle-class American plenty, who felt a real hatred of the machine and what it has done to us, and a homesickness for the garden that America once was and might still be. They were convinced that industrial civilization, once widely thought to be the solution for human problems, has actually been the cause of many of them, and has been the worst enemy of the continent from which we once expected millennium. America reduced to the gross national product can tell us, as Senator Kennedy observed, "everything about America, except whether we are proud to be Americans."

During the sixties there were a lot of Americans, particularly young, college-aged, draftable Americans, who were not proud of their country, of its public officials, of its international image, of its relentless equation of progress with economic growth, or of its unconcern with the expendable, whether its cost was in stripped acres of coal deposits or polluted rivers— or in Vietnamese lives. They were not devoted to a country which, rightly or wrongly, they felt had disfranchised them, nor to an adult world which they felt had misappropriated not only its own funds but their inheritance as well. Their collective bumper sticker read "Question Authority." That was very American of them; Americans have been questioning authority since Jamestown.

Their miscalculations were naive, even simple-minded. Neither blacks nor labor joined them as expected; as often as not they were held in contempt by those who were far more genuinely disfranchised. Their sloganeering was both shrill and simplistic. But they also had the perception, less generally shared by their elders then than now, that limits were being approached. The second serving had been called, and there was not much on the platter but the gizzard and the Pope's nose. They looked at a shrinking job market, rising housing costs, inflation, recession, overcrowding, and the declining cash value of a college education, and they began to drop out. It was not only the war in Vietnam. The impulse to question traditional American values and consider alternatives to upward mobility, materialism, and "success" was as much economic as political, and as much vaguely spiritual as either. If it was, like much American experience, utopian and romantic, it was also catching. By the early 1970s going back to the land, at first an expedient for young people at the height of an unpopular war, began to be a deliberate, unpressured choice for some with established careers and comfortably middle-class lives.

It was no march of lemmings to the sea, but it was, and still is, a movement with momentum. Not only people but businesses have been moving to the suburbs, the small towns, even the country, reversing the trend of nearly a century. We remain a highly mobile society, but our mobility today seems clearly in the spirit of Huckleberry Finn's lighting out for the territory.

There is both good news and bad in a rural migration, a mixed blessing as mixed for the newcomer hunting tranquillity and self-determination as for the townsman whose community is invaded. Those who come in from outside with the specific intention of exploiting an opportunity to make a profit are bad news for both. But at least part of the bad news for the natives is a change in the status quo so rapid that it can't be comprehended, much less resisted. The dialogue is not invented: "That hippie lawyer who moved in a year or so ago and got himself made a selectman, God knows how—now he's talking about Environmental Impact Reports. Where's he get off?" "You know those two queers who bought the Idle Hour and the radio station? Well, now they're showing those X-rated foreign movies down there, and playing Mozart all day long. I think - they're a couple of communists." "Say, I was up on the ridge road above Junior Simple's place, and I'll tell you, that long-haired freak who bought it is harvesting some kind of crop you sure won't find on the commodity exchange."

Newcomers change their location, and even some aspects of the way they live. They seldom change their ethics, morals, cultural values, politics, or social habits. To a conservative native, a Johnny-come-lately urban egalitarian with his talk of zoning, planning, and pollution controls is hard to take—especially when Johnny-come-lately smokes dope. It is even worse because Johnny often introduces a conflict between the head and the pocketbook. His appearance generally means an economic boost to the rural community. He brings outside money, and he needs services. He attracts others who also bring money and need services.

On the other hand, newcomers congregating in any numbers begin to reproduce the problems they fled from in the first place. They may bring in some services that the community never had and doesn't want. Or they become the growth, expansion, and development that they themselves deplore. Their children need schools, their sewage has to be dealt with, their roads need plowing, their lives and property need protecting. They bid up the price of land and houses, and taxes go up and up. Oldtimers can't afford to keep their own places. Somebody gets the idea of attracting tourists. Craftspeople follow the tourists, and more tourists follow the craftspeople. Recent newcomers begin to help put up signs that say "Visit our town, but please don't stay." In many places—say at Mendocino on California's north coast—the monster created is the monster fled.

Fortunately the pattern is not always so extreme. Well-settled and stable communities are sometimes able to maintain their character in the face of considerable invasions. And sometimes the invaded town can use some jacking up. However we romanticize the rural virtues and canonize simple folks, some sons of pioneers are as destructive and wasteful as their forebears were. The in-migrant often brings a wider experience with his preservationist opinions; and as in our summer town of Greensboro, Vermont, the invaded and the invaders may collaborate in creating a community that is good for both.

Rural America may well be where much of what has been lost during the last few decades gets reborn or rediscovered—things like family, community, occupational integrity, moral and social responsibility, a measure of self-sufficiency. The culture of narcissism finds it sterile soil. It is too quiet for the "me" generation. It offers more natural than manufactured diversion. But like so many American habitats, the small town is fragile. If its immigrants do not come to it with a degree of humility, with an understanding not only of its human ecology but of Paradise Lost as well, they can destroy it before it can gather itself and resist.

The environmental movement has had one abiding purpose: to assert the long-range public interest against short-term economic interests—in effect, to promote civilized responsibility, both public and private, over frontier carelessness and greed. Through a hundred years of effort it has accomplished some significant things. It has encouraged the setting aside of a magnificent (though still inadequate) system of national parks, monuments, historic sites, seashores and lakeshores and recreation areas, as outdoor museums, shrines, and playgrounds. It has helped to create the national forests, which not only hold reserves of saw timber and (sometimes) control their cutting, but, like the national parks, protect vital watersheds, preserve a habitat for wildlife, and provide outdoor recreation to millions each year. The wildlife refuges derive from the same preservationist thinking. And within all three systems, environmentalists have been instrumental in the creation of permanent wildernesses (read near-wildernesses) from which as a matter of public policy (not always respected by all the public) we deliberately withhold our roads, our machines, and our destructive intrusions and exploitations. Those islands of sanity, those clean and natural places where Americans may go, but must leave no tracks, may in another hundred years seem like the greatest achievement of the twentieth century.

Let us not forget the residual public domain, the lands that were too arid, high, rocky, steep, or otherwise unusable to attract settlers under the Homestead or other land acts. That public domain, exclusively in the western states and Alaska, is perennially the target of states'-rights forces. The ostensible reason for the latest of these, the Sagebrush Rebellion, as for the similar movements of the 1940s and 1950s, is "absentee-landlordism," bureaucratic control from Washington, suppression or frustration of local autonomy. The real reason is economic, not political. Those once-scorned BLM lands, useful at best for grazing at the rate of about one cow for every hundred acres, now show themselves to be underlain with coal, oil, gas, uranium, and other desirable and profitable materials.

There is a very great danger here. In the 1940s and 1950s only stockmen and loggers were after the resources within the public domain. Now enormous energy conglomerates backed by local politicians are after far bigger game, and control of far more profitable resources. Historically, from the early slavery debates to the present, every states'-rights movement has been dominated by local elites wanting to control local or regional resources. Washington doesn't always respond swiftly to local needs. By the same token it is far more disinterested than any state government can possibly be, and harder to dominate. No responsible historian can avoid the conclusion that, absentee or not, bureaucratic or not, imperfect or not, the federal bureaus have been better stewards than the supporters of the Sagebrush Rebellion would ever be. Krushchev said it: you don't set the fox to watch the henhouse.

Nevertheless, in the long view, it would be naive to expect that public ownership and management of a small percentage of American land can turn the American bulldozer from its course. Only the driver can do that, and the driver in this case is theoretically still the people.

Are they capable of so crucial a choice? Have we learned enough? Certainly we have learned something, and at its best the American environmental movement can give lessons to the whole world. But it would take a great optimist to deny that a large proportion of the American public, on the record, are not ecologically ignorant, they are ecologically lawless. The worst thing that can happen to any piece of land, short of coming under the control of an unscrupulous professional developer, is to be opened to an unmanaged public. The public agencies often do their best at control, and sometimes do well; but even the best-ordered and best-policed public lands, the national parks, are systematically endangered by the lawless, thus corroborating Mrs. Trollope. Liberty in the United States is still largely enjoyed by the disorderly at the expense of the orderly.

Too often, local authorities do not need a Sagebrush Rebel-

lion to assert their principles—they do the bidding of the speculators and developers. And yet how can we avoid the perception that every developer (whether individual or corporation,
whether with depreciation-sheltered bank loans or overflow oil
money or the profits of an illegal marijuana plantation) who in
search of profit tears up a hill or destroys a swamp or a mountain valley or skins off the topsoil with a bulldozer blade for his
subdivision, is as much a bandit as if he had presented a gun to
the public's head and walked off with its watches and wallets?
He operates on land-use assumptions that have been current in
America since 1608. The conditions that made him possible
have made him an environmental thug. The laws were made in
his interest, the public assumptions abet him. And if what he
does to us is not limited and controlled, we will be even more a
jerry-built wasteland in the twenty-first century than we are in
the twentieth.

There are Americans in the 1980s who understand these matters,
and who fight for more responsible public attitudes and more effective controls. But the impression that things have improved in
the past decade may be in good part illusion. What happened is
that environmental consciousness took center stage for a time;
conservation became respectable. The media paid attention
(though generally in the absence of something truly newsworthy)
to the Alaska pipeline, the snail darter (for comic relief), Three
Mile Island, the humpbacked whale, organic foods, Birkenstock
sandals. Now the earth has been escalated into the Whole Earth
and made available to every one through a mail order catalogue—
a commercial enterprise, a cause to celebrate, a topic of political
rhetoric, an issue of dinner-table debate.

But the pipelines are still built and the forests come down in
clear-cuttings and the coal is stripped and the aquifers are
pumped in the Santa Clara Valley, the Central Valley, the Owens
Valley. The air is still tan in Los Angeles. Instead of requiring a
brick in every toilet tank, we build another dam or canal to divert still more energy and water to grow yet more Hawaiian
blossoms in the desert. Instead of insisting on economical, func-

tional automobiles built by Detroit, we guarantee loans to a company that stubbornly refused to read the handwriting on the wall. Instead of a massive public transportation effort, we call for import quotas on the Japanese. Instead of a comprehensive energy plan, we have a new President and Secretary of the Interior who call environmentalists "extremists" and talk of the government's willingness to exploit the last-resort oil reserves off Big Sur and Mendocino, California. When the chips are down, environmental arguments get short shrift. When the energy pinch comes on, too many of us are prepared to sacrifice parts of Montana or Wyoming or Colorado or Utah—too many Montanans and Wyomingites or Coloradans and Utahans seem willing to allow their grazing land—to match the archetypal sacrifice area in California's Owens Valley. The justifications for synfuel plants in the land's most scenic country, or 3,000-megawatt power plants, or strip mines, are precisely the justifications that Theodore Roosevelt found for the rape of the Owens Valley.

We burn out rather quickly on most public causes—gun control, civil rights, women's liberation, prison reform, campaign financing, intelligence agencies, flower power—but environmental concern is not one that we can afford to burn out on. It is as central and as vital in our lives as democracy itself. And as much of a task, rather than a fact. It will take many more Love Canals, many more Four Corners plants, many more drowned Glen Canyons and bulldozed hills, many more summers when you can't find room to camp in the High Sierra, many more lights going out for endangered species, many more years of smogged air and paved-over countryside, before environmental concern either hardens into law that is both enforced and supported—or, better yet, is diffused through the major part of a population sobered by past mistakes and a wastefullness the New World taught us even while it was teaching us how to be free.

We are the most various people on earth, and every segment of us has to learn the lessons both of democracy and of conservation all anew. The Laotians and Vietnamese who in August

1980 were discovered poaching squirrels and pigeons in Golden Gate Park were Americans on the long road of learning how to *be* Americans. All of us are somewhere on a long arc between ecological ignorance and democratic responsibility. What freedom means is freedom to choose, but it takes a long time to learn *how* to choose, and between what options. If we choose badly, we have, not always intentionally, violated the contract. Democracy assumes, on the strength of the most radical document in human history, that all men are created equal, and that given freedom they can become better masters for themselves than any king or despot. But until we arrive at a land ethic that fits both science and human affections, until we achieve some common reverence for the earth that has blessed us, Americans are likely to be what Aldo Leopold in an irritable moment called them: people remodeling the Alhambra with a bulldozer, and proud of their yardage.

America is the world's greatest undeveloped nation, and by its very premises, nobody can develop it except its citizens. It is not enough to set government agencies to watch industry: government agencies themselves can be the agents of the industries they are supposed to control, and can themselves reflect the development attitudes. It was San Francisco that dammed Hetch Hetchy, it was the Forest Service that granted the permits for Mineral King and Ski Yellowstone, it is Los Angeles that is bleeding the Owens Valley dry, it is the Department of Defense that wants to install MX missile tracks under the deserts of Utah and Nevada and, for a delicate desert ecosystem sparingly hospitable to men, substitute an environment as sterile and as dependent on artificial support systems as a space ship.

It would promise us a more serene and confident future if, at the start of our sixth century of residence in America, we began to listen to the land, and hear what it says, and know what it can and cannot do.

Bibliography

This bibliography is only suggestive. Any list of books pretending to cover America's physiographic and climatic regions as well as something of the history of discovery and natural history could be almost indefinitely expanded. Beyond this beginning, a reader is on his own in a various, fascinating, and prolific literature.

The original publication date or manuscript completion date of older works is listed in parentheses following the work's title. The asterisk * identifies works cited in the text. The notation (O P) indicates the title is out of print.

THE NORTH AMERICAN CONTINENT

Human History:

Bakeless, John, *Eyes of Discovery: America as Seen by the First Explorers* (1953). New York: Dover, 1961. A survey of the major explorations of North America.

*Brinton, Daniel G., *The Myths of the New World: A Treatise on the Symbolism and Mythology of the Red Race of America* (1896). St. Clair Shores (Mich.): Scholarly Press, 1972. The religions of the North American Indians.

Commager, Henry Steele, ed., *Living Ideas in America.* New York: Harper & Row, 1964. Well-selected, firsthand accounts of the American experience from the colonial period to the presidency of John F. Kennedy.

Farb, Peter, *Man's Rise to Civilization*, revised edition. New

York: E.P. Dutton, 1978. A comprehensive survey of North American Indians from their origins to the twentieth century.

Fox, Stephen, *John Muir and His Legacy: The American Conservation Movement*. Boston: Little, Brown & Co., 1981. Especially valuable for its tracing of the preservationist ethic as against conservation-for-use advocated by Gifford Pinchot.

Handlin, Oscar, *This Was America*. Cambridge: Harvard University Press, 1969. Manners and customs as recorded by European travelers in eighteenth-, nineteenth-, and twentieth-century America.

*Holbrook, Stewart H., *The American Lumberjack*. New York: Macmillan, 1938. (O P) Once a logger himself, Holbrook re-creates the wilderness world of the colorful pioneers of the American forest from Maine to the state of Washington.

*Jackson, Helen Hunt, *A Century of Dishonor: The Early Crusade for Indian Reform* (1881). Williamstown: Corner House, 1973. Could be considered the *Uncle Tom's Cabin* of the long crusade to restore rights to America's natives.

McLuhan, Teri, *Touch the Earth* (1971). New York: Touchstone Books, 1976. A selection of writings by North American Indians that reveals their cherished values.

Marx, Leo, *Machine in the Garden: Technology and the Pastoral Ideal in America* (1924). New York: Oxford University Press, 1967. An analysis of the enduring conflict in our society between the desire for a rural paradise and an industrialized nation.

Morison, Samuel Eliot, and Commager, Henry Steele, *A Concise History of the American Republic*. New York: Oxford University Press, 1977. A solid history by two first-rate writers and historians.

Nash, Roderick, *Wilderness and the American Mind* (1967). New Haven: Yale University Press, 1973. A valuable study of the effect of the open continent on American thinking and attitudes, from the early view of the wilderness as hostile and forbidding to the modern view of it as the sanctuary of health and sanity.

*Turner, Frederick Jackson, "The Significance of the Frontier in American History." Washington, D.C.: *Report of the American Historical Association*, 1893.

Natural History:

Atwood, W.W., *Physiographic Provinces of North America*. Boston: Ginn & Co., 1940. (O P) The bones of the continent laid bare.

Brooks, Paul, *Speaking for Nature*. Boston: Houghton Mifflin, 1980. A history of the writers, famous or otherwise, responsible for the American tradition of nature writing.

*Carson, Rachel, *The Sea Around Us*. New York: Oxford University Press, 1951. One of our classic nature books that closes with this line: "For all at last return to the sea—to Oceanus, the ocean river, like the everflowing stream of time, the beginning and the end." Other important Rachel Carson titles that combine literature and science include *Under the Sea Wind*, *The Edge of the Sea*, and *Silent Spring*.

Huth, Hans, *Nature and the American* (1957). Lincoln: University of Nebraska Press, 1972. A lavishly illustrated account of three centuries of changing attitudes toward nature, both in literature and in painting.

Matthiessen, Peter, *Wildlife in America* (1956). New York: Penguin, 1978. A close look at our wildlife, both past and present, by the well-known novelist and naturalist.

*Shimer, John, *This Sculptured Earth: The Landscape of America*. New York: Columbia University Press, 1959. A good, readable account of how America's landforms were shaped.

Whitman, Walt, *Specimen Days* (1891). Boston: David Godine, 1971. The author of *Leaves of Grass* sets down his early memories of nature in various parts of the country.

NEW ENGLAND, NEW YORK, AND THE MIDDLE ATLANTIC STATES

*Adams, Henry, *History of the United States of America During the First Administration of Thomas Jefferson* (1880).

Ithaca, N.Y.: Cornell University Press, 1955 (abbreviated edition). Vivid social history before the opening of the West.

*Beston, Henry, *The Outermost House* (1928). New York: Penguin, 1976. The journal of a year spent alone in a cabin on Cape Cod's outer beach.

*Boyle, Robert H., *The Hudson River: A Natural and Unnatural History*. New York: W. W. Norton & Co., 1969. Section by section, human and natural history of one of America's most historic rivers.

*Bradford, William, *A History of Plymouth Plantation* (1630). Magnolia (Mass.): Peter Smith, 1960. One of the first responses to the American wilderness and the first account of sustained English settlement in America. Famous for its picture of the wilderness as bleak, dangerous, and forbidding, in contrast with later views that saw it as a place of liberation, freedom, and opportunity.

*Brooks, Van Wyck, *Makers and Finders Series (The World of Washington Irving, The Flowering of New England, The Times of Melville and Whitman, New England: Indian Summer*, and *The Confident Years: 1885-1915*). New York: E. P. Dutton, 1936 through 1946. A rediscovery of literary America from the forming of the Republic through the first quarter of the twentieth century by a distinguished literary historian and Pulitzer Prize winner.

Cole, John, *Striper*. Boston: Atlantic Monthly Press, 1978. An affectionate look at striped bass and at the fishermen connected with this endangered fish.

*de Crèvecoeur, Hector St. John, *Letters From an American Farmer* (1782). New York: Dutton Paperbacks, 1957. An early, idealistic account of the freedom and opportunity of the New World, and the first serious effort to answer the question, "Who is the American, this new man?"

Hay, John, and Farb, Peter, *The Atlantic Shore: Human and Natural History From Long Island to Labrador*. New York: Harper & Row, 1966. A poet and science writer describe the North Atlantic coast and its people.

Hoagland, Edward, *Walking the Dead Diamond River*. New York: Random House, 1973. Mostly essays about the Northeast wilderness, especially the Green and White Mountains and the rivers of Maine.

Holbrook, Stewart H., *The Old Post Road: The Story of the Boston Post Road* (1962). New York: McGraw-Hill, 1971. A life line through the New England of an earlier time.

Kalm, Peter, *Travels in North America* (1750). (O P) The account of a young Finnish botanist and friend of Linnaeus who visited America before the Revolution.

*Ogburn, Charlton, Jr., *Winter Beach* (1966). New York: Touchstone Books, 1971. A solitary journey along the Atlantic's winter beaches from Maine to the outer banks of North Carolina by a keen observer of nature and man.

Thoreau, Henry David, *The Maine Woods* (1864). New York: T. Y. Crowell, 1970. Thoreau's ideas translated to a wilderness wilder than Walden Pond.

*———, *Walden* (1854). New York: New American Library, 1973. The source and bible of much of American nature writing, as well as a doctrine of self-reliance, of nature against society, and of individual intelligence and integrity against coercive government.

Tocqueville, Alexis de, *Democracy in America* (1832). New York: Harper & Row, 1966. A Frenchman's penetrating analysis of American society.

THE SOUTHEAST

*Audubon, John James, *Delineations of American Scenery and Character* (1830), New York: Arno Press, 1970. Extracts from the writings of Audubon that accompanied his *Birds of America*. Though Audubon's travels took him westward up the Missouri and south to the Gulf Coast of Texas, his more characteristic wanderings covered the area from the east coast to the Mississippi and from Florida to Labrador.

Bartram, William, *Travels Through North and South Carolina, East and West Florida, the Cherokee Country, the Extensive Territories of the Muscogulges, or Creek Confederacy, and the Country of the Chactaws.* (1793). Charlottesville: University Press of Virginia, 1980. One of the most intriguing of American travel books, highly colored and romanticized, but full of curious and observant details. It was the basis for some of the images in Coleridge's *Kubla Khan.*

*Berry, Wendell, *The Unsettling of America.* San Francisco: Sierra Club Books, 1977. A poet and farmer from Fort Royal, Kentucky, makes the case for an understanding of ecology and presents a persuasive argument against agribusiness.

Beverly, Robert, *The History and Present State of Virginia* (1705), ed. by L.B. Wright. Chapel Hill: University of North Carolina Press, 1947. A vivid and romantic vision of Virginia and the Carolinas at the turn of the seventeenth century.

*Byrd, William, *Histories of the Dividing Line* (1729). Magnolia (Mass.): Peter Smith, 1970. Notes taken on the country and its inhabitants during Byrd's survey of the boundary between Virginia and North Carolina in 1729.

Caudill, Harry, *Night Comes to the Cumberland.* Boston: Atlantic Monthly Press, 1963 and *My Land Is Dying.* New York: E. P. Dutton, 1971. Two classics about the ravages of strip mining by a seventh-generation country lawyer from Whitesburg, Kentucky.

Coates, Robert M., *The Outlaw Years* (1930). Detroit: Gale Research Co., 1974. The history of the land pirates of the Natchez Trace.

Daniels, Jonathan, *The Devil's Backbone: Story of the Natchez Trace.* New York: McGraw-Hill, 1962. An account of the land and water of the wilderness trail from central Kentucky through Tennessee, northern Alabama, and Mississippi to Natchez.

Gilman, Charles, *Spain in America.* New York: Harper & Row, 1966. (O P) A compact summary from the time of Columbus through the explorations of de Vaca, De Soto, and Coronado to the emergence of the Spanish American nations in the nineteenth century.

Jefferson, Thomas, *Notes of the State of Virginia* (1788). New York: W. W. Norton, 1972. The notes of an American statesman on the geography, politics, flora, and fauna of his native state.

Teale, Edwin Way, *North With the Spring*. New York: Dodd, Mead, 1951. A naturalist's journey following the spring from Florida to New England.

*Vega, Garcilaso, de la, *The Florida of the Inca* (1560). Austin: University of Texas Press, 1960. The fullest account, written from the reports of participants, of De Soto's destructive and doomed raid on "Florida," which in his time meant the whole southeastern United States.

Warner, William W., *Beautiful Swimmer: Watermen, Crabs and the Chesapeake Bay*. Boston: Atlantic Monthly Press, 1976. A magical book for anyone interested in the Chesapeake Bay.

THE MIDWEST AND MISSISSIPPI RIVER

Bissell, Richard, *A Stretch on the River*. Boston: Atlantic Monthly Press, 1950. (O P) An ex-riverboat pilot records life among the steamboaters and bargemen in the period following World War I.

Chateaubriand, François-René de, *Atala* (1800). Paris: Classique Garnier, 1958. An American Indian is pictured as a noble child of nature by a French statesman and writer who reached America in 1791.

Leopold, Aldo, *A Sand County Almanac* (1949). New York: Oxford University Press, 1977. A modest Wisconsin-based nature classic that makes a persuasive case for the land.

Parkman, Francis, *La Salle and the Discovery of the Great West* (1879). Williamstown: Corner House, 1968. Romantic history at its best. La Salle emerges as a dominating, indefatigable, and ultimately tragic figure. He opened much of the country he traveled through—from the St. Lawrence to the Great Lakes, from the lakes into the Illinois and the Mississippi and down the Mississippi to its mouth.

Schoolcraft, Henry Roe, *Narrative of an Expedition Through the Upper Mississippi* (1821). New York: Arno Press, 1970.

The discoverer of the source of the Mississippi and the ethnologist from whom Longfellow took much of the material for *Hiawatha* reports on the water-soaked height-of-land in which our greatest river rises.

Twain, Mark, *Life on the Mississippi* (1883). New York: New American Library, 1961. Especially in its earlier chapters ("Old Times on the Mississippi") this reminiscence of a native son and ex-riverboat pilot is our best picture of life along the great waterway during the steamboat years from the 1830s to the Civil War.

THE MISSOURI AND THE HIGH PLAINS

Gregg, Josiah, *Commerce of the Prairies* (1844). Lincoln: University of Nebraska Press, 1967. An able and astute observer of the early years of the Santa Fe Trail and the trade that passed along it.

*Lewis, Meriwether, and Clark, George Rogers, *The Original Journals of the Lewis and Clark Expedition*, 8 volumes (recorded in 1804-1806). New York: Select Bibliographies Reprint Series. See also Reuben G. Thwaites's multivolume series on American explorers.

Mattes, Merrill J., *The Great Platte Valley Road*. Lincoln: Nebraska State Historical Society, 2nd edition, 1969. Full account, in great detail, of the route of the Oregon, California, and Mormon Trails up the Platte and North Platte Rivers.

Maximilian of Wied-Neuwied, *Reise in das innere Nord-Amerika in den Jahren 1832 bis 1834*. Published in English translation in Thwaites, *Early Western Travels,* Vols. XXII-XXV. New York: Dodd, Mead, 1906. See also *People of the First Man*, ed. Davis Thomas and Karin Ronnefeldt. New York: E. P. Dutton, 1976.

Parkman, Francis, *The Oregon Trail* (1849) New York: New American Library, 1965. A Boston Brahmin of genius reports on the Sioux frontier in the early years of the westward migration. The focus is on the area around Fort Laramie on the Oregon Trail.

Webb, Walter Prescott, *The Great Plains*. Boston: Ginn & Co., 1931. (O P) A landmark study of the geography, climate, peoples, and institutions of the Great Plains, especially as these have affected Anglo-Saxon settlers and imported laws and institutions. Webb's ideas to some extent derive from, but greatly extend, the ideas of John Wesley Powell; in turn, Webb influenced the work of Bernard DeVoto, among others.

THE ROCKY MOUNTAINS

Chittenden, Hiram, *The American Fur Trade in the Far West* (1902). New York: Augustus M. Kelley, 1935. The standard history of the Rocky Mountain fur trade.

———, *The Yellowstone National Park* (1895). Revised by Richard A. Bartlett. Norman: University of Oklahoma Press, 1964. The first full description of our first national park.

*DeVoto, Bernard, *Across the Wide Missouri*. Boston: Houghton Mifflin, 1952. An incandescent evocation of the mountain fur trade in its greatest days. Illustrated with the watercolors of the frontier artist, Alfred Jacob Miller.

Irving, Washington, *The Adventures of Captain Bonneville, U.S.A.* (1837). Portland, Ore.: Binfords & Mort, 1954. A somewhat romanticized biography of the enigmatic army-officer-turned-fur trader whose partisans roamed the whole West in the late 1830s and discovered, among other things, the Yosemite Valley.

Lavender, David, *The Rockies*. New York: Harper & Row, revised edition, 1975. A lively description and history by a historian who grew up in the mountain town of Telluride, Colorado.

Morgan, Dale L., *Jedediah Smith and the Opening of the West*. Lincoln: University of Nebraska Press, 1964. A fine biography and an informative account of the preeminent mountain man.

Murie, Claus and Margaret, *Wapiti Wilderness*. New York: Alfred A. Knopf, 1966. (O P) The life of a biologist in Jackson Hole, Wyoming.

Russell, Osborne, *Journal of a Trapper, or Nine Years in the Rocky Mountains, 1834-43. 1914.* (O P) Probably the most intimate and informative report on the life of a Rocky Mountain trapper.

THE COLORADO PLATEAU

*Bolton, Herbert E., *Pageant in the Wilderness: The Story of the Escalante Expedition to the Interior Basin* (1776). Salt Lake City: Utah Historical Society, 1950. (O P) The definitive account. Includes Escalante's journal translated and annotated.

*Dutton, Clarence Edward, *The Tertiary History of the Grand Canyon District* (1882). Layton (Utah): Peregrine Smith, 1977. The classic description of the canyon country upon which all later commentators have leaned. A geological monograph that is also great nature writing.

Fradkin, Philip, *A River No More*. New York: Alfred A. Knopf, 1981. A survey of the Colorado River from headwaters to mouth, from discovery to overutilization. Indispensable but sobering.

*Powell, John Wesley, *The Exploration of the Colorado River of the West* (1875). New York: Dover, 1961. The last great exploration within the continental United States. The report, besides being a good adventure story, is of scientific and historical importance.

Redfern, Ron, *Corridors of Time*. New York: Times Books, 1980. The story of 1.7 billion years of the Grand Canyon, with stunning photographic panoramas.

*Stegner, Wallace, *Beyond the Hundredth Meridian: John Wesley Powell and the Second Opening of the West*. Boston: Houghton Mifflin, 1954. A biography of Powell, with extended discussion of his work not only as an explorer but as a government scientist and prophet of western development.

THE SOUTHWEST

Abbey, Edward, *Desert Solitaire*. New York: Touchstone Books, 1970 and *The Journey Home*. New York: E. P. Dutton, 1977. A writer and part-time park ranger's words in defense of his beloved canyonlands.

*Bolton, Herbert E., *Spanish Exploration in the Southwest, 1542-1706* (1908). New York: Barnes & Noble, 1976. Reprints, with useful historical background, the narratives of the Cabrillo, Vizcáino, Oñate, Rodriguez, and other expeditions, in Texas, New Mexico, and along the Pacific coast.

*Dobie, J. Frank, *Guide to the Life and Literature of the Southwest*. Dallas: Southern Methodist University Press, revised edition. 1952. Literary history, especially strong on the life and times of cowboys and Texas rangers.

Fulton, Maurice G., and Horgan, Paul, eds., *New Mexico's Own Chronicle*, 1937. (O P) Essays on the various cultures of the Southwest—Indian, Spanish American, Mexican American, and Anglo American.

Garrard, Lewis H., *Wah-To-Ya and the Taos Trail*. Norman: University of Oklahoma Press, 1966. One of the liveliest firsthand accounts of the Southwest fur trade.

Graves, John, *Goodbye to a River*. Lincoln: University of Nebraska Press, 1977. A loving description of a river and Texas wilderness now gone.

*Hammond, George P., ed., *Narratives of the Coronado Expedition, 1540-1542* (1940). New York: AMS Press, 1972. Contains the known documents of the earliest Spanish penetration into New Mexico, including the indispensable *History* of Castañeda.

Horgan, Paul, *Great River: The Rio Grande in North American History*. New York: Holt, Rinehart & Winston, revised edition, 1960. A full, rich history of the Rio Grande and its significance in North American history.

Jennings, N. A., *The Texas Ranger* (1899), reprinted 1930. (O P) A report of lawlessness on the Texas frontier and the valor of the legendary rangers.

*Krutch, Joseph Wood, *Desert Year*. New York: Penguin, 1977. An easterner transplanted to Arizona evokes the natural wonders of the Arizona desert.

THE PACIFIC COAST

Austin, Mary, *The Land of Little Rain* (1903). Albuquerque: University of New Mexico Press, 1974. An authentic account of the once desolate mountain-rimmed desert country of California.

Doig, Ivan, *Winter Brothers*. New York: Harcourt, Brace, Jovanovich, 1980. A study of two students of the Northwest coast, a century and more apart.

Douglas, William O., *Of Men and Mountains*. Seattle: Seattle Book Co., 1981. A memoir of the Pacific Northwest by the indefatigable hiker and civil libertarian, the late Justice of the Supreme Court.

Irving, Washington, *Astoria* (1836). Portland, Ore.: Binfords & Mort, 1967. The first great adventure westward after Lewis and Clark, and the founding of the first American settlement on the Pacific.

Kroeber, Theodora, *Ishi in Two Worlds*. Berkeley: University of California Press, 1961. A biography of the last Yahi Indian of California who died in a museum of anthropology in 1916.

Lewis, Oscar, *High Sierra Country* (1955). Westport: Greenwood Press, 1977. The people and the land of California's Sierra by a distinguished anthropologist.

*Ricketts, Edward F., and Calvin, Jack, *Between Pacific Tides*. Revised by Joel W. Hedgepeth with foreword by John Steinbeck. Stanford: Stanford University Press, 1952. A classic work on the habits and habitats of the animals that live in one of the most perfect life zones of the world—the rocky shores and tide pools of the Pacific coast.

Starr, Kevin, *Americans and the California Dream*. New York: Oxford University Press, 1973. The liveliest recent history of California, ending with the Panama-Pacific Exposition of 1915. Much on literary and intellectual history as well as on the landscape and the westward migration.

Index

Andrus, Cecil, 128
Angulo, Jaime de, 190
Antelope Island, 88, 90, 91
Appalachian Mountains, 16, 22, 26, 56–57
Aquarius Plateau, 113, 115, 116, 125, 127, 130–131, 133
Arcata, Calif., Jambalaya in, 160, 163–164
Arkansas River, 8, 13, 16
Aspen, Colo., as unspoiled America, 51–53
Astor, John Jacob, 67
Audubon, John James, 26, 77

Bad Axe Bend, Wis., 66
Bartram, John, 27, 59, 210
Bartram, William, 9, 203
Bear River Migratory Bird Refuge, 85–87
Beartooth Mountains, 93–112
Beartooth Scenic Highway, 93
Bench Ranch, 95, 102–107, 111
Berry, Wendell, 145, 204, 226
Big Sur coast, 190
Bissell, Richard, 56, 73, 75, 76
Blackburn, Eugene, 127–130, 134
Blue Lake, Calif., E & O Club in, 160–163

Bollingen, Jim, 100, 105–106
Branger, Dave and Marge, 107–109
Brewerton, Lieutenant, 124
Bridger, Jim, 84, 86
Brimhall, Dean, 55, 126–128
Bryce Canyon National Park, 21, 129, 132–136
Buhne, Henry, 153
Byrd, William, 16

Cabeza de Vaca, Álvar Núñez, 9–11
Cabrillo, Juan Rodríguez, 5, 7–8, 23, 187
California, Gulf of, 8, 10, 21
Cape Mendocino, 7, 157, 186
Capitol Reef National Park, 55, 125–132, 134
Carson, Kit, 84, 90, 124
Cascade Mountains, 21, 22, 25, 152
Castañeda, Pedro de, 10, 11, 13, 23
Castle Valley, 117–120
Central Arizona Project, 180
Chalmers, Eddie, 70, 71
Champlain, Samuel de, 3, 5
Chandler Slough, Ill., houseboat living in, 73, 74, 76, 79
Circle Valley, 117, 121

Clark, George Rogers, 4, 8, 17
Colorado River, 20–21, 131,
    133, 180, 183
Columbia River, 9
Concerned Citizens of Owens
    Valley, 173–178
Cook, James, 211, 212
Cooper, James Fenimore, 55, 76,
    218
Coronado, Francisco de, 10–13,
    15, 19
counterculture, 41–43, 52,
    191–194, 195–202,
    226–230
coyotes, survival of, 204–206,
    213
Crèvecoeur, Hector St. John de,
    2, 18, 27, 59
Crow country, 93–112

Davis, John, 5
DeDecker, Mary, 174, 179–181,
    184
DeDecker, Paul, 178
Delta Queen, 60–69, 74, 76
Denver, Colo., 25, 50–51, 110,
    159, 224
DeSoto, Hernando, 5, 12–15,
    56, 57
DeVoto, Bernard, 2, 17, 41, 166,
    184
Dog Valley, 117, 120
Domínguez, Father, 83, 117
Drake, Sir Francis, 7, 8, 15
Dubuque, Iowa, 56, 59, 60,
    68–72, 73–78
Duff, James, 153
Dutton, Clarence E., 114, 121,
    122, 131, 133

Earth People's Park, 41–43
Eaton, Fred, 169–171

environment:
    American character determined
        by, 16, 25–26, 95–96,
        221–228
    cause and consequence in
        relationships with,
        208–212
    conservationists and,
        163–164, 173–181, 183,
        202–203, 208, 222–223,
        228–234
    defined, 202
    as heritage and resource,
        28–44
    industrial development and,
        109, 110–111, 128–130,
        230–232
    military and, 91, 92
    Native American views on,
        55, 96–99
    need for new ethos and, 27,
        184, 209–210
    "permissive society" as danger
        to, 197–203
    ranching and, 95, 99–112
    rapacity in approach to, 4,
        9–13, 27, 206–210
    real-estate speculation and,
        194–195, 231
    rural vs. urban needs and,
        166–185
    variety of marriages to,
        206–207
    way of seeing determined by,
        95–96
Environmental Impact Report
    (EIR), 175–177
Escalante, Father, 83, 117
Escalante River, 8, 116, 131,
    132–133
Eureka, Calif., 145, 152–154,
    158

exploration of New World,
    3–18, 56–58, 82–87,
    114–117, 186–190

farming, 202–203, 208,
    209–210
    American character and,
    26–27, 32–33, 37–38
Faulkner, William, 57
Ferndale, Calif., transformation
    of, 155
Fishlake-Manti National Forest,
    122–125
Fish Lake Plateau, 120, 122–125
Fletcher, Jim, 100–102
Fletcher, John Gould, 20
Flint, Frank, 172
Frazier, Linley, 196
freedom, America and potential
    for, 6, 25–27, 223–225, 230,
    232–234
Frémont, John Charles, 84–86,
    90
Frémont Island, 88, 90
Frémont River, 123, 133
Frost, Robert, 31, 36, 137, 205
Fruita, Utah, lost village of,
    125–127, 130

Gilbert, G. K., 82
Gilpin, William, 57
Golden Gate, 8, 23
Grand Canyon, 10, 20, 21, 130,
    211
Grand Island, Nebr., discovering
    America in, 46, 47–50, 53, 54
Grant, Ulysses S., 57
Gray Family, 30, 32, 37, 43–44
Great Basin, 21, 25, 80, 91, 114,
    117, 120, 166
Great Lakes, 4, 16, 23–24, 225
Great Salt Lake, 21, 80–92, 117

Gunnison, J. W., 120
Gunnison Island, 89
Guttenberg, Iowa, 67–69, 222

Hafen, Le Roy, 120
Hamilton, Alexander, 27
Henry Mountains, 116, 129,
    131, 133
Heyneman, Jack, 100, 103–107,
    108, 110, 111
Heyneman, Jim, 106
Heyneman, Susan, 95, 100, 103
Hill, Lewis and Nancy, 30,
    35–36, 42, 44
Hobbs, Thomas, 133–134
Holman, Chris, 100
Hudson River, 5, 8, 24
Humboldt County, Calif.,
    157–165

Inglesby, Doc, 125, 127
Intermountain Power Project
    (IPP), 128
Interstates, "discover America"
    and, 46–47, 50, 52
Inyo County, environmental
    issues in, 166–181, 184
Irving, Washington, 97

Jefferson, Thomas, 26, 27, 59,
    210, 226
Jolliet, Lewis, 4, 5, 8, 67
Jones, Howard Mumford, 3

Kelly, Charlie, 126
Kemper, Edward, 196
Kennedy, Robert, 221, 227
Khrushchev, Nikita, 231

Lambourne, Alfred, 89
Land, Edwin, 225
LaSalle, René Robert, 4, 5, 8, 16

Leopold, Aldo, 27, 96, 122, 209, 220, 234
Lewis, Meriwether, 4, 8, 17
liberalism, limits of, 201–202
Lippincott, J. B., 169, 170
Long Pond, 28–33, 43–44
Los Angeles Department of Water and Power (DWP), 167, 169–185
Louisiana Purchase, 17
lumber industry, 153–156, 159, 162, 231

McCauley, Hunt, 107
McGuane, Tom, 107
Mackay, Bill, 108–111
Mackenzie, Alexander, 4, 23
MacLeish, Archibald, 225
Manifest Destiny, 17–19, 33, 57
Marcos de Niza, 10
marijuana, 158–159, 161, 196, 200, 232
Marquette, Jacques, 4, 5, 8, 67
Marsh, George Perkins, 27, 222
Mattole River Valley, 159
Mexico, Gulf of, 8, 16, 57
Middle West, 45–79
    Wescott's definition of, 59, 99–100
migration, rural, 40–43, 145–151, 189–190, 226–230
Mississippi River, 5, 8, 12, 16, 21, 24, 26, 56–79, 209, 225
Mississippi Valley, 24, 26, 57, 59
Missouri River, 8, 24, 25, 26, 46, 58, 96, 209
mobile homes, 120, 148
Mono Lake, 181–183
Morse, Betty, 100, 102
Muir, John, 91–92, 117, 183
Mulholland, William, 169, 171, 172, 176

municipalization, dispute over meaning of, 171
MX missiles, land use and, 91, 92, 234
myths about New World, 2–6, 8–15, 18

national character, American:
    land in determining of, 18, 25–26, 95–96, 221–227
    nineteenth-century views on, 18–19
    in Vermont, 36, 42–44
national parks, 93, 97–98, 125–137
    concept of, 128, 184, 230
    traffic problems in, 46–47
    visitation drops and, 134–137
Native Americans, 74–75, 121
    Europeans killed by, 5, 9–10, 11
    fishing rights claimed by, 161–162
    Indians as a misnomer for, 3
    intermarriage and, 15–16, 74
    land as viewed by, 55, 96–97, 99
    legends of, 10, 11
    treaties with, 98
Nelson, Lillian, 173–178
Niagara Falls, 23, 25
Nicolet, Jean, 3, 4, 5
North America, geological change in, 19–23
Northeast Kingdom, Vermont as, 28–44
Northern Plains Resource Council (NPRC), 110
Northwest Passage, search for, 4–9
Norton, Vt., local people vs. Earth people in, 41–43

Oak Creek Canyon, 140–151
Octagon House, 70–71
Ohio River, 16, 24, 58
Ohta, Victor, 196, 197
Oñate, Don Juan de, 14, 139
Ottawa River, 4, 5, 23
Owens Valley, 166–185, 232, 233, 234

Pacific Coast, 152–203
Palisade, Colo., 54–55
Parkman, Francis, 16–17
Paunságunt Plateau, 116, 133
Pinchot, Gifford, 172, 185
plateaus, 113–137
Platte River, 25, 48, 58
Powell, John Wesley, 8, 27, 102–103, 116, 126, 132–133, 222
prairie, short- vs. tall-grass, 209–210
Prairie du Chien, Wis., 66, 67
Promontory Mountains, 84, 88
Pryor Mountains, 94, 111

ranches, 95, 99–112, 203
Reagan, Ronald, 202, 203
Redwood National Park, 154
Rickman, Tom, 202
Rio Grande River, 14, 21, 22
Rio Grande Valley, 12, 13
Rocky Mountains, 4, 16, 24–25, 50–51, 57, 93–112
Roosevelt, Theodore, 108, 172, 181, 185, 233
Rotten Belly, 96–99, 109
Royce, Josiah, 19
Ryan, James, 153

Sagebrush Rebellion, 135, 223, 230–232

St. Lawrence River, 4, 5, 15, 23–24
Salina Canyon, 117, 120, 121, 122
San Rafeal Swell, 21, 119, 120
Santa Cruz, Calif., 186–203
Schnebly, T.C., 141–142
Sevier Valley, 115, 117, 120, 121
Shelton, John, 152–165
Smith, Sylvester, 172
Spanish Trail, 116, 117, 120, 121
Stansbury, Howard, 83, 86
Steinbeck, John, 202
Stewart, George, 222
Stillwater complex, 109–110
Stoddard, Charles, 90
Straits of Anian, 7, 23
Stuart, Granville, 98
Stuhr Museum, 48–50

Table Cliff, 132–133, 135, 136
Taylor, Bayard, 36
Thompson, Almon, 132–133
Thoreau, Henry David, 223–226
tourism, 109, 136–137, 190
    foreign, 129, 132, 134–135
Twain, Mark, 18, 57, 58, 76, 77, 182

utopian communities, 68, 228

Verde Valley, 141–149
Verrazano, Giovanni da, 4, 5, 8
Vizcaíno, Sebastian, 7, 8, 18, 23, 187–188

Vogelman, Hub and Marie, 30,
    31, 32

Walker, Joseph R., 141
Wasatch Plateau, 116–117, 118,
    120, 121, 122, 137
Waterpocket Fold, 116, 125,
    127, 130, 131, 133
water use, 176–177, 184–185
Webb, Walter, 6, 15, 226
Wescott, Glenway, 59, 69, 99
White Mountains, 167, 181

wildlife, 62–63, 204–211,
    213–217, 230
Wilson, Lois, 173–177
work, pleasure principle vs., 53,
    109

Yellowstone National Park, 93,
    97, 222
Young, Brigham, 14

zoning laws, 120, 151

FOR MORE WALLACE STEGNER, LOOK FOR THE

All the Little Live Things
The sequel to the National Book Award—winning *Spectator Bird* finds Joe Allston and his wife in California, scarred by the senseless death of their son and baffled by the engulfing chaos of the 1960s.
ISBN 0-14-015441-8

American Places (with Page Stegner)
Introduction by Page Stegner
A collection of ruminations by the author and his son, Page, *American Places* reconciles the many images that exemplify Americans, America, and the land that made it all possible.   *ISBN 0-14-303974-1*

Beyond the Hundredth Meridian
John Wesley Powell and the Second Opening of the West
A fascinating look at the old American West and the man who prophetically warned against the dangers of settling it.
ISBN 0-14-015994-0

The Big Rock Candy Mountain
Stegner portrays more than thirty years in the life of the Mason family in this harrowing saga of people trying to survive during the lean years of the early twentieth century.   *ISBN 0-14-013939-7*

Collected Stories
Introduction by Lynn Stegner
Thirty-one stories, written over half a century, demonstrate why Stegner is acclaimed as one of America's master storytellers.
ISBN 0-14-303979-2

Crossing to Safety
This story of the remarkable friendship between the Langs and the Morgans explores such things as writing for money, solid marriages, and academic promotions.   *ISBN 0-14-013348-8*

Joe Hill
Blending fact with fiction, Stegner creates a full-bodied portrait of Joe Hill, the Wobbly labor organizer who became a legend after he was executed for murder in 1915.   *ISBN 0-14-013941-9*

On Teaching and Writing Fiction
Edited with an Introduction by Lynn Stegner
The beloved novelist, historian, and conservationist on the subject closest to his heart: the art of fiction—writing it, teaching it, living it. This unique collection of previously uncollected work addresses every aspect of fiction writing. *ISBN 0-14-200147-3*

Recapitulation
Bruce Mason returns to Salt Lake City not to perform the perfunctory arrangements for his aunt's funeral but to exorcise the ghosts of his past. *ISBN 0-14-026673-9*

Remembering Laughter
In the novel that marked his literary debut, Stegner depicts the dramatic, moving story of an Iowa farm wife whose spirit is tested by a series of events as cruel and inevitable as the endless prairie winters.
ISBN 0-14-025240-1

A Shooting Star
Sabrina Castro follows a downward spiral of moral disintegration as she wallows in regret over her dissatisfaction with her older and successful husband. *ISBN 0-14-025241-X*

The Sound of Mountain Water
Essays, memoirs, letters, and speeches, written over a period of twenty-five years, which expound upon the rapid changes in the West's cultural and natural heritage. *ISBN 0-14-026674-7*

The Spectator Bird
Stegner's National Book Award–winning novel portrays retired literary agent Joe Allston, who passes through life as a spectator until he rediscovers the journals of a trip he took to his mother's birthplace years before. *ISBN 0-14-013940-0*

Where the Bluebird Sings to the Lemonade Springs
Living and Writing in the West
Sixteen brilliant essays about the people, the land, and the art of the American West. *ISBN 0-14-017402-8*

Wolf Willow
A History, a Story, and a Memory of the Last Plains Frontier
Introduction by Page Stegner
In a recollection of his boyhood in southern Saskatchewan, Stegner creates a wise and enduring portrait of a pioneer community exiting on the verge of the modern world. *ISBN 0-14-118501-5*

Printed in the United States
by Baker & Taylor Publisher Services